D0848777

# Retrieving Democracy

# RETRIEVING DEMOCRACY
## In Search of Civic Equality

PHILIP GREEN

ROWMAN & ALLANHELD
PUBLISHERS

ROWMAN & ALLANHELD

Published in the United States of America in 1985
by Rowman & Allanheld, Publishers
(A division of Littlefield, Adams & Company)
81 Adams Drive, Totowa, New Jersey 07512

Copyright © 1985 by Rowman & Allanheld, Publishers

**Library of Congress Cataloging in Publication Data**

Green, Philip, 1932–
    Retrieving Democracy.

    Includes index.
    1. Democracy.   2. Equality.   I. Title.
JC423.G74   1985       321.8       8423798
ISBN 0–8476–7405–3
ISBN 0–8476–7406–1 (pbk.)


84  85  86  /  10  9  8  7  6  5  4  3  2  1

Printed in the United States of America

# CONTENTS

# ACKNOWLEDGEMENTS

This book argues for an egalitarian democracy, a society of truly equal citizens. It is preceded by my earlier *The Pursuit of Inequality* (1981), a critique of contemporary inegalitarianisms of race, gender, and class. Upon reading *The Pursuit of Inequality*, an English friend remarked to me, "Don't you find it strange that in a book in which every other word is 'equality,' you mention an elitist school like Smith College so often in your Acknowledgements?" The question did not disturb me at all; one encounters many British Marxists who continue to believe (incorrectly) that the only important inequalities are those of class; and that the struggle for equality between women and men is simply not serious.

Three years later, however, I am compelled to wonder what my English friend will make of the following sentence: For their generous help in providing me the time and assistance to complete this project, I want to thank, again, Smith College; the Institute for Advanced Study in Princeton, where I spent a very fruitful year in 1981 and 1982; and the Rockefeller Foundation, from whom I received a Rockefeller Foundation Humanities Fellowship during the year 1981.

I do think there are some interesting and provocative questions here, though not perhaps the one my friend would raise. It is not, as he might suggest, a compromise of one's revolutionary integrity to accept funding from the ruling class; unless in a sense so all-encompassing that the lapse begins the moment one cuts one's ties with "the people" (if one ever had any) and enters the academy (my friend is also a professor). That kind of purism is fatuous in the contemporary world. At the same time, it would certainly be fair to ask, "How can you object to capitalism, when it is capitalism, professor, that has provided you with the means to do your work? Is it not the chief glory of democratic capitalism, which you so nastily call (as will be seen) 'pseudodemocratic' capitalism, that it tolerates and even supports both criticism of itself and demands for its replacement by a different social system? About how many other contemporary social systems could that claim be made?''

Few or none, to be sure. And that is no small matter. As I insist in this book, any radical version of democracy that lacked the liberal political and constitutional institutions of the advanced capitalist states, or even that failed to improve on them, would be an unacceptable substitute. On the other hand, liberal capitalism does not have an unambiguous relationship to civic liberty. It supports civic liberty in that one way, and crucially undercuts it in so many others, as I shall point out at greater length later.

In a different vein the skeptic might also ask, with raised eyebrows, how seriously radical a critique can be that has been passed on by the Rockefeller Foundation (the Rockefeller Foundation!) as a safely academic project. That too is a question worth pondering for what it tells us about the state of social theory in the United States today. To put it simply, *all* serious critical intellectual endeavor among us is academic, for critical intellect here is detached (I cannot think of any exceptions) from any mass movement that might want to make use of it; to put its theories into effect. My purpose is precisely to be of ultimate, practical use. I have to admit though that the day when that wish might be granted is undoubtedly a long time off.

Meanwhile, the scholars at the Institute and the Rockefeller Foundation to whom I express my gratitude, who read my prospectus and saw it as firmly within the boundaries of professional scholarship, probably knew what I would be doing better than I did. I am not, for better or worse, a writer of party manifestoes. Still, I have always been fond of Keynes' famous remark that "The ideas of economists and political philosophers...are more powerful than is commonly understood. Indeed, the world is ruled by little else . . . Madmen in authority, who hear voices in the air, are distilling their frenzy from some academic scribbler of a few years back." I have no desire to inspire the kind of madmen in authority that Keynes was talking about; but my hope is indeed to be one of those academic scribblers who turns out to have been a voice, heard in the air, by those who now are excluded from authority, from power, and from the springs of social well-being.

More mundanely, a score and more of friends and colleagues gave me aid and comfort during this undertaking. Those who at one time or another read and commented on sections of the manuscript, or who otherwise gave useful advice, include Martha Ackelsberg, Bob Benewick, Fred Block, Bob Buchele, Molly Burke, Joe Carens, Joan Cocks, Bill Connolly, Steve Elkin, Steve Ellenburg, Bob Faulkner, Kathy Ferguson, Steve Fraser, Dorothy Green, Laura Green, Vivien Hart, Jennifer Hochschild, Allen Hunter, Craig Malone, Jane Mansbrige, Suzanne Marilley, Mike McPherson, Jenny Nedelsky, Barbara Nelson, Manuel Pastor, Nola Reinhardt, Carmen Sirianni, Dennis Thompson, John Wallach, Michael Walzer, Robert Paul Wolff, Sheldon Wolin, and Andy Zimbalist. Ann Hornaday, Rene Dziurzynski, Jackie Stevens, and Leigh Peake, all of Smith College, provided computer expertise, typing skills, and research and editorial assistance that have been beyond compare. More generally, but at least as importantly, I've been sustained for many, many years in contemplating our politics with the sorrow it deserves and in trying to imagine some different way of living our lives in the future, by the intellectual companionship and friendship of Pete Marin, Phil Pochoda, Norman and Elsa Rush, and Charles Sackrey.

Finally, the entire manuscript (in an earlier version) was read by Amy Gutmann; she was the equivalent of five ordinary readers. No one could have been as attentive, responsive, supportive, and yet as decisively critical at those many junctures where criticism was all too necessary. Since I found virtually all her suggestions to be well worth heeding she will, I fear, have to accept some small portion of the blame for whatever visible errors of commission remain. My debt to her is barely hinted at by these words; it is certainly not repaid.

Parts of chapters 1, 5, and 6 of this book originally appeared in *Politics and Society* as "Considerations on the Democratic Division of Labor," and are reprinted with permission. Chapter 3 originally appeared in *Philosophical Forum*, and is reprinted with permission.

# Part 1

*Introduction*

# 1

# SOCIAL EQUALITY AND
# POLITICAL EQUALITY

We live in a pseudodemocracy. We are certainly much better off than if we lived under tyranny, or were subject to the rule of impenetrable authorities, or were always in a state of fear that some group of colonels or admirals might decide to close down the few institutions of popular government we were struggling to maintain. What I call pseudodemocracy—representative government, ultimately accountable to "the people" but not really under their control, combined with a fundamentally capitalist economy—is thus preferable to most of the immediately available alternative ways of life of the contemporary nation-state. But it is not democracy; not really. I think most of us are aware of that. The subject of this book is democracy—what a democratic regime would look like, and what aspects of the way we live now prevent us from attaining it. My effort is to retrieve "democracy," a term with radical historical origins, from those who have made it into a prop for social stasis.

An argument for democracy, though, must be potentially attractive to a democratic majority: it must be potentially the subject of a mass movement rather than of merely intellectual speculation or vanguardist politics. Democratic mass movements, however, are easier to invoke than to describe. On one hand, the great historical shortcoming of populism has been its apotheosis of the people as a supposedly united mass against the elites, to the exclusion of a recognition of crucial class (and even more, caste) divisions among the peo-

ple themselves. Conversely, it has been an equally great failure of
Marxists to insist that the abolition of class (a rather vague goal to
begin with) would be all that is necessary to insure that caste divisions
and the power of governing elites would also wither away. Each of
these perspectives by itself is incomplete. In modern societies most
people are objectively united in their inability to effectively influence
elites; but the people are also subjectively divided by barriers of class
and caste. A viable democratic theory must recognize each of those
realities as a related but separable aspect of pseudodemocracy. No
single class (or caste) interest today constitutes a potential majority in
and of itself (as Marx thought the proletariat would); a vision of a truly
democratic society must therefore somehow subsume the interests of
a coalition of social forces.

The outline of any viable mass coalition in contemporary advanced
capitalist societies is clear. It will incorporate, at a minimum, three
sets of interests. First, there is the expressed or potential interest of
the traditional but declining working class and the new white collar
working class, in greater material equality and escape from the
consequences of obsolescence in full employment, workplace democracy, and social mobility (to move away from or move up within certain kinds of workplaces). Second, there is the interest of many
citizens of the liberal democracies in the classical liberal notion of
equal rights: in the fulfillment of the liberal revolution itself, quite apart
from any advances toward a more rational society, or a classless
society. This is the interest primarily of women, that is, of the
apparently increasing number of women who perceive themselves as
having such an interest; and of the members, both male and female,
of racial or ethnic minorities.

Third, throughout the liberal capitalist world (and some of the Communist world as well) there is a generalized movement for fuller participation in political decision-making: for political equality in the classical sense. In part this is the distinctive interest of educated elites; of
professionals and skilled white-collar workers employed in both public
and private bureaucracies, or even self-employed. It is a demand for
achieving some degree of control over the consequences of state and
corporate decision making: for being able to check, redirect, or plan
both the purposes of production and also the imposition on communities and families of what we might broadly call the "externalities" of
production (and reproduction). To some extent this demand is also
subsumed in the mobilizing ideas of feminism and ecologism. More

generally, this is the demand expressed, whether inchoately or explicitly, by the millions of persons engaged in grassroots mobilizations of all kinds--on the Right as well as on the Left. It is the demand to be equally involved in the authorization of a total way of life, and it is the fundamental political demand of democracy. Its potential constituency in every liberal capitalist society therefore also includes the traditional working class, excluded minorities, and even elements of the lower middle class that are so often described as the embodiment of right-wing authoritarianism in so much social science literature.

The necessary price of any mass coalition among these disparate social groups is a vision that incorporates elements of the traditional liberal agenda, the traditional socialist agenda, and the traditional and contemporary radical democratic agendas. At the same time, we must recognize that in these times the traditional socialist agenda has come to be of dubious political salience in comparison with the political demands of liberalism and radical democracy. Nothing can obscure the fact that much equalization has occurred in the capitalist world; and that this has been deeply desired by the great majority of the people in these societies.[1] However, the development of the social democratic welfare state has not been accompanied by any efforts to get people thinking of their social being as a realm more of cooperation and participation than of competition and withdrawal into the life of privatized consumption. Thus, the lack of broad popular support for recent egalitarian proposals (except perhaps in Sweden) is not surprising; but it does suggest that the discussion of equality, though it is in no way obsolete, ought now to take another tack. My approach, then, is to link these different outlooks by proposing that political equality is the primary demand of the citizens of the pseudodemocracies; and to argue that political equality, the real spirit of democracy—everybody to count for one and nobody to count for more than one—cannot be achieved without fundamental changes in the social and economic base; without a new commitment to social equality. The call for more democracy, and for enough social equality to achieve and undergird it, though obviously wishful is not necessarily unrealistic.

## II

Recent history confirms the logic of this approach. During the past two decades it has become clear that the classical democratic myth—that all individuals and groups belonging to the demos ought to have an equal say in the political decisions which concern them—is more vital than it has ever been. The democratic spirit has virtually exploded around the world with such force and visibility that even in the early 1980s, a time of retrenchment, it would be underlining the obvious just to begin to take note of the plethora of grassroots organizations and mass popular lobbies that bedevil representative government everywhere. It should not be at all difficult to sustain the argument, once the means can be found to present it to a public which is constantly being assailed by the idea that pseudodemocratic electoral politics is the real thing, that many of our central social institutions, and the antiegalitarian arguments used to justify them in welfare capitalist societies, are still totally incompatible with the institutionalization of political equality.

The point for egalitarians is thus to link the academic and intellectual ferment in the discussion of social and economic equality with the notion of political equality or democratization. A usable political theory demands that we make a connection between what ordinary people ordinarily want and the kind of society (or social invention) that the theorist allegedly wills on their behalf. Only in this way does it become possible for us to avoid imputing to ordinary citizens a form of social consciousness (radical egalitarianism) that they manifestly do not have.

From this perspective, it is not self-evidently pollyannish to claim that the extension of full political citizenship to all who desire it is a full-fledged historical demand with persuasive and genuine mass appeal. It is a revolutionary promise that is yet to be fulfilled but is an historically logical outcome of the popular movements that have produced universal suffrage: the rights to strike, organize, and bargain collectively; formal civic equality; and the continual proliferation of organs of local and community self-governance and mobilization. Therefore, although the tendency to democratization is validated by something much less than the kind of scientific law under which Marx attempted to subsume the alleged historical tendency to socialism, it is also much more than the product of my own private vision, or of the private vision of a cabal of egalitarian intellectuals. In that sense there is a real connection between the egalitarian theorist's view of the good polity and the visible desires of many millions of people. "Political equality" is a slogan that, although extremely difficult to realize, speaks to real popular demands that are constantly, if only inchoately and uncoordinatively, being expressed. The practical strength of particular versions of egalitarianism—of the moral vision that is outraged by the juxtaposition of wealth and poverty, power and powerlessness, privilege and exclusion, property amassed without working at all and hard work that produces no property—lies to a large extent in our ability to demonstrate the relevance and necessity of that egalitarianism to all those who long for the realization of democracy in the strong sense.

The pseudodemocracy of liberal capitalism is dialectically progressive: the pious utterance of its most hypocritical slogans illuminates the contradiction at its core for all to see. Thus the association of a program for redistribution and public control of resources with a program for democratic political equality is an association that offers the chance to justify effective action for change to the peoples of the pseudodemocracies, even those among them who presently think that the redistribution of the welfare state has gone far enough. The historical movement toward greater equality is not at all dead; it does, perhaps, need a new sense of direction. The sense of necessary and fundamental connection between the two kinds of equality, or two kinds of citizenship, that are usually kept carefully separated in official expressions of our public philosophy, has to be restored, if either is ever to be realized.

# III

In proposing now to set our sights on political equality as our primary goal, I am not proposing to ignore or denigrate the ideal of social equality, but rather to put it in what seems now to be a more appropriate perspective: as a necessary means to an end that most of us truly desire. What though do we mean by "social equality"?

The theory of egalitarianism I will be developing here follows a different direction from other contemporary efforts to chart a way out of the political and economic stagnation in which we have for some time seemed to be sunk. I do not write about democratic socialism or economic democracy or market socialism.[2] That is because a reading of the best expositions of those programs—expositions to which in many ways I am obviously and gratefully indebted—always ends on one crucial note of dissatisfaction; and not just dissatisfaction, but immeasurable dissatisfaction.

From all the discussions of workers' control, public representation on corporate boards, public planning, and the like, we do not get, finally, a *vision* of a different society operating according to fundamentally different rules. I want to explore a vision of social equality that *is* different; that does not recycle ideas that have already been tacitly resisted by large numbers of people everywhere.

My notion of social equality has three basic components: (1) constrained inequality, or a firm societal commitment to the idea of a modal income for all, around which deviant inequalities fluctuate, as the basis of a democratic reward structure: a modal income attuned to a full-fledged rather than a minimalist version of human need; (2) the democratic division of labor, or a division of labor designed primarily to empower competent, self-governing citizens, and promote the fulfillment of their human capacities among the greatest possible number of people, rather than to maximize the production of commodities; and (3) equal access to the means of production, or constitutional limitations on the ownership of productive industry designed to prevent any persons from amassing enough economic power or productive responsibility to confer unequal amounts of political power on them.

Although I shall be exploring the interaction among these various aspects of social equality, it is the idea of the democratic division of labor above all that is central to my vision. Socialists historically have proposed, and continue to propose, that corporate power and state power should be restructured, so that in our roles as workers and as citizens we may have equal influence in the decisions that determine the centers of our lives. But the traditional socialist agenda, on the whole, has failed to confront directly the question of how people with what appear to be widely varying capabilities will be able to participate in the complexities of decision-making for an advanced industrial (or postindustrial) society, on an equal footing. Notions of public or cooperative ownership, workers' control or industrial democracy and the like address issues of class and caste as though to equalize institutionalized power relations will be perforce to abolish class and caste.

Yet surely our experience tells us that those are fundamental, not residual phenomena: that inequalities of class and caste, and especially those that result in the division between mental and material labor, are not merely the result of unequal appropriation (of capital or the state), but are also logical ways of organizing diverse peoples to carry out tasks of extraordinary complexity. The restructuring of pro-ductive and administrative institutions is certainly a necessary precon-dition to creating a society of democratic equals; it is not a sufficient condition. Social equality must inhere in the division of labor itself, in the way people sort themselves out (or are sorted out) to accomplish their goals of production and distribution, if changes in the structures of power and authority are to have more than a cosmetic or symbolic impact.

In this respect, democratic socialists have at best an ambiguous attitude toward the phenomena of class and gender. With regard to class, this is true even of those who place their emphasis on radical notions of workers' control as the cornerstone of democratic equality. For what is never discussed by socialists or economic democrats of any kind is the very simple, yet extraordinarily painful question, of where the "workers" come from; how they got to be workers; and why that is what they want to be.[3] In the same way, (male) socialists hardly ever discuss how the sexual division of labor constitutes itself; how women get to fill the particularized social role of woman, and why that is what they want to do. These are not minor omissions, and it is not niggling to point them out.

If there is anything that is absolutely clear, it is that, in the first place, the authors of all these proposals (myself included) are not workers, have not been workers, and are not going to be workers, as that word is being used in all discourses about workers' control. We are intellectuals, economists, etc., proposing workers' control, but making no comment at all on whether intellectuals, economists, etc., are simply going to disappear in the good society. In the second place, it is equally clear that the authors of most of these proposals are men, but are making little or no comment on whether the social role of man we are so used to filling is also going to disappear in the good society.

Pseudorepresentation, party oligarchy, impervious bureaucracy, unresponsive planning, and male domination, are not a series of malign institutions that have been accidentally tacked on, as it were, to the contemporary division of labor in industrial societies. They are rather the expression (one might say the best expression, since it is also expressed in autocratic forms) of that division of labor. For the social division of labor among classes and sexes, and the technical division of labor among occupations, have become inextricably intertwined. Divide the world up into workers, professionals, managers, leaders, housewives, untrained conscripts in the reserve army of labor, etc., with no further thought to the matter, and what we are going to get is what we already have, in a mildly less offensive, mildly more responsive form. I don't think that is enough of a vision to inspire people to tear up a functioning system. The academy in every nation, communist as well as capitalist or social democratic, is full of social scientists who are impressively adept at explaining the necessity of elitism, rule by experts, and so forth. Any program that contains less than a full account of what is going to be substituted for elitism and the rule of (mostly male) experts, is finally going to be greeted with apathy. We can achieve some very valuable particular reforms in the name of economic democracy or democratic socialism, but not a truly new way of life for most people. By contrast, the democratic division of labor that I am going to advocate here, in combination with constrained inequality and the more traditional notion of democracy in the sphere of production, may seem to represent a considerable leap from the world of contemporary reality. I shall be making that leap, however, on behalf of a good deal more than an attenuated version of elite rule in political and productive organizations.

As all teachers of social science know, criticism of the pseudodemocratic status quo invariably elicits from students the protest, "Yes, all that is probably true, but what have you got to offer instead? We all know that real democracy is utopian." Marx's crucial formulation, that the future must be visible within the present if it is to appear as a nonutopian possibility, seems obvious enough on its face, but has in the end a fatal flaw. If the alleged future appears as nothing more that the embryo of one possibility in the midst of a host of stifling counterrealities, then that future will never be embraced by the mass of people, as the history of revolutionary moments, to paraphrase Marx, proves a dozen times over.

The ideal must be real to be a viable ideal, yes; but it must also appear to be potentially a viable ideal *before* any great number of people are going to take the trouble to make it real. What follows, therefore, is nothing more than an attempt to answer that perennial objection from my own students.

# Notes

[1] Compare the arguments of Christopher Lasch, "The Prospects for Social Democracy," *democracy*, vol. II no. 3 (July 1982), pp. 28–32, with those of Frances Fox Piven and Richard A. Cloward, "Economic Demands, Political Rights," on pp. 33–41 of the same publication. See also Piven and Cloward, *The New Class War: Reagan's Attack on the Welfare State and its Consequences* (New York: Pantheon Books, 1982). The fundamental discussion of the welfare state from a critical functionalist perspective is James O'Connor's *The Fiscal Crisis of the State* (New York: St. Martin's Press, 1973). Two excellent theoretical and historical discussions of the political character of the welfare state, both indebted to O'Connor, are Ian Gough, *The Political Economy of the Welfare State* (London: Macmillan, 1979); and Geoff Hodgson, "On the Political Economy of Socialist Transformation," *New Left Review*, no. 133 (May-June 1982), pp.52–66.

[2] See for example Martin Carnoy and Derek Shearer, *Economic Democracy* (White Plains: M.E. Sharpe, 1980); Michael Harrington, *Decade of Decision: the Crisis of the American System* (New York: Simon and Schuster, 1980); Oskar Lange and Fred M. Taylor, *On the Economic Theory of Socialism* (New York: A.M. Kelley, 1970); Bengt Abrahamsson and Anders Brostrom, *The Rights of Labor*, trans. by David McCune (Beverly Hills: Sage Publications, 1980); and Branko Horvat, *The Political Economy of Socialism* (Armonk, N.Y.: M.E. Sharpe, 1982). It is a telling point that Horvat's book, which of all these I find the most compelling, has no entry in its index for "division of labor."

[3] Andre Gorz is the most obvious exception to these remarks. See especially his essay on "Technology, technicians and class struggle," in Gorz, ed., *The Division of Labour* (Atlantic Highlands, N.J.: Humanities Press, 1976), pp. 159–89; *Socialism and Revolution,* tr. by Norman Denny (New York: Doubleday, 1973); *Ecology as Politics,* trans. by Patsy Vigderman and Jonathan Cloud (Boston: South End Press, 1980); and *Farewell to the Working Class.* trans. by Michael Sonenscher (London: Pluto Press, 1982). His notion of the "dual society" is especially provocative, and has much in common with the argument made in Part II of this book. Still, though Gorz has by now fashioned the most compelling critique of hierarchy among what he calls technical and manual workers, he has not yet engaged what I consider to be the fundamental question: in an egalitarian social formation, who would become manual workers or technical workers; how; and why? That is also true of the most original discussion of socialism by Americans, Michael Albert and Robin Hahnel, *UnOrthodox Marxism* (Boston: South End Press, 1978). Their treatment of gender, however, is better than that of any other (male) radical socialists.

# 2

# PSEUDODEMOCRACY

## I

An alternative formulation of the argument about linkage in the previous chapter, is to say simply that capitalism—the capitalist division of labor, the capitalist distribution of rewards, and the capitalist formation of the means of production—is incompatible with democracy in the strong sense: with the requirement that everybody should count for one and nobody for more than one.[1]

Capitalist societies are articulated around a complex set of relationships that has three central components: a social class structure that, though informal and apparently accidental, is necessary in its operations and real in its effects; an equally informal but equally real caste system comprising divisions of gender, and usually of race or ethnicity as well; and a formal separation between decision-making elites of all kinds and all other citizens. The decisive aspect of capitalist society is that it is impossible to attack this last division, the separation between elites and citizens, rulers and ruled, so long as the class and caste systems on which that separation is predicated remains intact.

## II

The caste-and-class structure of liberal capitalism is not adventitious but definitive. One can only hope to become a capitalist because there will be workers to employ who are not capitalists, and a class of marginal workers, or a reserve army of labor, whose presence will restrain the wage demands of those employees. Conversely, one becomes an employee knowing that one cannot also be an employer of labor; and as a member of a racial or otherwise marginalized minority, or of the female sex, one fundamentally understands one's special connection to the reserve army of labor without necessarily being aware of the existence of a Marxian vocabulary within which to conceive it. Finally, one hopes to become a member of the "professional managerial class," or the middle class of highly trained professionals, precisely in the expectation that one will not be a worker, a seller of abstract labor power: that one will escape from a class that exists, ideologically, primarily to be escaped from.

The central tactic of the exponents of liberal capitalism has always been not to deny the existence of this structure; but rather to deny that this structure—the social division of labor—necessarily determines the development of a similar structure within the strictly political institutions of liberal capitalist society. They suggest that when majority resignation, apathy, or tacit withdrawal from the polity replaces active majority participation in a capitalist society, it is to be understood as a side-effect of human nature, or the reality of large-scale organization: that the structural demands of capitalist production are, so to speak, innocent bystanders.

To be sure, the social division of labor and the political division of labor are not identical; but their resemblance and interpenetration are more than merely metaphorical. To lead the kind of life we want to lead, the resources we need are time, skill or knowledge, money, and property. Those are exactly the resources we need in the political realm as well. The first three give us access to the world of public decision making; the last, if we have enough of it, insures that public decision makers must treat our activities as a paramount focus of their decision making.

Thus in the political realm human capital in the literal sense—real capital such as belongs to the capitalist class—exists in a dual form. First, insofar as the control of money and property enables us to buy or command other people's time and skills, inequalities in the distribution of economic capital are virtually reproduced in the distribution of political capital. Those who by virtue of their social position, have direct personal access to the political realm are more likely to get the chance not only to express preferences about outcomes but also, much more decisively, to express preferences about which outcomes other people should get to express preferences about.

Second, economic capital reproduces itself in the political realm with an even more decisive inequality. It stands for effective control of the channels for the production and distribution of those goods and services the loss of which, if they suddenly became unavailable in the accustomed amount, might deprive political institutions of their legitimacy. The people who exercise that kind of control do not need to seek access to politics; access seeks them. Behind all the other resources of the capitalist class lies the ultimate resource of prior possession of social necessities. In every capitalist society a multitude of laws, usages, and rulings have for many generations dispensed well-being in its favor; its extensive command of time, money, and skill pales in significance by comparison. In the U.S., when some marginal group arranges a march on Washington, the news media treat it as a major spectacle; but if the purpose of such events is to influence governmental actions then the real truth of capitalism, as I.F. Stone put it, is that "the rich march on Washington all the time." The interest of the capitalist class as a whole is the apparent general interest of society as a whole in capital accumulation. Thus, for example, the wages and powers of a sector of organized labor may increase, but usually only because the laborers involved work for the owners of a crucial sector of capital. Contrarily, the incomes and powers of owners and managers neither increase nor decrease because they work with organized labor or any particular segment of it. The fury of American liberals at Charles Wilson for his injudicious remark (when he was nominated to be Secretary of Defense-designate in 1952) that "What is good for the country is good for General Motors, *and vice-versa*" [emphasis added] has always manifested a good deal of self-deception. The injudiciousness of Wilson's remark lay precisely in the fact that he was speaking the unpleasant truth.[2]

### III

Thus the political upper class, or capitalist class, has the greatest resources in time and money to spend on behalf of its interests. Many of its interests are already deeply entrenched in law, and its methods for protecting those entrenched interests have become so intertwined with the accepted means for maximizing the general welfare that the costs of tampering with them will often seem too high even to those who positively hate the existing distribution of power.

It is also true, of course, that the professional/managerial class as well has a very disparate access to political opportunity, compared with the working class.[3] Many of its members who lack productive capital do possess realizable political skills: the trained capacity to exercise authority, make decisions upon which other people depend, negotiate among conflicting interests, do research, argue effectively, work with compilations of esoteric materials, write well, etc. Although it was not always the case, clearly now to be in this position one almost necessarily has to be a member of the educated middle class—a professional or a semi-professional (or the educated wife of a professional man). Usually (that is, statistically far more often than could be accounted for by chance) it helps to have been born into that class. Those of us in that class who wish to place those skills in the service of political power will rarely be turned away. On the contrary, even if the ground rules and mores of liberal capitalism permitted the visible direct rule of the capitalist class (which on the whole they do not), that class would still be unable to manage the fortunes of state and economy without turning over most of the actual work and thus, necessarily, decision making, to activist members of the professional class.

The political position of the working class, however, is quite different. Let us think of the working class in the broadest possible sense, as consisting of all those persons who neither own investable capital nor possess the kinds of highly trained skills that define the members of the professional/managerial class. (Thus uneducated housewives would be described as "working class" in this understanding). Because the members of this class do not, as individuals, possess the kinds of resources (money, property, intellectual or organizational skills) that are useful to those who, at any given moment, exercise political authority, the political existence of the class as a whole, often divided against itself in any event, is encompassed almost entirely by the formal institution of voting: of expressing preferences in the most direct possible way. But this necessary reliance on sheer power of numbers, of aggregated individuals (assuming they can be successfully aggregated) has a decisive impact: an impact much like that of receiving a wage rather than a salary or profit.

Let us put it this way. If all the capitalists in any capitalist social order abstained from voting on election day, it would probably make no difference at all in the outcome of the elections, or in the policies to be implemented afterwards. Capitalists do not depend on votes to underpin their power and influence; the other resources at their command are considerably more decisive. The educated middle class has voting power to add to the skills it can rent out, especially as modern economies shift in emphasis from blue-collar to white-collar work. The real strength of this class, though, still comes from its social rather than its political position; as a class, what is most important about its voting power is that the choice of whom to vote for is usually a choice among members of this class.

For both those classes, though clearly for one more than the other as a class, the factor-shares model of neoclassical economics works well in the political realm—with hardly any metaphorical component at all. The capitalist gets political profit, the possessor of skills gets the political version of economic rent. But the factor-shares model works for the average voter, as for the average worker—and they are mostly the same people—in a different way. Voting power, unlike capital or skill but much like labor power, creates products that pass out of our grasp as soon as we have made them. In the political realm these products are not commodities but rather are officeholders; and, as Rousseau argued two centuries ago, the moment we install them is the very moment in which we lose whatever power we had over them. Those who possess little or nothing beyond the vote are thus political wage earners, and their labor-power does not earn a return equivalent to a capitalist's (or a professional's) political investment. How in good conscience could it, since to vote, or even to write a letter to one's representative, is to do virtually nothing by comparison to what the possessors of capital or of skill can do? The voter's product is alienated precisely because the voter's political labor is alienated: because voters are not able to engage in the kind of political work necessary to make it their own.

This alienation of the voter's commodity from the voter is perfectly compatible with all the seemingly egalitarian decision rules of procedural democracy; the structure of capitalism is decisive in this realm as well.

It is not simply that there is a hidden conspiracy of the wealthy and their skilled servants to place some issues "on the agenda" rather than others; or that some people find access to decision makers more difficult to obtain than do others. Above all, pseudodemocracy confirms the rationality of the existing political class structure, which means that for most of us it confirms the rationality of being apolitical and leaving politics, aside from the individually meaningless act of voting, to others. As a mass phenomenon, of course, voting is far from meaningless. For any specific individual, however, there is perfect rationality in the perhaps apocryphal remark attributed to Edward Banfield: that he never votes in national elections because statistically there's a better chance that he'll be run over on the way to the polls than that his vote will affect the outcome.

In sum, then, when we compare all social classes with regard to their ability to deploy time, money, skill, position, or (as in the case of the strike weapon, for example) coerciveness, we see that though each of those classes possesses some useful degree of one resource or another, the political upper class is especially favored with regard to every one of those resources, and in comparison with every one of the other classes. The kind of economic and social inegalitarianism that contemporary capitalism manifests, in other words, makes the notion of equal citizenship among social classes a chimera. From any individual worker's standpoint, the others in politics, though they may have his or her interests more or less at heart, are roughly the same as the others in economic and social life. If equal participation is what we prescribe, it is as impossible in political life as on the shop floors or in the offices of a capitalist society.

None of this is to say that power is limited to the wealthy through their representatives. At the individual level, anyone (almost) with enough drive can indeed "make it." But some make it with hardly any personal effort at all, others only through their own and their neighbors' intense activity; others only through the activities of strangers remote from them—some at the cost of badly needed financial resources, others only at the extreme cost of their lives or liberties.

Certainly, capitalism as the unalloyed rule of the capitalist class is historically a losing struggle, if not as dramatically and decisively as Marx asserted. The discrepancy between the many who work hard for a passable and insecure living, and the few who need not work at all to maintain their grotesque wealth, always threatens to undermine the rule of capital, setting limits past which mass disaffection from the capitalist system will set in. Capitalism comes to be a continual compromise that by fits and starts, and more so in one nation than another, is gradually being compromised into something else. Since the introduction of universal male suffrage, the history of capitalism can be read as one of a progressive decline of the unchecked power of the capitalist class, though much more so in some societies (e.g., Sweden) than in others.[4] In several liberal capitalist nations, parties of organized labor have been successful enough in the parliamentary arena to help bring about the elimination of structural poverty; a great extension of equal opportunity to those who used to be at the bottom of the social class order; the provision of a broad and fairly firm security net for most of those who for one reason or another are threatened with economic disaster, and the development of industrial democracy or codetermination schemes that have made the employer-employee relationship much less unalloyedly hierarchical.

Furthermore, in all liberal capitalist societies the economic upper class is not a true ruling class, for its members do not govern merely by virtue of their membership in that class. They participate in actual governance much more disproportionately than do the members of any other economic class, but they still must either be recruited or work their way into political or administrative activity. On a class basis they share governance with, and on a numerical basis are outnumbered by, those political and civic activists who are recruited, or recruit themselves, from the professional and small-business class. All of these together form a governing political elite. In most Western European nations (though hardly at all in the U.S. or Japan), representatives of the organized working class have been co-opted into this elite, as part of an overall corporatist social compromise, or (as in Great Britain and Italy), through the ties of labor to a political party that either sometimes governs or sometimes is able to exert direct influence on government.[5]

Thus economic classes and political classes are not coterminous. The employees of the state apparatus, the governing elite, cannot as a totality be defined as a part of any one political class. They are drawn primarily from the professional class, though, and the significance of that fact is ambiguous. On one hand, political activists often attain position or power only insofar as their ideas and skills are useful to those with more real social power (control of capital) than themselves. On the other hand, they not only develop some degree of power as a collection of discrete individuals, they also may develop some cohesion as an elite. As a whole or (more often) in part, they may come to be at odds with segments of the capitalist class, since governing elites have their own specific class or occupational interests. From unionized civil service workers to professional consul-tants, they develop their own sense of an identity between their own demands and what become alleged needs of the state.

Beyond such relatively narrow concerns, moreover, governing elites are the subjects of conflicting cross pressures that are built into the very notion of their formal independence from the ruling class. From one direction, pressure is put on the governing elite by the demands of international politics, and especially the demands of international capital, which may not be at all compatible with the desires and needs of national capitals. From another direction, government steadily attracts to it those who wish at least to play a mediating role between social classes, and sometimes to truly represent the unrepresented. Furthermore, the need of the upper class, even on those occasions when it effectively controls the state, to counter Marxist or populist propaganda by presenting the state as a nonpartisan social arbiter, ensures that some targets of that presenta-tion will be taken in by it enough to start playing their assigned roles in earnest. One of the great resources of the upper class, its ability to convey an aura of ideological disinterestedness, is potentially self-destructive when employed too often. Gradually, for this reason as well as straightforward technical and organizational needs, the state assumes a somewhat independent character.

From a perspective of commitment to egalitarian social and politi-cal change, it is essential to emphasize this potential openness of the capitalist state with respect to the ambiguous class and political interests of those who manage it. To leave our description of the capi-talist state at that, however, would be misleading. For purposes of understanding the existing constellation of power and influence, and the strength of the forces of resistance to fundamental change, it is equally necessary to insist that there are strong factors militating in the direction of political stasis, or even antidemocratic resolutions of particular crises, in the management of the capitalist state.[6] Even leaving aside the obvious and, in an inegalitarian society, understand-able susceptibility of the working class (or elements of it) to appeals for national struggle in place of class conflict, the governing elite itself has an indeterminate political agenda. Independence might mean independence on behalf of peaceful class integration or even more political and social equality. But the partial independence of a governing elite from a weakened or fractured capitalist class may also mean, under the right historical circumstances, a more authoritarian state based on some combination of repressive and technocratic solutions to a crisis in capitalist society (or in the capitalist world system). Thatcherism and Reaganism certainly look like harbingers of such a movement.[7]

Such grim prognoses aside, there remains a strong enough relationship between economic and political class in capitalist pseudodemocracies to make the status quo always a safe outcome to predict with respect to the distribution of political power. For better or worse, the independence or relative autonomy of the governing elite is always dependent on circumstances. In Fred Block's words:

> Not every extension of state power will survive beyond those periods in which state managers have special opportunities to expand the state's role. After a war, depression, or period of reconstruction, the business community is likely to campaign for a restoration of the *status quo ante.* State managers in these periods will be forced to make some concessions to the business community in order to avert a decline in business confidence. However, the state managers also want to avoid the elimination of certain reforms important for the stabilization of the economy and the integration of the working class. Self-interest also leads them to resist a complete elimination of the state's expanded powers. The consequence is a selection process by which state managers abandon certain reforms while retaining others. In this process, reforms that are most beneficial for capitalism will be retained, while those whose effects are more questionable will be eliminated ... (the)ultimate outcome is determined by intense political struggle.[8]

In that struggle, as Block points out, state functionaries are very vulnerable compared to capitalists. If economic policy fails in a social order marked, as is liberal capitalism, by separation between politics and economics, a particular government is much more likely to bear the brunt of the blame than is the entire corporate order. In addition, many factors aside from considerations of economic and political pressure tug those among the professional class who are state managers in the direction of reconciliation with the expressed needs of capital. Even though many of its members have doubts about the justice or efficacy of capital's unlimited sway, on the whole they are as committed as are capitalists themselves to maintaining the profoundly significant class barrier between their work, and that which is done by the working class whose interests they often claim to represent. The rule of privilege—and that is the essence of capitalism—can protect itself by encouraging lesser forms of privilege that leave the fundamental social structure intact. But when they appear linked they reinforce each other, in that the working class is robbed both of possible allies and, more importantly, of potential skilled leaders. Until democratic activists can inspire a broad coalition of both classes and castes, the professional class (which is also inevitably the leadership class) will continue to be drawn toward alliances with capital. Only a critique of capitalism itself, that promises to reward professionals with independence from economic hierarchy in return for their greater submission to democratic controls from below, might break that alliance and empower a more effective democratic movement. Certainly that will never happen while capitalism is perceived by professionals as insuring their interests rather than stifling the expression of their needs.

Further, while the governing elite governs, it certainly does not rule. Even where representatives or organized labor have been added to it, it must share rule with the economic upper class and their direct representatives in politics, for the reasons we have already discussed. Only some form of the democratic socialization of the property it controls can strip the capitalist class of that inherent power and transfer it to an equal citizenry. The overriding truth about liberal capitalist societies is that if the collective resource of the vote is to be used in such a way as to reduce extreme economic inequalities and put notions of greater equality on the agenda, that can only happen to the extent that the primary institutions of capitalism—private corporate enterprise and the treatment of labor as a commodity under the unilateral command of ownership and management—are successfully attacked by it. Only in so far as organized workers and their allies force capitalist societies to cease operating according to the traditional rules of capitalism can they begin to bring about an equal involvement in governance, and thus begin to demolish the most substantial bulwarks of pseudodemocracy.

The upper class, confronted with the need for self-defense, is able to mount a massive defense of an entrenched system which distributes the control of productive property. Much of its wealth and power, furthermore, reside beyond any particular set of national boundaries; the capitalist political system (and a political system is what it becomes when it transcends those boundaries) is more modernized, less parochial and, thus, in many ways more authoritative, than the institutions of pseudodemocracy themselves. The electoral system ultimately offers every class or group the chance to argue for the degree of equality or inequality it favors; but the chances for success for the various groups are, by the very nature of the social system, distinctly unequal. The upper class in capitalist societies rules or has real and regular access to rulers, but is not ruled. Members of the other classes as such (other than those co-opted into organized political life), in greater or lesser degrees are ruled but do not, except very occasionally, rule; and have only irregular access, at best, to rulers.

Therefore, to say that the other classes have achieved political equality in having entrenched positions to defend, just as does the upper class, would be to treat language with contempt. One might as well say that bicycles and automobiles are both entrenched in New York City: cyclists having the privilege of riding in Central Park on Sundays without fear of being hit by automobiles, and motorists having the privilege of riding everywhere else all the time without fear of being hit by bicycles.

The existence of free elections and a formally neutral state apparatus is one among several necessary preconditions of a successful struggle for political equality. But the logic learned by popular movements of the past, that political reform without structural economic change has only limited potential, is inescapable. Political equality will exist only when the benefit to all citizens from the institutions of representation, solidary organization, and interest-group lobbying, varies only as their numbers vary. From that perspective, though political class and economic class and caste are not coterminous in capitalist social orders, they overlap enough and in significant enough ways to justify the conclusion that capitalism and political equality are incompatible. The exclusion of what is considered merely private productive decision making from the ambit of democratic majority rule, institutionalized as a divorce between the economic and the political, divides the community into two classes. The first is a class of real citizens who, whether they pose as owners, managers, or public servants, make decisions about the fundamental productive concerns of the community. The second is a much larger class of pseudocitizens who are debarred from participation in the making of those decisions.

All citizens can be equally likely to have their needs or interests represented only when the rule of "private" capital has been abolished. Here is the core of the linkage between social and political equality.

# Notes

[1] Of course capitalism, especially liberal capitalism, is obviously not the only social formation that is incompatible with democracy; with political equality. On the contrary, liberal capitalism probably offers a more likely avenue to political equality than most of the available alternatives. Writing from Eastern Europe, for example, a radical democrat would have to take a much different tack from the one I have taken here. See, e.g., Rudolf Bahro, *The Alternative in Eastern Europe* (New York: Schocken Books, 1980); and Andras Hegedus, *Socialism and Bureaucracy* (London: Allison and Busby, 1976).

[2] In a study of the tortuous history of the nationalization, denationalization, and renationalization of the British steel industry, Doug McEachern notes that the industry, "which struggled most, and had an institute to co-ordinate [sic] its actions, was not in the long run able to protect its interests though it was well aware of what they were." British capital on the whole was aware that many sectors of the economy would gain rather than lose if the declining steel industry was shored up by nationalization. Free enterprise ideology caused it to equivocate, though, so that on this issue the capitalist class as a whole "lacked any effective form of organisation [sic]" and "did not act." Still, in the end "they had their interests secured by the actions of the governments." That is the nature of class power. See McEachern, *A Class Against Itself: Power and the Nationalisation of the British Steel Industry* (Cambridge: Cambridge University Press, 1980), p. 192.

[3] My use of the term professional/managerial class is taken from Barbara Ehrenreich and John Ehrenreich, "The Professional-Managerial Class," in Pat Walker, ed., *Between Labor and Capital* (Boston: South End Press, 1979), p. 45. Of all the literature of the past two decades on "the new class," the Ehrenreichs' essay is the most persuasive, and I am deeply indebted to it.

[4] See John Stephens, *The Transition from Capitalism to Socialism* (Atlantic Highlands, N.J.: Humanities Press, 1980).

[5] On corporatism and social democracy, see Leo Panitch, *Social Democracy and Industrial Militancy* (New York: Cambridge University Press, 1976), and "Trade Unions and the State," *New Left Review* No. 125 (January-February 1981), pp. 21–44; Adam Przeworski, "Material Interests, Class Compromise, and the Transition to Socialism," *Politics and Society,* vol. 10 no. 2 (1980), pp. 125–154; and Phillipe Schmitter, "Still the Century of Corporatism?," *Review of Politics*, vol. 36, no. 1 (1974), pp. 85–131. See also Schmitter and Gerhard Lehmbruch, eds., *Trends Toward Corporate Intermediation* (Los Angeles: Sage Publications, 1979), especially Bob Jessop's "Corporatism, Parliamentarism, and Social Democracy."

[6] On this point, Bertell Ollman's "Theses on the Capitalist State," *Monthly Review*, vol. 34 no. 7 (December 1982), pp. 42–6, are particularly pertinent.

[7] See the general theoretical remarks of Erik Olin Wright, in his "Capitalism's Futures," *Socialist Review* No. 68, vol. 13 no. 2 (March-April 1983), pp.77–126; and the more chilling discussion of Theresa Amott and Joel Krieger, "Thatcher and

Reagan: State Theory and the 'Hyper-Capitalist' Regime," *New Political Science*, vol. 3 no. 8 (Winter 1982), pp. 9–36.

[8] The quotation is from the best recent discussion of the limitations on class rule, Fred Block's "The Ruling Class Does Not Rule: Notes on the Marxist Theory of the State," in *Socialist Revolution*, No. 33, vol. 7 no. 3 (May-June 1977), pp. 6–28. See also Block's "Beyond Relative Autonomy: State Managers as Historical Subjects," in *Socialist Register 1980*, ed. by Ralph Miliband and John Saville (London: Merlin Press, 1980), pp. 227–42; Eric Nordlinger, *On the Autonomy of the Democratic State* (Cambridge: Harvard University Press, 1980); Margaret Levi, "The Predatory Theory of Rule," *Politics and Society*, vol. 10, no. 4 (1981), pp. 432–65; and Theda Skocpol, *States and Social Revolutions* (New York: Cambridge University Press, 1979).

# Part 2

## *Social Equality*

# 3

# PROLEGOMENA TO ANY FUTURE THEORY OF SOCIAL EQUALITY

---

## I

It is one thing to say that we must forge a linkage between social equality and political equality; quite another to argue that social equality itself is sustainable as a mode of the production and reproduction of a materially satisfactory way of life. Does not market economy, in which the level and nature of production is set by competition between the owners and managers of capital for the resources of consumers, necessarily produce more or better than might a democratically controlled economy, in which production was oriented and surplus product (profit) appropriated and disposed of, according to the equal choices of all participants in the production process?

To answer this question, let us proceed, as did Marx in his manuscript on alienated labor, from an "actual economic fact." Neither the discipline of the market nor the cajoling of welfarist and planning institutions is working well today in the capitalist world. Capitalism indeed seems to have reached its moral limit, even if its material limit remains, in principle, the sky. In the advanced capitalist world no imaginable tinkering with existing institutions seems likely to overcome what now looms as permanently recurring stagflationary inertia, modified only by the painful cycle of boom (but shorter and shorter booms) and bust.

The capitalist division of labor and mode of organizing the means of production, that is, is no longer clearly a technical solution to the problem of efficiency in the production of commodities and the realization of their value (as in the analysis of Max Weber, for example). The problem of the capitalist division of labor evinces itself in various ways. It is manifest in the rise in what comes to be taken for granted as a permanent level of unemployment and concealed underemployment everywhere, even in those nations with a commitment to full employment. The defect of the capitalist division of labor is also evident in the difficulty all capitalist nations are experiencing in absorbing the labor of women, as that becomes more valuable in the workplace than in the home; and in the explosive shuffling in and out of the work force of masses of cheap labor, whether in the form of immigrants from abroad or internally colonized peoples at home.

Above all, the breakdown of productivity in our particular civilization of production and consumption is signalled in the growing inability of either the state or private capital to pay out an overall social wage sufficient to contain the escalating psychic, political, and material costs of the capitalist way of life. This difficulty is visible everywhere. Thus, increased social investment in higher education begins to cheapen the value of that education without liberating either human or nonhuman forces of production. Or as the provision of health care becomes more and more technologically advanced, no system for delivering that care seems able to withstand the tremendous pressure that the new technologies place upon delivery costs—a phenomenon that exists in the apparently unrelated realm of, for example, police work as well. Or, the external diseconomies of production (e.g., pollution of various kinds), are spewed forth at an increasing rate, but we have more and more difficulty in finding techniques for dealing with those diseconomies that do not threaten to disemploy productive workers. Yet more broadly, demands for job protection within national economies threaten to aggravate already existing manifestations of international instability in the exchange of both currencies and goods; domestically, the protected wages of unionized labor and the less protected wages of the ununionized and state dependents confront each other in an opposition that produces seemingly insoluble problems in putting the unemployed or underemployed back to productive work.

## II

It is the legal and social rootlessness of capital; the division of legal status and authority between ownership/management and labor; and the technical division of labor within industries, that are directly responsible for these dilemmas: for the existence of a gross national product that does not increase and may even now diminish gross satisfaction.

Thus, to start at the core of the social division of labor of capitalism, the preeminence of absentee ownership as a social relation of production generates escalating uneven regional development in the form of capital flight and the repatriation of profits. Millions of people within nations, hundreds of millions or billions in the world, are devastated by the right of absentee ownership to relocate productive capacities where it will, unaccompanied by any requirement that those who benefit from the process compensate those who have suffered from it.

Since the end of the nineteenth century, for example, the Appalachian economy has been tightly integrated with and even central to, rather than separated from, the American economy as a whole. It has been, and is now, a very profitable sector of that economy. There were immense returns to be earned by the coal and lumber of Appalachia, and they were earned, but not by the residents. The simple fact about Appalachia (as about many other underdeveloped regions) is that it has been an exporter of resources and capital, and an importer of consumer goods: a recipe for the poorhouse.

But that regional self-destruction did not occur because, due to some cultural lag—some enclave mentality—the people of the region chose it for themselves. On the contrary. Appalachia was denuded, over the protests of its people, by absentee owners; it was the very integration of Appalachia into the American capitalist economy that sealed its fate. It was not an aversion to hard work or to cost accounting that created regional backwardness, but the conscious maintenance of those regions as areas for resource exploitation by those with the legal, financial, and often military power to do so.

It may well be that regional imbalance is a law of economic development. By any reckoning, though, the people of Appalachia, whose coal and timber were essential to American economic development for more than half a century, should have been able to strike a much better bargain for themselves than they actually did. However, the people of Appalachia had nothing to bargain with, nor the power to strike any bargain for themselves, good or bad. Their past and present underdevelopment is the result of nothing more than that simple fact: what they "had" they did not have, for it legally belonged, and still belongs, to somebody else; to a national or even international capitalist class that repatriates its profits elsewhere.[1] The legal right of absentee ownership to appropriate all proceeds from the use of capital is as capable of creating poverty as wealth.

In what sense are we to say that such a history, which can be multiplied endlessly, is an example of an efficient capital market in action? Free market theorists are very lax when it comes to specifying the boundaries within which market optimality is to be assessed. In truth, only within the entire world system does the market optimize productivity and thus (allegedly) well-being.

This is a promise which will surely by now seem derisory to most of its putative beneficiaries, for it is of little interest to specific groups of people in specific regions who suffer disbenefits from the operations of capital. There is no a priori reason to believe that the people of, say, Youngstown, Ohio, or Wheeling, West Virginia—especially those among them who shift helplessly in and out of the reserve army of labor—will ever see their share of the social utility that supposedly accrues from the closing down of steel plants or coal mines or other productive enterprises in those or other such locations, and the shifting of their operations to lower-cost areas overseas. Free market theory is a theory only about the virtue of being able to buy consumer goods or real property cheaper (and, in the latter case, sell them dearer); it has nothing to say about the virtue of having or not having productive employment in the communities within which our lives are rooted.[2]

## II

The division of status and authority between ownership/management and labor, in addition to producing goods and services for our consumption, also necessarily produces disutility within the sphere of production itself.

Within the sphere of production under capitalism, social class relationships are formalized as they are not in the sphere of consumption,
and the realization of well-being for one class inevitably involves the
realization of comparative misfortune for another. Or, to put it
another way, within the sphere of production the people who determine the contours of "efficiency" are not the same people who
experience the results of that determination. And although capitalist
enterprises may compete to see which can give potential consumers
the best life—in the very narrowest sense of that phrase—they rarely
compete to see which can give its workers the best life; quite the contrary: unless "best" is defined as most conducive to profit-making for
the employer.

Thus, to take an example that is obscured by most rhetoric about
the costs of environmental protection, in the case of many external
diseconomies of a firm's operation, it is almost certain that the corporate directors themselves are not in a position to bear any of the
burdens of the diseconomy they create. If pollution kills fish, that is
not in streams or lakes that the directors (or top management) fish in.
If the air around an industrial plant becomes unbreathable, that is not
air that those same directors and top managers (and absentee owners) are going to have to breathe for more than a few seconds a day.
If improperly disposed wastes breed serious toxic effect for generations after their disposal, we can be sure that those wastes have not
been disposed of where those who made the policy decisions about
disposal live.

Contrarily, the neighborhoods that are seriously affected by these
kinds of externalities are precisely the neighborhoods that most of the
workers at a particular plant reside in. We can offer as an almost
unquestionable hypothesis that the lower down in a job hierarchy, the
more likely is a given worker to be directly subject to any destructive
diseconomies of its operations.

We cannot leap from this observation to an automatic conclusion
that if there were no such division of authority in a plant external
diseconomies would be abolished.[3] But one thing is certain: the
necessary calculations of cost and benefit would be made quite differently by people who knew that they themselves would bear the full
costs of whatever they decide. People's decisions as to what constitutes the efficiency of production, therefore, will be entirely different

depending on whether or not they belong to a social class that lives without having to bear the social consequences of its own actions.

Similarly, the appropriation by capital and its representatives of special powers to determine the conditions of production, and (subject only to occasional regulation by the state) to define the best working conditions for a given process, has a differential impact on the way we experience capitalism's efficiency.

As with absentee ownership's right to appropriate and denude communities of capital, or to replace skilled laborers with machinery, it is apparent here that the sense in which managerial prerogative makes for social efficiency is again a very limited sense. Given an arranged division of labor by which ordinary workers are deprived of all integrated knowledge of the productive process, of course management will always be able to argue that its analysis of the conditions of improved productivity (probably the only available analysis) is correct.

But this way of considering the issue begs the question. Increased productivity raises profits and thus—given a certain political or sectoral strength of labor—wages. Wages, however, are not an end in themselves, but a means to an end. From the worker's point of view, that end is "the good life," or at least as good a life as can be lived while being a worker. The largest part of that life, good or otherwise, is lived away from the workplace and tends to be defined wholly as the purchase of various kinds of satisfaction by means of one's wages. But another large part of that life—on the average, half of most people's waking hours—is lived on the job or at the workplace itself. Although the wages one gets are to some extent a valid index of the kind of life one will be able to lead away from work, they are in no way a valid indicator of the relative pleasures or pains to be obtained during those many hours spent at work.

Furthermore, efficiency in this particular instance is measured by different standards not only for different social classes, but also for different groups of workers (as those of different races or sexes). A workplace hierarchy in which white male workers are relatively privileged and black workers disprivileged may seem useful to employers, and may marginally maximize the utilities of the whites; yet it is also likely to diminish overall social utility, by obstructing potential increases in demand, or creating resistances to what would otherwise be progressive changes in workplace organization. Similarly, a healthy and safe workplace for men is not necessarily a healthy and safe workplace for women (and their potential offspring); working arrangements that are convenient for men are not necessarily convenient for women who have children. Since, moreover, the putative children of women in this situation are also putative future citizens, a social order that permits them to incur some of these risks, or takes no care for their well-being while their mothers are working, is depleting its future human resources, in some cases at an appalling cost. Employers who take advantage of female workers' greater productivity (which is usually nothing more than their inability to avoid working at lower wages than do men at the same jobs), but are unwilling to pay the costs of accommodating their particular human requirements, degrade a significant part of the social order in the name of the narrow standard of efficiency.[4]

In all these various ways, then, social well-being is fractured rather than unitary. Even the way in which capitalist economic theory teaches us to think about "inflation" reinforces this dissolution of social utility. Let us remember that, according to neoclassical economic theory, although raising wages without correspondingly raising productivity is inflationary, that is only the case when the wage increase is received as an increment to one's buying power in a marketplace for goods or services which has not itself expanded. Wage increases in the form of a better work life or physical environment are not necessarily inflationary, therefore; they are only inflationary if workers or management choose to pay for the improvement not by cutting back on excess profits but by raising the price of their goods. If all workplaces everywhere at once were democratized and humanized, conditions of work and reward equalized, and external diseconomies brought under some control; and if in most cases prices were raised to accommodate this change, that would by definition be an inflationary event. But in that case how could we call the resulting inflation inefficient, or unproductive, since it would merely result from a determination by economic actors that, given the various purposes of their economic activities, they had been undercharging for their goods or services in the first place?

The cases of external diseconomies and working conditions are thus the obverse of each other. In the first case the nonwork lives of most members of "a firm" are excluded from consideration when efficiency is to be assessed; in the second, their lives at the workplace

are excluded. The net result is the same. The market ideology of efficiency that most of us accept as a given, so defines its subject as to
exclude from its ambit, arbitrarily, the vital interests and needs of an
entire class of citizens, wherever those needs and interests conflict
with the pursuit of profit by a much smaller class of owners and
managers.

Moreover, my distinction between those various forms of conflict
within the capitalist division of labor has been entirely artificial, as can
be seen in one exemplary instance. The displacement of labor in the
coal mines by giant power shovels (aboveground) and automatic continuous mining machines (underground) has been destructive of
those American communities that used to find work in the mines, by
robbing their inhabitants of local opportunities for employment.
Aboveground, largescale strip mining denudes yet other communities
of their ecological support systems. Underground, continuous mining
also threatens greatly to increase the incidence of black lung disease
(from the dust stirred up by the perpetual running of the machines)
and of serious accident as well. The machines not only create a new
kind of danger from their tremendous vibratory power, and not only
create new electrical hazards in the mines, they also rob experienced
coal miners of the early warning signals of danger that their own
senses of touch and hearing used to provide them with. Though mining has always been thought of as an extreme social situation, it is
extreme only in the physical effects of these phenomena, not in the
extent of their interrelationship. This is what can happen when technological progress is defined by a dominant class, to the exclusion of
any input by the people most directly affected (except on those infre-
quent occasions when the interests of the two groups actually coin-
cide).[5]

In sum, the efficiency of free market economy is a very peculiar
kind of "efficiency." It is defined solely with respect to the most narrow range of human capabilities and rewards—marginal differences
in our consumption patterns. That definition shuts out as though
they did not exist the actual range of values which, for most people,
economic activity is ultimately intended to serve. There are many
cases in which the free market in capital imposes inefficiencies of a
broad, destructive kind—of class, caste, and regional inequality—on
specific localities; and it is specifically the capitalist division of labor
that creates, allocates, and renders people defenseless against these

inefficiencies. Even from the standpoint of maximizing overall social utility—a standpoint which capitalists invariably claim as their own—the sphere of production becomes an arena of group self-protection, and sometimes internecine warfare; rather than one in which the most socially desireable mix of productive effort and worktime allocated to it, can be rationally agreed on by all.

## III

Additionally, the capitalist division of labor brings about, again as a concomitant of its normal operations, a massive misallocation of resources. As Harry Braverman has shown, from the beginning of the era of modern monopoly capitalism—the era in which the national and then multinational corporate form has extended its sway over all sectors of economic activity—the proportion of workers engaged in essentially unproductive activity, whether within the industrial, agricultural, and extractive sectors themselves, or through the development of an ever-burgeoning commercial sector attached to them, has risen sharply as a proportion of all workers. As he puts it, the servant of a capitalist is not "a productive worker, even though employed by the capitalist, because the labor of the servant is exchanged not against capital but against *revenue*. The capitalist who hires servants is not making profits but spending them."[6]

We would have no doubts about the meaning of this metaphor if we thought of the "servant" as a valet, hired by the capitalist out of profits, and thus paid with money that could otherwise have been reinvested in the business. In this literal application of the metaphor the capitalist begins to imitate the feudal lord with his parasitic retinue. But suppose that instead of a valet, butler, footman, etc., the capitalist hires (1) a patent lawyer, an industrial spy, an overseas representative, a public relations consultant, an advertising agency, a market analyst; or (2) a personnel director, an industrial psychologist, a floor supervisor, a cost accountant, a labor relations department, an administrative staff to keep a paper record of productive activity; or (3) a tax lawyer, a financial advisor, an investment counsellor.

None of these people are actually increasing the amount of product generated by the setting in motion of a given capital. Their jobs are various, but have *un*productivity in common. The first group of employees from the aforementioned list is put in place to help the firm market its product, whether locally, nationally, or internationally, in competition with other similar firms and products; or to take over or merge with other firms to the end of increasing combined joint pro- fit margins. The purpose of these people is not to stimulate produc- tion or to increase the productivity of labor as applied to machinery (that is the function of engineers, technical analysts, etc.), but rather to protect a firm's market share, or displace some other firm's share, for any given amount of product. They move into action only after productive efficiency has already been maximized relative to a given input of labor and technique.

All of this pseudolabor has come to seem somehow natural and necessary to us, but it is only natural to and necessitated by a market economy characterized by a particular division of labor. With respect to the question of efficiency, that is, the group of administrative employees engaged in the struggle for and rationalization of markets do what they do because the anarchically competitive character of the capitalist market system requires their activity to give it a semblance of stability and security; not because their jobs are a given of advanced technology.[7]

The claim that this kind of activity increases overall social utility is, in principle, no different from the claim that we can increase gross national product by first introducing a poison into all water supplies, then engaging in a crash program to train and employ millions of doctors, pollution control experts, filter operators, toxicologists, etc. All of that massive new investment would certainly lead to a vast jump in GNP, but we would not dream of saying that social utility had been increased, or economic efficiency maximized, without first mak- ing an independent judgment as to whether we had really needed to poison our water supplies in the first place. The concept of efficiency could not even be addressed coherently except in that normative context—a context which many actors within the capitalist division of labor work very hard (and expensively) to prevent us from ever consid- ering.

As for the second group of jobs from the above list, they share a different purpose, but one also having little to do with productivity or efficiency in the conventional sense. On the one hand, the purpose of many of these jobs is to enforce political rather than technical discip- line. Except where labor is extraordinarily docile, or where the ground rules of capitalism have been departed from far enough as to give self-administering work teams a great deal of cooperative control over their own job performance (as to some extent at, e.g., Volvo in Sweden), costly hostility potentially exists between the classes of those who work on or with capital and those who own or manage or control it. Thus some of those jobs—though many, many more of them in the U.S. than in, say, Japan, which requires far fewer supervisory personnel to get the job of production done—exist for no other reason than to police, mitigate, or otherwise cool down that potential hostility. This kind of supervisory and personnel management activity conduces to efficiency only if we demand this kind of division of labor and thus this variant of class conflict in the first place. As long as both the social division of labor and the technical division of labor separate social classes from each other morally and physically, then as Marx wrote "capital is constantly compelled to wrestle with the insubordination of the workmen." It is a costly wrestling match, nor does capital always win it, a fact reflected in the costs of sabotage, absenteeism, strikes, working-to-rule, alcohol and drug abuse, and all the other outcomes of sublimated resistance that appear at their most costly wherever the ground rules of the capitalist division of labor are most stringently followed.

As for the third category of jobs, they are truly an immense elaboration of the role of the lord's valet; and courtier, and jester, and bailiff. It is astonishing to reflect on how many jobs and institutions exist only because there are wealthy individuals or private firms to pay for them; and how much the costs of social services in general are distorted by the private market of the corporate rich for housing, legal, medical, and financial services, first-class transportation opportunities, education, leisure, and so on. In a tidal wave of lavishness, there comes into being a sumptuous class, extending far beyond the mere capitalist class in its numbers, that lives by devoting its services, for excessive fees, to the class that lives off the surplus. This sumptuous class exists not because of normal human intercourse but in spite of it; it exists only because of the sheer immensity (amounting in the U.S. to hundreds of billions of dollars a year) of freely disposed profit.

In addition, because of the power of corporate wealth to define the conditions of prestigious and sometimes simply acceptable service, the providers of these services must strive to have their activity take on the same character as it has in its most luxurious and bureaucratized form. Services that could be inexpensively distributed on a voluntary or cooperative basis are turned into commodities distributed by immensely expensive bureaucracies. The cost of these

activities, from the expense-account lunch to big-time college athlet-
ics to the endless duplication of computerized office services, can
only be measured in the billions of dollars each year in the American
economy. The result is a skewed cost-benefit curve, in which the tail
(the expenditures of the wealthy on their services) wags the dog (the
expenditures of the rest of us).

# IV

To put all these points, summarily, another way, it is true that, in the
aggregate, the so-called "law of supply and demand" that is the stuff
of capitalist economic theory really does work. Prices rise when
demand exceeds supply, and vice versa. However, the demand that is
spoken of so casually is not, in capitalist societies, the demand of
individual human beings. It is the demand of organized economic
resources, the unequal distribution of which is primarily determined
by the unequal distribution of capital; by the laws of ownership and
control, and the associated customs of reward and distribution. No
particular relationship of demand to supply, or of needs to the willingness and ability to work, is inevitable; all such relationships are particularly dependent on the public laws, not inexorable scientific laws, of
political economy.

   One concrete example out of the many thousands we could
choose will illustrate the reality of economic relationships, or laws.
For many years a gigantic office building in the center of London
stood virtually empty while its owner, who had built it out of the profits
made from other speculative ventures in real estate, waited to find a
single tenant willing to rent the whole building, meanwhile taking a
useful tax loss on his failure to get a return on his property. The peculiar tax laws of corporate capitalism had an effect on the history of
Centre Point, but only to the extent of supporting its owner in his
obsessive desire to rent it to a single tenant. Without the help of those
laws, he would simply have rented some though not all of the single
offices to whomever would take them, perhaps taking a loss, but one
that given the rest of his resources he could easily afford. The building site would still have been unavailable to homeless human beings.
(In fact he finally did do this).

One would assume from what neoclassical economists say that there must have been a greater demand for office space in London than for housing at the time that Centre Point (as it is called) was built. Yet we know that that is not so, since there are now and were then thousands of desperately homeless families in London, and apparently an unexpected shortage of luxury office-building tenants. Had the latter existed, though, their "demand" for the building would have been much greater, expressed monetarily, than that of any number of prospective low-income tenants, since they possess capital which is so much more valuable than mere wages (or welfare payments). The human demand for housing exists, but cannot be expressed with appropriate sums of money, and therefore it does not exist. It is not, as economists would say in their evasive language, "effective demand." The law of supply and demand, then, means that the needs of those without ample resources get subordinated to the desires of those who have plentiful resources. Nothing about this comparison requires an arbitrary moralistic definition of need, either. All we mean by it is that a place to live is something that a person without a home must have (in our kind of civilization), and for which there is no substitute; whereas a new office, while more pleasing to its tenants than an old or overcrowded one, is not something they must have, and is something for which they can easily find a substitute.

A scenario which makes this distinction between economic demand and human need graphically clear is one in which we ask ourselves this question. What would have happened had we offered some homeless or slum-dwelling families on the one hand, and the corporate inhabitants of a slightly outdated office building on the other, the (then-vacant) site of Centre Point with either housing or office space to be built on it: the property to be conceived of as a prize to be rewarded to whoever would work at helping to build it six days a week, ten hours a day, for five years without vacation (a sort of urban homesteading act, in effect)? Can there be any doubt who would have won that prize, that is, who would have turned out to have the greatest demand if we measured it by human effort rather than by financial resources? And can there be any doubt that in every capitalist society there are a hundred, a thousand, a million Centre Points; that immense and proliferating waste, rather than the rational husbanding and development of resources, is the capitalist way of life?

We are all cognizant of the counterargument, that any equalizing change in the capitalist division of labor would—since capitalist economies already operate at what must be a peak of productivity—have the effect of cutting into profit levels, which are the market's more-or-less accurate indicators of the tax we must levy against current income on behalf of the future. In this perspective, the drive to profit only secondarily distributes wealth and income; primarily, and necessarily, it spurs and disciplines the very economic activity we all depend on even while some of us (such as myself) are excoriating its effects. Without profit, there can be no investment. Without the appropriate rate of profit, there cannot be an appropriate rate of rein- vestment. Above all, the class that lives by creating opportunities for and appropriating profit is the only class that can be relied on to seek and maintain appropriate profit levels, since that is its business—its life. If workers, as in my earlier discussion of workplace humanization and control, were to have to choose between cutting profit or cutting current consumption in order to realize their goals, they would cut profit—since that is not the kind of return that their class lives by—and would gradually bring about net social disinvestment; they would run society down in the service of raising wages and thus consumption. The rate of profit therefore indexes general social utility appropriately.

That argument is clearly circular: capitalists are only the class that lives by maintaining profits, and workers by maintaining wage levels, as long as we live in a capitalist society. Since we are raising the pos- sibility of living in a different kind of society, it is pointless to characterize people by the traits they exhibit in this one. But there is more to be said on the subject of profit, who earns it, and what is done with it. Profits in fact are but one form taken by the overall social surplus that must be created if progressive economic behavior is to be possible. In confusing surplus in general with profits in particular we not only hypostatize the ground rules of capitalism; we fail to understand the real function of capitalist profits beyond their serving as an incentive to save.

Profit, or the claim which capitalists make on the returns, consists not only of investment in the largest sense, but also of the excess con- sumption of the capitalist class; and not only of the capitalist class, but also, as I have noted above, of all those well-paid servants of capi- tal who would not exist as such in a different social order; and not only of the servants of capital, but as well of all those workers who staff the institutions that have been created to serve the needs primarily of corporate capital and personal wealth. That is why the standard exercise in which defenders of the status quo divide up the after-tax income of millionaires and show that, as a social dividend, it would add hardly anything to the income of all individual wage earners, misses the point. It is not millionaires who siphon off income that could be better spent by the rest of the public, but rather the structure of monopolistic and oligopolistic private capital that distorts the income flow; in particular that aspect of the structure which permits the disposition of profit to be largely uncontrolled. For this reason it is quite true that there are diminishing marginal returns to the redistribution of income in capitalist societies, and these are reached pretty quickly (though the immense difference between levels of poverty in the U.S. and in Sweden demonstrates that even in capitalist societies, important redistribution is possible). To speak of a democratized division of labor is to speak not of the redistribution of income, but of the reordering of the economic institutions that generate income for distribution in the first place.

Not only does capital misappropriate profit to its own use from the standpoint of other citizens; it also allocates and thus potentially misallocates what is reinvested for the future. The potential for misallocation is immense. The controllers of capital and thus the distributors of profit compete with each other to make the most attractive payout to shareholders (and bondholders). The competitiveness of the promised payout, however, is measured relative only to the short-term gains to be realized. Unless some public planning agency is entrusted with effective power to do so, no capitalist institution exists to compel the subordination of short-term to long-term rationality. When spokesmen for a corporate giant such as Exxon, with more after-tax profit (in absolute dollars) to distribute than any other economic institution in the world, complain that profits are too low to support needed reinvestment, they mean rather that there are more promising short-term gains to be realized elsewhere. There is no one to make them represent the public's interest in the long run, so capital flows willy-nilly.

Thus, aside from a fragile expansion in government employment, most of the jobs created by the logic of the capitalist division of labor in the U.S.during the 1970s were in the relatively low-paying service sector, while other jobs that could have been created were exported elsewhere. The effect of most of that activity was to spend surplus rather than to regenerate it, and so to depress the average wage and the average standard of living of Americans (without significantly bettering the lives of peoples elsewhere).

Given this total structure, arguments about whether capital needs an average rate of return of 6 percent or 12 percent or 20 percent to insure an appropriate level of reinvestment, are frivolous. It is impossible to separate out those portions of the profit of, say, Exxon that go to needed reinvestment in energy resources and development; the purchase at inflated prices of competing energy resources (totally useless from a social standpoint); the building of luxury real estate developments; the rearrangement of assets to take advantage of tax codes; the subsidization of grotesquely expensive and socially pointless television commercials; or the fees of the surgeons, attorneys, accountants, etc., who service Exxon's major shareholders, executives, and their families. What is certain, however, is, again, that unfathomable wasting of resources is built into this structure, in the fundamental sense that ordinary people equally and consciously setting out to plan their own lives in a situation of uncertain and limited resources would make the lowest possible priority of all such expenditures. None of these expenditures add pleasure to the average life; many of them are concealed taxes on it.

It is rational that investment capital that might otherwise be earmarked for resource development will indeed flow into luxury real estate or fast-food chains if the latter promise a greater flow of short-term profit. But that is an indictment of how the market works, not an explanation of it. Most of those alternate channels are the creatures of monopoly capital itself, not of human nature or voluntary collective human endeavor. In their absence, the claims on profit as a proportion of total product, and thus the need for it, would be considerably less than we think necessary. The rationality of the free market for capital is a purely internal, shortsighted rationality; it has nothing to do with what any group of thoughtful, disinterested, and informed people would be willing to consider worthy of the name. Capitalists are no more guaranteed than anyone else to allocate capital wisely. Their track record is better than that of commissars and aristocrats, but is hardly so impressive that we must despair of finding alternative ways of doing their work.

# V

At the same time that the capitalist way of life inflates the claim of profits on the total social product, it often also, and just as seriously, inflates the claim of wages (that is, of workers as opposed to owners). Thus the capitalist division of labor multiplies its own (and our) difficulties. The reason is the directness of class conflict under capitalism, even at its most subdued (or subjugated). Workers of all kinds, and owners, are different classes of people making competing class claims on the same product. But whereas workers represent the claims of the present on that product, owners, who by economic theory are said to represent the claims of the future, also speak for extremely differentiated and palpably greedy and parasitic claims on the present as well.

In the abstract, it is undoubtedly true that a society cannot live beyond its means, that "sufficient unto the day is the evil thereof" is a self-destructive slogan, that "waste not want not" is sensible policy. But owners, or governments representing them, cannot in good faith make those arguments unless they practice, as they rarely do, their own self-restraint as a class. As for workers, they need never confront their own responsibility for the future, since in legal fact they have none, having been separated from the means of production and thus from any obligation to "take care" for them. (In that respect almost all contemporary economies share a fundamental, built-in irrationality.) The competition between the claims of present and future appears instead as a competition for rewards or power between classes, marked by envy, bitterness, and spite. For a while this wasteful competition, which is the sole underlying cause of continuing inflation in capitalist societies, may be dampened down, as class relations are constrained by a temporary spirit of compromise or by sheer coercion. But except where remnants of traditional culture severely constrain expressions of purely utilitarian behavior, no class compromise—formal or informal—can be expected to last for long, once tested by external or internal strain. If the only public philosophy unthreatening to the ruling class is that more is better than less, faster is better than slower, and bigger is better than smaller, we will all ultimately insist on the application of that philosophy as the criterion for judging the performance of all social institutions.

Contrarily, workers as owners, that is to say as citizens, would have to confront the conflicting claims of present and future; would have to respect the natural rate of profit in the form of a reasonable set of expectations about the needs of the future. If they had the responsibility to do that, they might be much more willing to practice conservation, thrift, and the husbandry of resources, than is now the case; for now they are constantly bargaining in a purely self-interested way with an opposed class who, having that responsibility all to themselves, quite evidently make little credible effort to carry it out. As R.H. Tawney remarked over half a century ago, "Eminent persons who are not obviously producing more than they consume explain to the working classes that unless they produce more, they must consume less."[8] That discrepancy rarely goes unnoticed. Economic crises must be far advanced indeed, or a tradition of class collaboration well established, or the repeal of democratic rights far gone, before the thin will heed the clarion call of the stout to tighten their belts.

## VI

No technological fix exists for any of these dilemmas. In every case technological improvement, while perhaps promising an ultimate increase in overall social well-being, now generates instability and conflict. The source of this paradox, of these actual facts, is not hard to find. Where the ability of a large proportion of a national labor force to take advantage of technological improvement is thwarted either by lack of access to its benefits, or by labor market barriers against putting those benefits to productive use, then class divisions, and racial and sexual divisions as well, must be profoundly deepened. In the presence of that tendency, every further application of economic rationalization, either in the production of goods or in the delivery of services, only makes matters worse.

There is a deeper social reality that lies behind this "actual economic fact." The efficiency or productivity of the capitalist division of labor also necessitates the squandering of an immense amount of human resources for which we all receive no compensation, not even as consumers.

As a long line of business historians have now documented successfully, a good deal of so-called technical innovation has been introduced and adopted by workplace managers, not for the purposes of improving productivity, but for the quite different purpose of reproducing social class divisions within the workplace, so that the technical division of labor there comes to replicate the social division of labor between owners and workers.[9] So it is ensured that the owners of firms, and their hired managers, do not lose control of the production process to those skilled and potentially knowledgeable workers who actually do the productive work.

The contemporary version of job creation, which seems now to be endemic in almost all capitalist societies, thus casts an ironic light on the classical notion that economic progress sloughs off unattractive, unproductive jobs by substituting machinery for them. On the contrary, expensive machinery is on the whole substituted for expensive workers; cheap workers are very desirable for capital:

> The paradox that the most rapidly growing mass occupations in an era of scientific-technical revolution are those which have least to do with science and technology need not surprise us. The purpose of machinery is not to increase but to decrease the number of workers attached to it. Thus it is by no means illogical that with the development of science and technology, the numbers of those cheaply available for dancing attendance upon capital in all of its least mechanized functional forms continues to increase at a rapid pace.[10]

Thus, egalitarians who find themselves embarrassed by the question, "Who will do the 'dirty work' in the good society?," should begin their answer by asking instead, "Who will do the 'dirty work' in capitalist society?" On the whole the answer is women, minorities, and foreigners; an answer which puts the contention that the capitalist division of labor maximizes social utility or overall welfare in a somewhat different perspective. The class structure of capitalism is becoming, just as Marx (prematurely) thought it would, a fetter on the productive forces it encompasses.

The traditional, skilled (white male) proletariat is in severe decline in advanced capitalist societies, and a new, only questionably productive white-collar proletariat is on the rise, but those societies continue to reproduce the proletariat, or persons prepared to be nothing but proletarians, as though that were still the motor force of production in a post-industrial or knowledge society. What is reproduced and perhaps even enlarged, therefore, is an obsolescent class that is only prepared to do relatively unproductive labor which is constantly in danger of being eliminated; and relatively unprepared to do what could be genuinely productive labor if production were socially planned. This obsolescent proletariat and reserve army of labor, moreover, is socially costly to reproduce and maintain far beyond the productive capacities of proletarian labor in advanced capitalist societies; especially because of its skewed class, racial, and gender composition. This fact is the root cause of what conventional economists designate as rising structural unemployment—a phenomenon which their theoretical model is unable to explain.

At the same time, the knowledge class, the class that through its activities could be creating the mode of production of the future, is fettered by the obsolescent social relations of capitalism. Waste is its most salient product; its collective trained intelligence is used only grudgingly by capital, with little attempt either to enlarge it at a rational pace, or to put it to work to develop the new mode of production in as coherent and useful a manner as possible.[11] The proletariat, or at the very least its children, ought to be joining the knowledge class, that is, applying its own intellectual abilities to the organization of production, and thus expanding the sphere of the new technology, in planned conjunction with the phasing out of the old technology. Because capitalists, even with the state at their partial command, cannot plan in this way (because they cannot produce for use rather than for the skewed and distorted marketplace) the fetters on production and on social reproduction remain. This thesis may seem similar to the notion of "stalemate" in capitalist societies as developed by such analysts as Michel Crozier, Felix Rohaytn, and Daniel Bell. It should be emphasized, however, that those and similar critiques share the characteristic of attributing "stalemate" to an obsolete and irrational class-struggle mentality; and their gist is invariably that if the major economic interest groups—especially organized labor—would but overcome their irrational fixations on the past and understand the need for a new "austerity," or even a religious revival, then the stalemate could be overcome and capitalist reconstruction could begin.[12] Needless to say, egalitarian social analysis does not begin with a call for the working class to discipline itself (or be disciplined). Rather the version of stalemate I have developed here emphasizes the costly obsolescence of social relations of domination and subordination, competition and exclusion: of capitalism itself. And my purpose in the opening chapter of this book was to sketch the outlines of a democratic mass movement that might unchain those fetters.

What stands behind all these considerations, of course, is the larger, the fundamental question: do we really believe that the great majority of people are incapable of mustering the intelligence and mastering the skills necessary to take responsibility for the productive use of labor-saving machinery? It is not possible to make even a marginally relevant statement about the efficiency of the capitalist division of labor without reflecting at length on all the implications of that question.

We must remember that it is not nature or the distribution of human capital but the designers of the corporate capitalist system and its component parts who have established the categories of manager and laborer, expert and layman, as necessarily consisting of the few and the many. What version of social wellbeing or productivity is allegedly maximized when we economize on training people to do the most rewarding job they could possibly do?

The question is rhetorical. But let us suppose for a moment that all those children who are very predictably going to grow up to be dominated by the short-run perspectives that Edward Banfield calls the hallmark of "the lower class," were, from a very early age, indentured, with the cooperation of their parents or guardians, to a major corporation. The terms of the agreement would be as follows: in return for regular attendance and satisfactory performance at schools chosen by their future employer, and peer association limited to those similarly indentured, they would be guaranteed entry to a high-level training program or professional school (or both). Short of adhering to one of the intellectually dubious theories of genetic determination that have recently attained currency, can anyone doubt that the number of people turning out to be qualified to do professional or executive work at some level would be enormously increased?[13] As a democrat, I do not propose indentured servitude as a substitute for the "free labor" market; I offer this modest proposal merely to provide a stark illustration of the difference between the effects of "nature" and of social convention. The capitalist labor market stands for a reduction rather than a maximization of the potential amount and variety of human intelligence to be applied to the solution of technical and organizational problems. We concentrate on developing the capacities of a minority to the utmost, and neglect the chance to develop the capacities of the majority. This practice proceeds in the name of economizing; but the belief that we can possibly be maximizing overall social intelligence, and thus overall social utility in this way is better classified as a bizarre superstition.

## VII

Is it possible to induce people to work as hard as they need in order to get what they want in any other manner? That is the real question. In the end, the shaky ground upon which all defenses of the rationality of the capitalist division of labor finally stand, is that only exposure to a risky labor market that may equally reward or penalize them, will get people to work as hard as they ought to.

This grimly practical and moral theory (if you don't work you won't eat) would, perhaps, work as well as any other or maybe even better: if it could be put into practice. But all our history—the collective history of the industrial world—shows that it cannot. No people have tolerated the free market in labor for more than a few years at a time without undertaking to hamstring it with varieties of protective legislation or trade union organization. That is not because modern men and women are faithless to the work ethic. Rather, the work ethic as a capitalist ethic is too visibly indefensible: too obviously betrayed by the class arrangements of capitalism, which ensure that on the whole the harder one works in terms of sheer physical effort, the less one earns; and that the people with the most are the ones who actually work the least.

Capitalism therefore persists not by the faithful adherence of its public and private servants to its principles, but instead by muddling along, mixing the discipline of the market with the cajoling of welfarist and planning institutions in the varying degrees visible in the liberal capitalist world. None of these mixtures is working extraordinarily well at the moment; none gives strong promise of leading us to a better way of life, or even a more materially pleasurable one. Those societies—namely the U.S. and Great Britain—most tolerant of the free labor market's sheer savagery toward those in an unfavorable market position, are hardly advertisements for it. Paradoxically, it is almost certainly the case that only in a more egalitarian society that had displaced envy as a primary social attitude, tamed profit to visibly social uses, and provided a level of fundamental welfare sufficient to allow every person an equal opportunity to make use of equal opportunity, could a genuine work ethic be the popular norm. Particular national economies may manifest countertendencies for a while; but now economic and social well-being, let alone the search for democracy, require a solution to the problem of the contemporary division of labor. That solution will be either imposed in its authoritarian form of coerced class compromise and the supersession of class interest by the development (again) of aggressively nationalistic identifications; or it will come about as the result of the search for a more democratic way of life.

## Notes

[1] See for example Herbert C. Reid, "Appalachian Policy, The Corporate State, and American Values: A Critical Perspective," *Policy Studies Journal*, vol. 9 no. 4 (1980–81), pp. 622–33; Henry D. Shapiro, *Appalachia on Our Mind* (Chapel Hill: University of North Carolina Press, 1978); and John Gaventa, *Power and Powerlessness* (Chicago: University of Illinois Press, 1980). The definitive study of regional misallocation in capitalist societies is Stuart Holland, *Capital Versus the Regions* (London: MacMillan, 1976).

[2] On "capital flight," see Barry Bluestone and Bennett Harrison, *Capital and Communities: The Causes and Consequences of Private Disinvestment* (Washington, D.C.: Institute for Policy Studies, 1980). See also *Shutdown: Economic Dislocation and Equal Opportunity*, a report prepared by the Illinois Advisory Committee to the United States Commission on Civil Rights, June 1981. The study points out that capital flight also aggravates barriers of caste, as minorities suffer from its consequences disproportionately.

[3] But for an argument that does attempt to persuade us of this, see Hugh Stretton, *Capitalism, Socialism, and the Environment* (New York: Cambridge University Press, 1976).

[4] For an overview, see Carolyn Teich Adams and Kathryn Teich Winston, *Mothers at Work* (New York: Longman, 1980).

[5] I am indebted for this account to Duane Lockard of Princeton University, who is engaged in a full-length study of the history and politics of coal mining in the United States. See also Michael Yarrow, "The Labor Process in Coal Mining: Struggle for Control," in Andrew Zimbalist, ed., *Case Studies in the Labor Process* (New York: Monthly Review Press, 1979), pp. 170–192.

[6] Harry Braverman, *Labor and Monopoly Capital* (New York: Monthly Review Press, 1974), ch. 10, and pp. 411–12.

[7] Of course not only capitalism is characterized by swollen, unproductive bureaucracies. So is Communism or state socialism, even more so, but its bureaucracy is of a different nature, being populated instead by planners and their entourages, party cadres, middlemen and expediters, etc. This conquest of Communism by authoritarian and exceedingly wasteful bureaucratism is a sign of how incomplete has been its separation not only from the statism which preceded it (in the Soviet Union especially) but also from the capitalist world system and mode of production.

[8] R.H. Tawney, *The Acquisitive Society* (New York: Harcourt, Brace, 1920), p. 130.

[9] See David F. Noble, *America by Design* (New York: Knopf, 1977); and Alfred Chandler, *The Visible Hand* (Cambridge: Harvard University Press, 1977). See also

Stephen A. Marglin, "What Do Bosses Do? The Origins and Functions of Hierarchy in Capitalist Production," in *The Review of Radical Political Economics,* vol. 6 no. 2 (Summer 1974), pp. 60–112, and Katherine Stone, "The Origins of Job Structures in the Steel Industry," ibid., pp. 113–73.

[10] Braverman, p. 384. Robin Blackburn and Michael Mann, in *The Worker in the Labor Market* (London: MacMillan, 1979), note on p. 280 that 87 percent of several hundred workers studied by them in one job market "exercise less skill at work than they would if they drove to work. Indeed, most of them expend more mental effort and resourcefulness in getting to work than in doing their jobs."

[11] I take the term "knowledge class" from Fritz Machlup, *The Production and Distribution of Knowledge in the United States* (Princeton: Princeton University Press, 1962).

[12] See Michel Crozier, *The Stalled Society,* trans. by Rupert Swyer (New York: Viking Press, 1974); Felix Rohaytn, "Reconstructing America," *New York Review of Books,*, 28, (March 5, 1981), pp. l6ff; and in a different vein, Daniel Bell, *The Cultural Contradictions of Capitalism,* (New York: Basic Books, 1976). My own notion of stalemate has been put very well by Fred Block and Larry Hirschorn: ". . . the transition to a post-industrial society creates a profound social crisis: contemporary capitalism is ripe for a transition to post-industrial society, but existing social relations block the release of new productive forces, creating social and economic stalemate." See their "New Productive Forces and The Contradictions of Contemporary Capitalism: A Post-Industrial Perspective," *Theory and Society,* vol. 7 no. 3 (1979), p. 364. A similar argument is made by Alan Wolfe, *The Limits of Legitimacy* (New York: Free Press, 1977), Part II. Block and Hirschorn, and Wolfe emphasize, as I do, the necessity of a mass movement to undo the paralysis to which we are now subjected.

[13] Edward C. Banfield, *The Unheavenly City Revisited* (Boston: Little, Brown, 1974), ch. 3. For a critique of the erroneous notion that IQ testing has demonstrated the existence of group variations in human intelligence that are both immense *and* innate, see Philip Green, *The Pursuit of Inequality*, (New York: Pantheon Books, 1981),chs. 2–4, and Stephen J. Gould, *The Mismeasure of Man* (New York: W.W. Norton, 1981).

# 4

# CONSTRAINED INEQUALITY

---

## I

The problem I have identified in describing the contradictory social structure of capitalism is, in short, the problem of inequality: that rational social planning, a rational pace of technological innovation, and rational distribution of the social product and the labor needed to produce it, are impossible among unequals. Contrarily, the self-presentation of capitalism, through its philosophers and ideologists, is that whatever its shortcomings, the capitalist division of labor is the outcome of the interplay among impersonal market forces; that it in a sense represents the collective wisdom of a population whose members express that wisdom by putting different prices on different forms of labor.

Let us consider the credibility of this story (for that is what it is) by contemplating instead a different story. What might happen if we all could come together (in a collective meeting place rather than through an impersonal market) to decide, democratically, on the structure of incentives and rewards we should create in order to ensure that our society could be as productive as possible without being humanly unpleasant? The first rule of procedure, obviously, would have to be that no one should be coerced by the force of arms or the pains of social circumstances into doing a job that others were unwilling to do. That is simply to define what we can mean by a truly free agreement about what is truly rational among a population of people with equal opportunity to make determinative economic choices.

The question is, do we think we would agree, if we all had an equal voice, to create a society in which corporate managers, baseball players, lawyers engaged in the furtherance of business competition, and sellers of pieces of paper conveying the right to draw dividends from a business, were rewarded with 20 to 50 times the income of skilled craftspersons? Would we unanimously agree (or even a majority agree) to make immense distinctions between wage labor and salaried work, so that anyone doing the former must be inhibited and restricted in the enjoyment of various aspects of social life by comparison with anyone doing the latter? Would we agree that some people should receive thousands of times what others do without doing any work at all? Would the people themselves replicate the present distribution of incentives and rewards if they were able to start over again from an advanced base of industrial and commercial activity, and if all jobs had to be filled voluntarily?

These questions, being rhetorical, are unanswerable. Anyone can believe anything by way of answer to them. But there are some general principles and some concrete examples worth reflecting on just the same.

To begin with, class differences, except at the extremes, have much less to do with income than they do with the nature of one's relationship to work itself. At the extremes, a wealthy person can buy the services of others to do his or her unpleasant tasks; a very poor person will be unable to avoid doing those tasks for a very low rate of pay. But what makes for class differences among the nonrich and the nonpoor is that some jobs or occupations carry with them the opportunity for being one kind of social person rather than another. Those who work with flexible working hours, have input into the definition of their own job, have regular access to higher decision-making authorities and regular association with others like themselves, and generally are encouraged to take intellectual responsibility, necessarily belong to a different class than those who punch a time clock and are viewed by their employers and society as simply interchangeable wage laborers—no matter what they are paid in a monetary form. A stockbroker who will eventually be paid $100,000 or more a year, and a young graduate doing manuscript editing in a publishing house who may some day rise to an assistant editorship in the twenties of thousands, have much more in common with each other than either has in common with a machinist, though the latter's wage be about equal to the editor's; and both of them are much more likely than the machinist to wind up being someone of significance in a political association, to have a child who becomes a professional, etc. And that is so despite the fact that a machinist may have to have more innate intellectual skill than a person filling either of the educated middle class positions.

Thus the necessity of class is almost invariably mistated by inegalitarians, who concentrate their attention on the secondary matter (except for the very rich and poor) of income differentiation rather than the more fundamental matter of lifestyle differentiation. Clearly, nothing about incentives or rewards or economic practicality would keep us from defining the role of a machinist to include the requirement of some higher education, on-the-job training devoted to enabling him or her to appropriate the entire job process intellectually, the provision of flexible work time, of a salary rather than a wage, participation in democratic decision-making processes at some level of the enterprise, and so on. These are all political aspects of the so-called economic system; to implement or not to implement any one or all of them is a strictly political decision. In that sense we are able to say that if people did have the opportunity to create their own structure of incentives and rewards, there is no reason to believe that the most critical determinants of social class differentiation would seem to them to be part of the merely economic facts of life.

If all jobs provided the opportunity for leading what we nowadays consider both the work style and the life style of an educated middle-class person, then differentiated incentives to do socially differentiated work, if any were necessary, would have to be strictly monetary. We can't say how great they would have to be but we can speculate about their relation to what, in our own society, we accept as rational differentiations. Let us then think about the rewards structure of, say, the coal industry. It is perfectly clear that that industry is always going to need many more miners than sales managers (or executives of any kind). Moreover, the job of the miner is one of the most dangerous and unpleasant that society has to offer, and certainly much more so than that of sales manager. If no one knows to what job he or she is fated beforehand, but rather everyone were truly free to choose, then it would be much harder to find miners than to find people to arrange the distribution of the coal after it is mined. Nor are these considerations countered by the necessities of training and compensation for foregone income for the sales manager.

Again, a fixation on our own way of doing things to the neglect of general possibilities could lead us to misunderstanding. In our society sales managers have five to seven years of higher education and miners generally have none. That is because of the way we have arranged to treat those jobs socially, not because of anything inherent in them. On one hand, there is nothing intellectually inherent in most middle-range executive jobs that couldn't be learned through some combination of business school and executive apprenticeship; the liberal arts education that most middle-level administrators get is a symbol of their social status rather than a genuine prerequisite to it. On the other hand, miners require no higher education or extensive training only because we do not expect them to participate—in fact, prohibit them from participating—in the definition of their job responsibilities, day-to-day decision making, etc. That has to do with the ownership and control of capital, and our philosophy of ownership and control; not with the nature of the job.[1]

In a society in which coal mines were owned publicly and managed democratically, there seems every reason to believe that people choosing freely would pay the miners more than the associated middle-level executive personnel. To be sure, the more democratically organized the economy, the more onerous become the tasks of management, so that oddly enough the necessary wage of the top managers, from a purely functionalist standpoint, might be higher in a socialized than in a privatized economy. That would hardly be true, though, of the writers of ads for cosmetic manufacturers, sales directors for bowling accessory supplies, etc., who in capitalist societies today can earn several times the wage of miners but would surely not be assigned that level of reward if we were really free to choose.

This intellectual exercise, then, is a test of the assertion that the free market merely arranges the doing of what we all really want to do anyway. How far the actuality of what the free market has accomplished is from what would be a recognizably democratic version of choice, is exactly how far we are from having ever really consented to the nondemocratic division of labor we all now live under.

## II

Where, though, should the definition of a society of equals begin? Clearly, if we are seriously interested in political equality we must in some sense or other desire a classless (and genderless) society, that is, a society of citizens who, if they share inequalities, share only those inequalities that do not translate into political stratification. Our purpose has to be to discover what kinds of inequalities are or are not acceptable, given that basic requirement. (This chapter, however, is specifically about class. The question of gender equality is taken up in chapter 5).

The principle I propose is the principle of Constrained Inequality: that whatever work people do should receive roughly the same socially standard reward at similar phases of their life-cycles. If the democratic majority, via whatever techniques are available to it, chooses to reward what it considers to be special merit or effort (see my discussion below) or to provide additional incentives for what it considers to be especially necessary and difficult work, that will be its choice. The democratic principle, however, is the principle of a standard, decent reward for a standard, decent effort. In that way not only would everyone be provided with roughly the same resources for active citizenship, but the inevitable differentials in reward or earning power would appear as a series of deviations from an expected social norm, rather than (as now) proposals for a social norm appearing as deviations from an expected array of sharply differentiated social-class divisions. This is the most meaningful way in which to realize the principle of constrained inequality: and it in turn forms the requisite basis for any labor market that can possibly lead to the fullest possible development of all rather than some.

I do not speak, it must be acknowledged, of absolute equality, of society unmarred by any form of socially differentiated wage labor; just as in the discussion of the democratic division of labor that follows, I do not speak of the abolition of all forms of functional differentiation; of bureaucracy; or of every last vestige of either the social or the technical divisions of labor. It is only with hesitation that I have come to advocate the relatively rather than the absolutely classless society. The simple truth, however, is that strategic reflections about what most people really do desire aside, I do not see how any of us now can meaningfully advocate the creation of what Marx would have

considered a truly classless society: a society in which the revolutionary project of human liberation has been completed.

We must start from where we are. There are certain fundamental,
apparently unavoidable, and in any event historically confirmed
presuppositions that, once we accept them, compel us to adopt a
much less demanding version of relative rather than absolute classlessness:

1. The relationship between people and nature is and will be mediated by complex and rarefied technologies.

2. The relationship between people and the products they create,
and thus between producers and consumers is necessarily mediated
by intermediate organs of distribution and valuation.

3. The relationship between people and their neighbors is not on
the whole one of face-to-face interchange, and therefore requires, on
occasion, mediation by people who specialize in such mediations.

4. The relationship between people and the objects of their
knowledge or esthetic appreciation is necessarily mediated by an
intermediate group of people with a more complex and sophisticated
understanding of those objects, and of how to work with them.

5. The relationship between people and the cultural milieu into
which they are born is not unproblematic, but rather constitutes a
continual process of adjustment and resistance, of which the outcome can never be certain; therefore, neither the family nor any other
primary social relationship can substitute for organs of impersonal,
negotiated cooperation.

It follows from these presuppositions that elimination of the social
division of labor, and thus of variable monetary reward for varying
tasks, is impossible. We necessarily have relations to each other as
citizens different from or transcending our mutual relations as workers. We require institutions for the mediation of political relationships
that are not themselves simply derived from work relationships; and
that in many cases neither imitate, reflect, nor even flow from work
life. Such, for example, are relationships between parents and children, workers and nonworkers, men and women, teachers and students, experts and their clients, the healthy and the disabled, producers of resources and commodities and the producers of services, the
producers of private pleasures and the producers of public pleasures,

the builders of structures and the users of structures; or more broadly,the community as an imagined whole in confrontation with similar communities that engage in different, perhaps opposed kinds of organized behavior elsewhere. Not only will such relationships not be imitative of work relationships; given the presuppositions I have enunciated, they will be complex, ambiguous, and fraught with ten-sion and conflict. The complexities, ambiguities, tensions and con-flicts may be mitigated by appropriate institutions in a democratically organized society; but they will never disappear.

Moreover, transcendent political relationships aside, industrial democracy is an unsatisfactory model even for all workplace relation-ships themselves. When we speak of democracy in, say, a factory, we are on the whole committing ourselves to a mode of rule-bound, impersonal, and bureaucratized decision making. The relationships among production teams and work councils may be democratic rela-tionships, but they will also ultimately be bureaucratic relationships. Modern bureaucracy and modern democracy develop hand in hand; we cannot imagine serious decision making as a permanent referen-dum.

But rule-bound, impersonal, formalized bureaucratic relationships are just what we do not seek in many realms of work, including most of those I have mentioned. The relationship between the professional and paraprofessional, the master and the apprentice, is a relationship established with the purpose of giving immediate, tangible, specifi-able satisfaction (not an impersonal commodity) to a third party—a client rather than a consumer—who often is present during the prac-tice of the relationship itself. Such relationships, therefore, cannot simply be regulated by union rules, but must be dictated by cir-cumstances; and circumstances will often require dictation, or even dictatorship. At the same time, and conversely, any idealized version of that relationship must, quite in contrast to what we expect within the factory, be predicated on its being able to call upon bonds of warmth, humaneness, and mutual respect. But it is much harder to generate mutual respect and care within the limits of hierarchical authority than it is to generate respect for the law within the limits of majority voting and impersonal rulemaking (which is one reason for the increase in personnel services); and it is much harder to negotiate the master/apprentice relationship, especially if it is our hope that apprentices can someday become masters, than it is to negotiate the relationship between one kind of skilled production worker and another.

In short, whereas in the factory we may be able to contemplate democratizing most aspects of the technical division of labor and thus attenuating if not abolishing much of it, in the other work world our desire must be to make the equivalent relationships transitory, or reflective of purely voluntary choices by those who participate in them, as well as more humane; but not to abolish them, and often not to democratize them more than minimally.

In addition, relationships between the immediate producers of a good, no matter how constrained by impersonal democratic, bureaucratic, or leader-follower institutions they may be, are not relationships based on the exchange of abstract values. The interrelationships among production planners, engineers, quality inspectors, and a production team of skilled workers, may be technically very complicated; but in the sense that they require nothing from anyone beyond attention to the object of production and its qualities, they are also simple. Whether democratically or autocratically, workers can interact with each other directly. But that is not true of abstract exchange relationships, which must persist, no matter how many products or services we withdraw from the marketplace, as long as there is more than a simple social division of labor. The mere existence of money, or whatever we choose to substitute for it, conjures into being the possibility of exchange between people who never see or know each other, but whose actions affect each other's well-being decisively. That web of actions and their effects can't be mediated by the rules of direct democracy or cooperative working arragements, because the latter require for their meaning an actual, personal interchange that does not and cannot exist in the realm of abstractions. That realm is the realm we have come to think of as the realm of politics, in which x negotiates with y about z on behalf of a, b, and c: in which, that is to say, exchange creates group interests irreducible to individual points of view, thus demanding layers of institutionalization that will be opaque to most individual men and women.

My claim is not that resources and goods are necessarily scarce; or that people inevitably treat each other wickedly; or that human society is in any sense necessarily a war of all against all, and never a community of publicly shared values. It is only, rather, that there is an organizational requirement embedded both in the human rational, scientific project (defined however unaggressively and unpatriarchally we would define it), and in the realities of human population. The society of transparent social relationships is beyond our attainment. My ensuing description of what we might be willing to call a "classless society" is contained by that organizational requirement. It is also, though, intended to stretch the bounds of that requirement as far as may be humanly possible.[2]

### III

What is the underlying principle that buttresses the critique of the capitalist division of labor? From our standpoint that principle seems clear. A democratic society will be one that rewards humanly expressed need before economically effective demand, and it will do so because its essential rule is not "one dollar, one vote" but "one person, one vote" where by "vote" we mean not literally the ballot but whatever is the sum total of the various legitimate ways of exerting desire publicly. That is not to say that a democratic society substitutes an endless round of politics for the economic marketplace, but rather that politics must, to the greatest extent possible, be insulated from marketplace criteria.

Nor does this mean that democracies would draw the line between economic and political institutions more sharply than do pseudodemocracies. On the contrary, it is the artificial distinction between the two that inhibits the inhabitants of capitalist pseudodemocracies in their attempts to function as citizens. Equal citizens, as they turn their attention from the earning of incomes to the arena of public decision making, will perforce leave their social inequalities behind them; that is, those inequalities must be so minimal that their effects can only be trivial.

As a first approximation, this suggests that all citizens must have either the minimal resources or access to the minimal resources necessary to become active citizens or to derive, through others, the benefits of active citizenship. For this abstraction to take on some flesh, we must give a more precise account of how much social inequality, or what kinds of social inequality, would render that transformation impossible of attainment—as it is now in capitalist societies. In turn, those aspects of the (capitalist) division of labor that necessarily sustain such inequalities are the aspects of it that must be changed for democracy to exist.

We could begin this account almost anywhere, but the rule of parsimony seems to dictate that we begin by asking the simplest, yet most all-embracing question: are there, in fact, any inequalities of the marketplace that will not necessarily translate themselves into political inequalities?

The immediate answer is that of course there are. If all we know about a distribution is that it's inegalitarian, that is trivial knowledge. The notion of political equality is indifferent to the existence of relative individual wealth, as long as that wealth is based neither on the exploitation of workers nor on extortion from consumers, and as long as it cannot be translated into political influence. Thus, if a people were to decide, upon serious reflection, that the price of a desired amount of technological advance is the provision of an economic incentive to inventors, and rewarded them with a payment enabling them to buy all fleshly pleasures and more, no political harm would eventuate. It could not be said that society was allowing a separate, potentially powerful class to develop in its midst. Only in societies structured around a conflicting politics of consumption do onsumption differences, or differences inherent in control over the means of consumption, translate into political distances the way relations to productive work do. The inventors would merely be unemployed at a high level of compensation.

The same considerations apply to those who make their personal fortunes by marketing their personalities or entertainment skills to the public at large. Only a politically pointless moralism objects to the special reward that such persons can gain in capitalist society (or even in contemporary Communist society, though less of that reward takes a monetary form). There can be no objection that they are unproductive, for so are the providers of all services that enrich life rather than reproduce the conditions of production. Someone who chose to spend scarce resources on a season's ticket to watch the graceful Baryshnikov dance, or the graceful Dave Winfield play baseball, rather than spend it on weeky visits to a chiropractor for the relief of muscular soreness or a psychiatrist for the relief of depression, would certainly be making a defensible choice.

We lose sight of the insignificance of this kind of inequality, I think, because we usually assume the conditions of capitalism in thinking about it. In those conditions, what is striking about the wealth of a Dave Winfield—or, to use Robert Nozick's famous example, Wilt Chamberlain—is its social context. As an esthetic matter, the existence of riches in the midst of poverty is always offensive (except to those who are tone-deaf to considerations of decency). But the wealth of the beautiful individual lies mostly outside the causal nexus of "poverty amidst plenty"; and all the more so if we have effectively abolished poverty.

In this context, it is worth thinking a little more about Wilt Chamberlain. In Nozick's argument (from *Anarchy, State, and Utopia*), Chamberlain clearly deserves his wealth since we can easily imagine basketball fans voluntarily contributing part of their ticket price to him personally to pay for the privilege of watching him. We could not prohibit them from doing that, Nozick says, without interfering with "capitalist relations among consenting adults."[3] By extension, therefore, it is such free relations that ultimately produce the wealth (as mediated by the team franchise). Unfortunately, this line of reasoning misses the point of the entire critique of capitalism since Marx. Those are not capitalist relationships Nozick is describing, they are the simple relationship between a buyer and a seller that has existed from time immemorial. Capitalist relations, as Marx tells us, are specifically relations through which a worker produces surplus value for an owner. Marx himself repeatedly said that in the sphere of circulation or consumption—the sphere inhabited by Chamberlain, his teammates, and his fans—there often actually is a fair exchange of equal values between sellers and buyers, in that otherwise no deal would be struck. That is precisely not true of the asymmetrical relationship between the sellers of labor power and its buyers, who legally monopolize the power to set the labor of others in motion within the sphere of production. In that sphere, and only in that sphere, because of the structural inequality between the parties, we cannot assume genuine consent on the part of an individual worker to any agreement reached between himself and an employer.

Let us reverse the question, then. Is there really no inequality of income earned from the provision of services to consumers that would be unacceptable to the democrat? The answer is, of course: such inequalities in material resources as would (to paraphrase Rousseau) enable some citizens to buy the political activities of others, are unacceptable.[4]

The kind of wealth that could conceivably be earned by a Baryshni-kov, a Winfield, or a Thomas Alva Edison, from a grateful though democratic populace, can never be such as to produce political power, because political power, outside the premodern context of direct domination and subordination, is structural and contextual.[5] Since the earliest days of modern capitalism, it has taken more than mere money to obtain political power: it has taken corporate wealth based on corporate control. There have certainly been men rich enough to buy political office or political officeholders— Rockefeller, Hunt, etc.—but their wealth is not the kind that can ever be gained from voluntary consumers in Nozick's sense; it comes only from the exploitation of essential social resources, or employees, or both. The wealth of a Dave Winfield pales by comparison. In a democratic society it will enable him to buy nothing but a public relations agent, a good time, and a reputation for doing charitable works. All in all then, it is excess wealth based on structural economic power, and no other kind, that a democratic society must abolish; which means that it is the structural power, not the wealth, that needs to be directly attacked.

Thus, when a defender of democratic capitalism writes, for exam-ple, that "democratic capitalists hold that every person of talent—musical, intellectual, economic—should have every opportunity to discover and develop his talents," he has said nothing that (the gender pronoun aside) could not be agreed to by "democratic social-ists" as well. Even the belief "that natural and developed inequalities enhance the common good of all," and that societies without economic genius" are "poorer in every respect for such a lack," is not necessarily peculiar to "democratic capitalists."[6] What is really in question is the extent of the special rewards, if any, deserved by "economic genius"; and the extent of the special incentives, if any, required by it. We do not reward talented musicians or intellectuals with far-reaching rights of ownership over the activities of thousands or millions of other people, nor do we think that the promise of such rewards is necessary to encourage them to develop those talents. The search for mastery is undoubtedly a real human desire; but the prom-ise of unlimited wealth, on the record, inspires only the search for mastery over the pursuit of wealth itself. For decades the members of the Rockefeller family have controlled the Chase Manhattan Bank and Standard Oil of New Jersey (Exxon), and have achieved collaborative control of several equally vast enterprises. In what sense is this a fitting reward for the enterprise of the original Rockefeller? In what sense is the promise of that kind of power an essential incentive to would-be developers of economic talent? None that has been demonstrated: around the world innovation in the development of potentially useful goods continues to spring forth from people who clearly have had no such expectation in mind.

Take control of the Chase Manhattan Bank and Standard Oil away from the "Rockefellers," with everything that implies about control over our own fates for the rest of us and they can be left free to go out and engage in as many capitalist relations as they can find other adults to freely consent to; and they can be paid whatever return their efforts deserve. We can be sure that if that decision is made democratically, the return will not be such as to cause us to tremble for the preservation of our own equal liberties or community spirit.

As for the maintenance of political equality in the face of a free rein for the flowering of "economic genius," the only additional requirements we must add are traditional to all modern egalitarian visions. They are, first, that people who have earned individual wealth during their lifetimes, be prevented from passing on to their children, either via in vivos gifts or via inheritance, so much of that wealth as to constitute their children as members of a privileged, luxury class through no effort or accomplishment of their own. Second, that some system amounting either to progressive taxation or to special encouragement for philanthropic works be always on hand, to prevent any persons from accumulating such inordinate wealth as to enable them either to buy favors from public agencies or to buy the skills and efforts of representatives in some special degree. These are the ways in which we prevent the condition of sharply unequal worldly endowments from becoming commonplace, while permitting unequal attainments. This, in other words, is how we constrain inequality.

Two comments can be added about these provisos. First, these are questions about which we need say nothing more than that democratic majorities will settle them by their own lights in different democratic societies. I am only suggesting here that in principle those provisos are required by tolerance toward the accumulation of individual wealth, and we can only dispense with them by ending that tolerance.

Second, too great an infatuation with the elegance of Nozick's reasoning about the justification of individual wealth may lead us to for-

get that direct contributions to those we admire could not easily produce the kinds of wealth that such people earn in contemporary capitalist societies. Their salaries do not come from the direct or even
indirect contributions of fans or clients, but are rather due entirely to
the antecedent existence of immense private corporate structures, or
mass communications oligopolies (especially in television). Neither of
these could exist as they do in a society of political equals; and thus
the kinds of nonproductive investments that such wealth-
agglomerating institutions are now able to make would not exist
either.

## IV

It seems more complicated, at first glance, to describe how we would
construct institutions designed to do the opposite: to generate that
fundamental equality around which inequality is to be constrained. To
state our purpose, though, is to go a long way toward solving this
problem.

What egalitarians must desire is to create a secure floor above
which everyone has the material resources adequate for citizenship,
and beneath which no one willing to make whatever effort they're
capable of (or no effort at all if they are physically or mentally helpless) will be allowed to sink. An exercise often engaged in by theorists
of the good society is to start listing the goods and services that
ought to be freely and equally available to all citizens; that ought not
to be allocated by marketplace criteria if we wish public life to be free
of marketplace corruption.

Such lists, though, which often start innocuously enough with obvious candidates like health care and education, soon begin to get out
of hand.[7] How much health care? How about housing, food, and
transportation? If a question seems difficult to answer, the most useful approach is often to rephrase it. Let us then ask not what are the
basic needs of equal citizenship, but how we know when we are in
their presence. From a democratic standpoint we know we are in the
presence of human needs because humans have expressed them. Of
course, ordinary people as well as plutocrats can demand more than
they need or deserve.

How would a community of equal citizens measure need and
desert? Only one standard is possible among equals. For those able
to work at any task recognized as socially desirable, their willingness

to engage in at least the minimally ordinary amount of such work would demonstrate both their desert and their need together. (Consider my example of urban homesteading). What we deserve we deserve because we participate in the common life; what we need is what others like us have said we need in order to be able to lead the kind of life that citizens of our society are expected to lead.

What I have done here by way of defining constrained inequality is to combine in one standard Marx's two formulations, "From each according to his/her ability, to each according to his/her work;" and "From each according to his/her ability, to each according to his/her need." No doubt there are problems with this conception. But all in all, distribution according to this version of need—the social need of maximizing the possible occurrence of acts of citizenship— does not conjure up a vision of any moral dilemmas other than the ones that already exist in our own pseudodemocratic polity. To return to our original question about marketplace provision and public provision, it would seem that distribution by need in this sense would have to replace marketplace criteria in the provision of (1) the decent minimum of goods and services necessary for the maintenance of an average amount of physical and mental well-being ("security"); (2) the services which make training for and participation in work life and other forms of civic life possible; and (3) the resources, above all information, time, and the skills of experts, necessary to realize the goals of that participation.

The last named type of resource is distributed by political rather than economic institutions. Access to them has to do mostly with the relationship between representatives and constituents, experts and clients, rather than with the relationship between work and reward; I discuss these relationships in Chapter 9. The second of the three kinds of need we generally call education or training. The case for removing provision of this type of good from the marketplace in a democracy is unassailable: not because education and training couldn't be distributed via a market mechanism, but because in a democracy the qualities of citizenship will not be for sale. Equal citizenship rests on a certain kind of equality in educational treatment, and a democracy can no more sell fundamental education for citizenship than a theocracy could sell eligibility for salvation.

It is the first category of goods and services, the decent minimum, that poses the problem for us—a problem that can't simply be disposed of by saying, let the public provide. It is not obvious that removing needed goods and services from the market will be either economically or politically efficient. How much, in the end, can we ask public bureaucracies to do before we overstrain their capacity and undermine their legitimacy? The beauty of nonmarket morality is that it enables us to appreciate the degrading wretchedness of the notion that as a matter of right (not just accident) the ability to live our lives should be dependent on the caprice of chance or the power of others; it also reminds us how socially self-destructive, how subversive of voluntary human cooperation, is an unrestrained free market. On the other hand, the beauty of the market—often overlooked by its critics—is that it enables us to bypass, in a noncoercive manner, all those impossible choices among proliferating versions of the good.

Moreover, in a seeming paradox, rational social planning requires the concomitant existence of a market mechanism to be fruitful. Goods should be allocated according to their market price if irrationality is not to take hold of the allocatory process. By the same superficially paradoxical token, however, a market mechanism requires the concomitant existence of a public philosophy of equality,and of some public agency or agencies of planning and (re)distribution, to make sure that the system of allocation is responsive to human need rather than to momentary fluctuations in supply and demand.[8] Otherwise a free market in commodities may render equal citizenship impossible.

It seems that we must somehow combine the operations of the market with a morality not based on the market; with a morality that emphasizes need, cooperation and mutual care. There is, I think, one and only one way to come close to doing this. Furthermore, having rephrased the original question we are now in a better position to see what it might be. The problem is in knowing what the basic needs of citizenship are. The answer was that we will accept their expression by actual people as the best, if not the only evidence. It is clear that application to public or communal agencies is the most direct way in which people can provide such evidence. It is equally clear, however, that we will be leaving too much room for the occurrence of distortions in the allocation of resources, or for the development of new patterns of depersonalization, paternalism, and dependency, or even of domination and subordination, if we institutionalize public allocation wherever we think we confront a "basic need."

Can the marketplace alternatively provide believable evidence of people's basic material needs? The answer is that it can, if and only if market decisions about the allocation of their consumption by individuals are made by equal or at least nearly equal individuals. Then and only then could we say that the marketplace mechanism is merely efficient, rather than being amoral, unfair, subversive, and often degrading as well. Thus the answer to the question about which institutions are most necessary for creating a welfare floor, in other words, is precisely that *constrained inequality*—constitutionally embedded prior restraint on inequality of reward—is the very best such institution.[9]

Within the boundaries, therefore, of severely constrained and primarily functional inequality, different communities will find different mixes of goods and services to take off the market, through social insurance, subsidy, free provision, or other forms of public allocation. These choices will be based partly on moral traditions and historical experience, but above all, on structural constraints. A society in which geographical mobility is a regular occurrence, so that there can be no reliance on kin to care for those who have become too old to work, could not fail to provide some kind of nonvoluntary old-age insurance. Similarly, societies which value complex and expensive medical technology must come up with procedures for allocating it on a fair basis; the existence of widely differentiated costs among different facilities and techniques makes marketplace allocation intolerably risky and intolerably unfair, and thus public health insurance could not be left off any such community's shopping list for public provision.

Beyond such basic arrangements, people would presumably make their own choices what to buy or not buy. The point of constrained inequality is that it's socially more efficient to minimize inequality in the first place, rather than to let the marketplace create inequalities as it will and then have to invent contradictory (and bureaucratic) institutions of redistribution. The fewer the kinds of goods that have to be provided through nonmarket mechanisms, the better; but only so long as the market is truly a forum for expressing diverse tastes rather than for institutionalizing the war of all against all, the rule of dog eat dog, the morality of every man for himself and may the devil take the hindmost.

## V

How, though, can inequality be constrained in any practical sense? What might a "socially standard reward" be, or how might we conceptualize it, in a relatively classless society?

Given the presuppositions about organizational complexity that I have already identified, it is clear that the consumption of commodities and services paid for out of a money wage (after taxes) must remain a central aspect of social existence, even in a fully democratic society. On the other hand, the legislating of wage levels is surely much more undesirable even than the proliferation of public service agencies. If any proposal is perfectly designed to make public agency or government a perpetual target of resentment and obloquy, it is a proposal for government to regulate incomes, and thus to engage constantly in the determination of who deserves what.

What the ideal of equality requires, then, is legislation only of the principle that some socially standard reward, or narrow range of rewards, be available to every citizen who desires it, and who engages in some socially approved task or tasks. Beyond that general principle, though, certain obvious questions of equity demanding more than a mere statement of principle instantly suggest themselves.

To begin with, assuming the continued existence of some variant of the noncommunal family structure with which we are most familiar, we can't avoid making some kind of distinction between a family wage and an individual wage. That is, it seems reasonable that the social guarantee for a single parent with a child should be more than for a single person; for a couple with a child should be more than for a childless couple; and by the same token for a couple with a child should not be twice as much as for a single parent with a child. The opposite of such a scheme would be unreasonable: any income structure that is oblivious to the needs of children is oblivious to the most fundamental of all human needs, and would hardly consititute much of an improvement on the free labor market of capitalism. Provisions for communal daycare and for shared parenting would be an important form of family income in themselves (though there will undoubtedly always be many old-fashioned husbands and wives who mutually prefer not to take advantage of them). Still and all, children have costly needs that go well beyond mere physical supervision and emotional support, and no community of people striving for equal citizenship together could fail to want to meet those costs somehow.

Conversely, it is doubtful that any community of equal citizens would agree to fully support two nonhandicapped adults who were willing to engage in no activity other than caring for a child or children. It's hard, though, to imagine any but disturbed persons voluntarily behaving in this manner, and legislation against this prospect would be egregious. A good talking-to from neighbors would be much more to the point; and we should be able to assume that in a society dominated by cooperative work organizations and activist citizens, more people would be willing to act like neighbors. In any event, there is no need for a social theory that proposes general modes of conduct to take account of every possible extreme, and I mention this one only as the first and last example of the kind of tangential social problem that I will ignore from here on in.

The remaining issues of equity or inequity within a fundamentally egalitarian regime, all have to do with the question of differential reward for different kinds of work or workers. In every such case a close analysis suggests that we need have no dogma for dealing with such matters; we need have only a general understanding of the principle of the social standard of constrained inequality, and a consistent view of what consititutes democratic decision making, in combination with that further basic aspect of social equality I have called, "equal access to the means of production."

Although I have not yet discussed the question of ownership and control at length, it is clear that the implementation of equal access to the productive sphere must require a significant public sector of production and employment. The implication of this confluence between a public sphere designed as the foundation of equal citizenship, and a legislated standard reward, is that the goods and service industries making up the public sphere would by definition be well-paying. If the democratic public creates a public or cooperative economy out of its pursuit of civic equality, rather than as a rescue operation for sunset industries, then it will hardly legislate an inferior reward structure for itself. We can only assume that a group of citizens are trying to implement political equality among themselves because that is what they desire, not because they fell into it via an invisible hand while really engaging in purely self-interested endeavors. The consequences of imagining the standard reward as a socially high or at least moderate reward average are, however, profound.

In the first place, in such a circumstance the drift on below-average or below-standard earnings should necessarily be upward, that is, toward equalization. Anyone in the private sector earning below the standard could better himself or herself by seeking public-sector employment. We do not need the complications of economic models to tell us what the likely effect of that structural fact would be, both on incomes and on working conditions (in the largest sense) as well. The resulting natural drift, moreover, would have the happy side-effect of obviating the need for coercive and divisive legislation to equalize incomes.

In a more elusive but probably just as real manner, furthermore, above-average earnings would be subject to a downward drift, and with the same happy side-effect. Whoever would be doing work socially defined as deserving or requiring above-average compensation, many of them would be doing it in the public sphere. They would have been brought up to be citizens of a democracy and thus to think of the public world as a good if not the best world. But in the public sphere all employees, or collaborative owners, would already be receiving a compensation defined not only as adequate but also as socially standard; as sufficient for sustaining the good life. It is unlikely that such a public would tolerate demands for extreme differentiation by those engaged in serving it. Thus, there would exist a group of people defined as public service workers, possibly being paid slightly more than the average rate of pay. They would constitute a reserve army of labor in an ironic fashion. This reserve army would have the effect of keeping down the compensation of similar persons in the private sector, since some public sector workers would always be available to be bribed away from their public employments into the private sector for only marginally superior compensation. Thus, a guaranteed, standard wage, conceived as the modal rather than the average or minimum wage, would in and of itself be the great equalizer, without coercive distributions of income. [10]

A similar conclusion about the benign effects of an open labor market that is free within the limits of certain constraining general rules, pertains to the problem of potential regional differentiations in income distribution. Within any social entity thinking of itself as a united sovereign community, there are likely to be regional disparities, mostly geographical but perhaps cultural as well, that make one area seem more desirable and another less desirable as places in which to live and work. In the absence of enforceable prohibitions against immigration or emigration across protected boundaries, potential workers, requiring the socially standard reward, will freely migrate to areas of what they consider to be greater amenity. If enterprises in those areas are to maintain the general, necessary level of reinvestment—there's no reason why that should vary with amenity— and yet pay more workers per unit of output a socially standard wage, then that standard must fall. In theory it should fall to the point where citizens become indifferent to the choice between regions. (In practice a perfect equilibrium will rarely be reached, since regional identities, or national identities in a single world order, will inhibit some people from moving to an alien environment no matter how attractive its amenities.) A single national guaranteed wage, therefore, would require constant readjustment to counteract that tendency. Moreover, it's not clear whether readjustment would actually be appropriate. Perhaps certain amenities really do compensate for foregone monetary rewards; perhaps not. Who is to decide? That is not the sort of issue a national legislature wants to spend its time debating. Here too then is a decision that the market ought to be allowed to make. And the same consideration applies to sectoral inequalities, such as the windfall profit that might be earned—and could be divided up in the form of year-end bonuses, income supplements, etc.—by producers for whose particular good (or service) demand had sharply and unexpectedly risen. In a developed and diversified economy, however, that kind of inequality could only be temporary and marginal most of the time: and if it was more than that a democratic citizenry could always make the choice to tax it away.

In the normal course of events, in addition, there will also be what we might call cyclical inequalities attached to any nonutopian division of labor, as people move along career axes, master new skills, or simply grow older. Most such inequalities are trivial, since they would befall everyone in a democratic economy. Certain traditional reasons for differential compensation do require additional discussion, though.

Two of these—special rewards for what is judged to be special merit and compensation for foregone income—do not cause any difficulty, for they in no way seriously violate the general principle of constrained inequality. As I have already argued with respect to the reward of inventors, there is nothing inconsonant with democratic principles in the recognition of merit by a democratic majority. Democratic citizens might very well prefer other emblems of honor to monetary reward, but where they do choose the latter no imaginable principle of civic equality is violated. As for foregone income, considering that no training period we have lasts longer than about one-fifth of an adult's potential work life, the most highly trained professional—say a neurosurgeon—would on the average have to earn only about 1.25 times as much as a semi-skilled laborer, toward the same age of retirement, in order to make up for earning time lost to studies. No community of rational men and women, I think, would find income variations in that neighborhood, or even somewhat larger, unacceptably deviant from the general ideal of equality.

The problem of compensating people for entering unattractive or onerous occupations that have been judged by the majority to be socially necessary is more complex. How would a democratic citizenry be able to handle this kind of differentiation?

Let us return to coalmining and managing as examples of the kinds of occupations that might raise serious problems for the restraint of inequality within a democratic social formation. Loosely speaking, those two examples represent physically and mentally onerous work respectively. There are good and obvious reasons for not worrying about the effects of equality on parcelling out work of the former sort: physically dangerous work. If the people who are doing that work do require special compensation, it is because they cannot translate what they are doing into any other sort of social utility: their work is too debilitating. For that reason, in an egalitarian society one would expect coal miners, deep-sea divers, etc., to demand not so much more pay as more leisure or educational opportunities: more time to be spent either not working at all or learning how to do some other kind of work. Transiency on one hand, and inefficiency through overstaffing on the other, are the problems that should confront us with respect to this kind of work. In fact I think that it is indecent to conceive of offering more money as an inducement to do dangerous work, and I imagine that any society of equals would feel the same. We don't want to bribe people to do more dangerous work; we want them to make it possible for them to do less of it.

Therefore, the prospect that such jobs will have to be treated differentially is not so much that we would create a new and privileged class as that we would have to build considerably lower productivity for essential work into the system. One of the ways in which we link social equality to political equality is by sharing the costs and opportunities of doing different kinds of work that the community wants done; otherwise some people would be effectively debarred from the activities of equal citizenship. Anyone who thinks that coalmining, for example, is too important to be treated equally should rush out to volunteer for a job in the mines.

Professional jobs raise different and more serious questions, perhaps, since some such jobs (lawyer, manager) do accrue other forms of individual utility fairly regularly.

However, we don't want to violate the principle that central public authority should do no more than promote and maintain the idea of a social standard, for to do that is to set down the fatal path toward the bureaucratic allocation of labor. It is one thing to say that democracy cannot exist unless the freedom of the capitalist labor market is attenuated and restrained. It is another thing entirely to subject what ought to be simple economic transactions to the dead weight of abstract political bargaining and distant administrative and bureaucratic implementation, every time the demand for some particular kind of labor shifts.

The obvious alternative is that enterprises or communities should engage in their own democratic decision processes about just how much bribery of those who can't be appealed to on other grounds is too much. To put it another way, equal citizens themselves must decide the point at which they'd rather forego having some task done by the most apparently qualified people rather than compromise their equal citizenship. That sort of communal decision making about differential rewards will hardly threaten to reproduce our contemporary structure of vast inequalities. Given (1) an egalitarian public philosophy; (2) a market mechanism that moves people toward areas where the socially standard reward is lower but not too much lower; (3) a market mechanism, in the form of the socially standard public sector reward, for restraining the rewards of specialists and experts in the private sector; and (4) prohibitions against the transmission of inequalities across generations: then there is no obvious reason why inequalities in reward should ever be anything more than what we have said they can be and still be consonant with democratic equality: constrained.

This optimistic appreciation of the problem of unequal compensation still does not confront what might be the most serious difficulty facing a society of political equals. It is another thing entirely to know how to respond when privileged workers whose privilege consists of their willingness to do some especially undesirable job, start exercising their special economic muscle. That threat is not of the creation of a new class (prohibitions against the inheritance of wealth will prevent that) but of interest groups demanding special favors from the political system itself, in the form of restrictive licensing or other regulations designed to preserve unequal rewards at the highest possible level. In our own society the examples of truckdrivers or the building's trade unions in our large cities, or of doctors, come readily to mind.

The specific dilemma that would confront a democratic society would be this. The more extensive the public sphere—the sphere in which the socially standard reward is available—the more likely it is that a threat to withhold labor in order to gain more favorable treatment will be perceived as a threat against the national or regional or local community itself, which will be the ultimate employer. In every nation in the world today, it is more difficult for public service workers to strike legally than it is for private sector workers. How could a democratic society, in contrast with our own pseudodemocracy, resolve the conflict between the right to strike and the public interest in restraining inequality?

The conflict is fundamental. The right to strike—a right embedded at the deepest level of constitutional grants and prohibitions—is central to the notion that no occupational minority be made to bear, unequally, the costs of providng a socially necessary (or desired) good. What it means to bear those costs "equally" will always be a subject for potential negotiation and ultimate disagreement. The "right to strike" is nothing more than the right not to be ordered to work under conditions which others, but not oneselves, have agreed on as a fair resolution of the disagreement. Thus, denial of the right to strike is the implementation of forced labor. Unfortunately, recognition of a right to strike is potentially the recognition of a regime of unrestrained inequality among occupational groups.

The obvious solution to this dilemma will not satisfy those for whom the regime of political equality must be a utopian blueprint, or else be emotionally deficient. The obvious solution is that there is no solution. Democracy doesn't do away with conflict, not even fundamental conflict. Even in a society of perfect equals we can imagine conflicts about "rights" that might escalate into pitched battles: the rights of smokers and nonsmokers, pet owners and animalphobes, those who adorn the exteriors of their homes and those who prefer to devote their time in other endeavors, etc. Civic equals may have much to fight with each other about, and there will never be any guarantee that the right side, whatever that might be, will win. Still, if the worst crises of distributive justice we can conjure up when thinking about its likely course of development, are conflicts over the extent of marginal privilege for those who do functionally necessary work, we would be living in an almost infinitely more just society than the one we live in now. Citizens dedicated to political equality are going to be philosophically and temperamentally averse to any inequality of any kind that doesn't require much stronger justifications than the kind of justification we habitually accept today.

# Notes

[1] In the machine tool industry, one observer notes, "[t]here is nothing inherent in (numerical control) technology . . . that makes it necessary to assign programming and machine tending to different people (that is, to management and workers respectively): the technology merely makes it possible . . . Management philosophy and motives—reflecting the social relations of the capitalist mode of production in general and a historically specific economic and political context in particular—make it necessary that the technology be deployed in this way." David F. Noble, "Social Choice in Machine Design: The Case of Automatically Controlled Machine Tools, and a Challenge for Labor," *Politics and Society,* vol. 8 nos. 3–4 (1978), p. 340.

[2] For a somewhat similar, much lengthier, and altogether brilliant discussion of the limits and possibilities of "the classless society," see Carmen Sirianni, "Production and Power in a Classless Society: A Critical Analysis of the Utopian Dimensions of Marxist Theory," *Socialist Review* No.59, vol. 11 no. 5 (September-October 1981), pp. 33–82.

[3] Robert Nozick, *Anarchy, State, and Utopia* (Oxford: Basil Blackwell, 1974), pp. 161–64.

[4] In *Spheres of Justice* (New York: Basic Books, 1984), Michael Walzer suggests that the central component of our shared understandings about social justice is that the accrual or even monopoly of power that is appropriate within its own sphere should not be transferable to a sphere within which it is inappropriate: e.g., it is legitimate for money to buy commodities, and even for a lot of money to buy a lot of commodities; but it is illegitimate for money to buy political influence. This is, I think, a tremendously useful suggestion, although the notion of "shared understandings," detached from any mass political movement such as I describe in chapter 1 above, is questionable. However, Walzer does not pay sufficient attention, I think, to the prospect that the civic realm can probably never be safely insulated from a material sphere in which the pursuit of money and commodities are tolerated as the dominant human activity. For a further discussion of this point see chapter 7 below.

[5] This is not to say that wealth and the concomitant potential to consume are of no political relevance; quite the contrary. Fred Hirsch especially elucidates the structural imperatives of liberal capitalism which force citizens to pursue affluence and consumption as necessary conditions of full economic participation, yet simultaneously and necessarily limit the number of successful participants to a minority. See Hirsch, *Social Limits to Growth* (Cambridge: Harvard University Press, 1978).

[6] Michael Novak, *The Spirit of Democratic Capitalism* (New York: Simon and Schuster, 1982), pp. 203–04.

[7] The strengths and weaknesses of a serious program for distribution according to need are revealed in Howard J. Sherman, "The Economics of Pure Communism," *Soviet Studies*, vol. 22 no. 1 (1970–71), pp. 24–43. The most telling argument against Sherman's very persuasive brief is that no one who's had the experience of living in a liberal society of any kind could possibly take it seriously.

[8] This is the basic principle of market socialism, of course; see Lange and Taylor, cited in Chapter 1, note 2. In thinking about the distinction between allocation and distribution, I have benefitted from an unpublished paper by Richard Krouse and Michael MacPherson of Williams College, on "Rawlsian Justice and Economic Systems: The Case of Market Socialism."

[9] My notion of an initial equality not subject to the market, and a subsequently fluctuating inequality generated by a regulated market, is similar to Ronald Dworkin's version of initial "equality of resources." He contrasts "equality of resources" to "equality of welfare," which, he argues, would be impossible to define coherently. This problem of analytical coherence is a linguistic analogue to the practical political problem I point to in footnote 7 above. See Ronald Dworkin, "What Is Equality? Part I: Equality of Welfare," *Philosophy and Public Affairs* vol. 10 no. 3 (Summer 1981), pp. 185–246; and "What Is Equality? Part 2: Equality of Resources," ibid., vol. 10 no. 4 (Fall 1981), pp. 283–345. My argument and Dworkin's are also both similar to Walzer's distinction between "simple equality" (which most commentators would call "absolute equality") and "complex equality:" the former requiring an endlessly intrusive state, the latter only a regulated market. See footnote 4 above. The difference between the egalitarianism I am developing here and Dworkin's (so far as he has stated it previously) and Walzer's, is in my argument that equality in the division of labor and a significant extent of social ownership of the means of production, are prerequisite to any market arrangements that could be compatible with democratic civic equality. See Chapters 5 and 6 below. For an argument more similar to mine in this respect, see William Ryan, *Equality* (New York: Pantheon Books, 1981).

[10] See Nozick's comments on "patterned distribution" in *Anarchy, State, and Utopia*, ch.7.

# 5

# THE DEMOCRATIC DIVISION OF LABOR

---

## I

The notion of constrained inequality implies a paradox, which we may sum up in this way (and thus see that it is not a paradox): to maintain a useful and nonharmful free market in the buying and selling of goods and services we must severely circumscribe the traditional free market in labor, without at the same time restricting the freedom of laborers.

With this consideration, we necessarily move beyond the very limited notion of constrained inequality. The principle of constrained inequality tells us how to reward useful labor, in such a way that everyone will be rewarded with the material resources necessary to engage in a democratic version of social life. That principle is a necessary condition for the maintenance of an egalitarian polity. But it is not a sufficient condition; for we need some kind of understanding that the labor we do will be considered useful labor. Furthermore, and perhaps above all, we need to create institutions that will help us to develop, through our labor, the capabilities for a respectworthy commitment to civic life. It is not roughly equal reward for socially valued activity that makes equal citizenship possible, after all. It is the prior guarantee of socially valued activity for all that accomplishes this. Only people who know that as a matter of right they will be enabled to make a living are in a position to think freely about how they want to live. For that right the capitalist labor market substitutes for some classes of people a security based on birth (social class); but for most people only the painful task of continually demonstrating their ability to "make a living" in a competitive, uncaring marketplace. That aspect of "the free market" can never coexist with political equality, for the permanently secure and the permanently insecure cannot be political equals. Thus, we are led logically to the essential core institution of social equality: what I call the "democratic division of labor."

The best way to understand the democratic division of labor, and especially its egalitarian political implications, is to compare it with its antithesis, the capitalist division of labor. Rhetoric about equality aside, what is the deepest source of the conflict between capitalism and democracy? From the standpoint of capitalists, the maximization of profit through the exploitation of labor power is the goal of life activity. To be successful, this process requires the incessant production of commodities, and the incessant reduction of noncommodity goods (above all, different types of labor) to the status of commodities; however, profit can only be realized if there also exists a supply of potential consumers who will never cease to demand those commodities, and who must therefore sell their labor power to employers in order to be able to become and remain consumers. From the standpoint of those who work for a living, attempts to find satisfaction in work will necessarily conflict with the conditions of profit maximization; the goal of our life activity becomes, primarily, the attempt to find satisfaction outside of work, in the very consumption of commodities that capital demands for its satisfaction. Overall, the spirit of capitalism is to produce commodities; and the more commodities, the better.

The spirit of democracy, contrarily, is to generate capable citizens; and the more capable citizens (that is, the greater the proportion of the inhabitants who are political equals), the better. That is the deep sense in which democracy and capitalism are antithetical, and this antithesis goes far beyond what is usually meant by the simpler claim that monopoly capital has to be publicly controlled for democracy to be realized.

Why are the priority of producing commodities, and the priority of generating citizens, antithetical? If our goal is the production of more and better commodities, then people are but a means to that goal. The purpose of commodities themselves is allegedly to produce the good life, but the method of maximizing commodity production demands that the interests of some concrete people be sacrificed to the needs of that production.

Where total social value (utility), though, is measured by the amount of commoditization that takes place; and commodities in turn are produced through the realization of a surplus in their production: then social value is achieved through the production and realization of that surplus. All our lives are thus in thrall to the constant need for rationalization in the production process. Less productive methods are bad, for they do not maximize commoditization. Methods of production that enhance other values are irrational if they do not also enhance a narrowly defined productivity. The rules for such productivity enhancement are very simple. Regardless of whether we call our political economy capitalist or socialist (or something in between), those rules require that less efficient workers or work methods be replaced by more efficient workers or work methods; that workers be replaced by more efficient machines at a rate of compensation punitive enough to keep productive workers from volunteering for it; and that work organization overall be in the hands of those best equipped within the system's operating procedures, to ensure the production of a maximum surplus. The welfare state in capitalist societies then introduces unemployment insurance, retraining programs, workplace humanization, codetermination, etc., to ease the daily blows to well-being and self-esteem that are a necessary concomitant of those rules. But all the welfare state innovations in the world cannot eradicate the chasm between those who are subject to action, and those who impose it on them.

This is how we should understand the gap between what Marx called "mental" and "material" labor. In essence, the differentiation between those two forms of labor is not the difference between the activities of working with paper and working with machines; or using one's mind and using one's hands: most types of labor are done most productively when conception and execution are conjoined. Rather, the fundamental division is between those who plan their own or others' work routines, however carried out; and those who follow routines that have been planned for them. (Skilled industrial workers, of course, often resist and modify the routines that have been imposed on them by management. Whatever the degree of success they achieve though, resistance to the division of labor is a far cry from participation in organization of it.) This arrangement of the gap between mental and material labor, is the form of alienation that is probably experienced most powerfully and painfully by most people today.

This mode of alienation is attendant upon a hegemonic ideological framework imposed on all of us, willy-nilly, with our "consent," by those capable of imposing such frameworks. In some sense everyone is victimized by this ideology, but certainly the old and new working classes most of all, and, the costs of social envy being what they are, most expensively of all. At the heart of this hegemonic ideology is an acceptance of the narrow notion of "productivity" defined above. Most people accept that productivity in this sense is both real and necessary; that, consequently, efficiency requires sharp restrictions on the proportion of people admitted to what are defined as the most productive arenas of work; and that "efficiency" also requires a very restrictive distinction between productive labor and those realms of social existence—education, homemaking, leisure, civic activity— that are to be considered essentially non-productive. This, then, is also the ideology that justifies the maintenance of obsolete class and caste boundaries and relations: the capitalist division of labor.

In part, obsolete boundaries are maintained within the social construction of productive work at workplaces themselves. Workers learn to develop the capacity to please employers, and nothing more. That is the purpose of whatever education or training they undergo in the course of their work lives; learning how to perform a particular task better, or more intelligently, is only incidental. Artisanship is never directly rewarded by employers; tinkering with the tools of production and the blueprints of what is to be produced—the real heart of the experience of a craft—is almost always an offense against the rules of corporate authority.

But it is the notion of non-productive activity that is the strongest force in maintaining class and caste boundaries. The institutional expression of a value system that places the production of goods above the empowerment of citizens, can be seen most clearly in the mutual separation of education and family or home from work in both theory and practice. This separation is articulated with the basic class divisions of capitalist society, and also with the division between the sexes. As such, it is not only emblematic of the attendant separation of work from leisure and especially from civic activity. In a profound way, it also incorporates that fundamental political separation.

Put most sharply, practices of work, whether the work is of production or reproduction, are constituted as though their sole function is
to produce goods or services. Improving the capacities of the person
who does the work is never treated as relevant, unless it is the capacity to do the work itself (or the next highest level of work) that is
being improved. In the latter case, we call the improvement vocational or professional "training," and treat it as something separate
from general education; it is not available to all those who might
benefit from it, but only to those whose benefit might accrue to the
advantage of the firm that provides it. The empowerment of competent citizens, on the other hand, is relegated to the realm of general
education. It is not taken seriously there, however, precisely because
it is not a kind of training of which the ultimate effects can be measured monetarily. Thus, in almost all capitalist societies, what we
might call "civics" education has the lowest priority of all within the
educational endeavor, and is anyhow itself so defined as to be education for passive reception of politics (including the politics of workplaces) rather than active immersion in them. Nor would it make very
much sense to spend a lot of time training people for civic activity,
since the average person will never have to exercise real civic responsibilities. And for most of us outside the small professional political
class, when we finally do engage in civic activity it is during time
taken off from or added on to work or home: which retain their priority for most people who can't afford any different set of priorities. Our
productive work lives are structured so that for most of us work time
converts into civic time, even on the job, only with the greatest difficulty or not at all.

Correlatively, certain labor markets themselves (comprehending
relevant institutions of education and training within that term) are so
restricted as to insure the formal or informal exclusion of large, predefined groups of people. Thus, the supply of certain types of positions
or careers is kept limited relative to the demand of people who might
like to fill them, if given the opportunity. The result of this type of restriction is that some occupations take on the aura of privilege or even
of mystery: enrolling the acolyte in a way of life that must be unavailable to the majority, who come to be stigmatized (all together) as a
kind of lesser breed. The privileged class that comes into being via
these restrictive mechanisms is a social class because its way of life
is exclusive; and it is a political class because whatever institutions of

representation or party may exist generally, the mass of people have been effectively removed from the possibility of any rational intervention in the determination of policies affecting the practices of that class. They are deprived of social possibility; society is deprived of their possibility. This is to say that, wholly aside from the structural contribution that a reserve army of labor and a fragmented labor market make to the reproduction of capitalism, what most decisively separates the unemployed or the poorly employed from the well-off middle or upper class is what also distinguishes the skilled blue-collar working class from its social and political "superiors": the inability to do socially respected mental labor, or to participate effectively in the kinds of civic activity that require the manipulation of ideas or knowledge. Aside from the division between owning and not owning means of production, that is, the critical division of labor is between those who do primarily mental, and those who do primarily material, labor.

The democratic division of labor, that is the empowerment of citizens as a highest priority, must therefore be so organized as to facilitate removal of the barriers between most people and (what are now) privileged careers in the knowledge class; but should be only typical work experiences in a class open to all. In all contemporary societies the division of labor is centrally articulated around a particular kind of relationship between the triad of institutions that we call work, education, and family. So too, our model of a democratic division of labor must be articulated around a particular relationship, although a much different one, between those three fundamental institutions.

What we must then do, acknowledging all the pitfalls of attempting to draw abstract blueprints for a nonexistent social order, is to describe an economy in which the activities of citizenship would be the primary goal of child rearing and education rather than a byproduct; in which mutual mobilization on behalf of our perceived needs or interests or versions of the good is a goal to be achieved rather than a catastrophe to be avoided.

This is the way in which free laborers have to be rescued from the free labor market. Our description cannot be in any way realistic with respect to the kind of life we all participate in today, since my purpose is precisely to present a new vision. On the other hand, in all capitalist societies it becomes harder and harder to create enough satisfying work to go around; while at the same time, as I have noted, the costs of human waste mount: the waste of untrained minds and unmastered skills. Looked at in this perspective, I would claim, this vision is not irrelevantly utopian.

# II

Let us think, as a convenient shorthand, of what we might mean by a policy for the full development of human capabilities in a society of equal citizens: of how, that is, "the guarantee of socially valued activity for all" might be realized. Even in those contemporary social democracies most committed to the Keynesian version of full employment of exploitable labor power (for that is what Keynesian full employment really is) people in different social statuses find grossly unequal opportunities when they confront the labor market together. The college or graduate student and the high-school graduate (or dropout); the housewife and the career woman; the full-time worker and the involuntarily unemployed or part-time or temporary worker; the employee of a progressive, competitive industry and the employee of a declining, obsolete and noncompetitive industry; the participant in the primary labor market and the participant in the secondary labor market; the (male) member of the dominant social group and the minority group member or alien: depending on which of those several statuses the individual inhabits, he or she will find a much different fate and have a strikingly greater or lesser chance to be an effective citizen, whether in good times or in bad. To bring about, instead, truly equal opportunity will require a complete break with our accustomed ways of thinking about labor and the labor market, in several decisive respects.

The problem we confront is that there is a dialectical relationship between what happens to people on the labor market, and their own characters and qualifications. Most of the time, the people who are trapped in the dead ends of the job structure are there because their capabilities are thought (by potential employers) to be unsatisfactory for anything better. Their capabilities are likely to be unsatisfactory for anything better because they long ago quite rationally concluded, on the basis of observing the experience of others like themselves, that there was no point to trying to engage in the costly effort of serious self-improvement. (That will not be true of pure victims of discrimination, who do less well than they ought to, on the basis of their qualifications in any career line). By and large, our educational accomplishments as children inexorably set us on particular and divergent career paths. Those paths are divergent because, reflexively, their nature is thought to be appropriately defined by the nature of the education that has preceded them. We enter the life of opportunity, of the pursuit of happiness, at what appears to be the foot of an upward spiral; but before we have gone very far along it closes as a vicious circle.

An egalitarian labor market, then, as opposed to the free labor market, would enable us to bridge the gap between mental and material labor in such a way that people's total life experiences are not mutually alien, mutually opaque, and ineluctably bound to generate relationships of domination and subordination. By the same token, we must be enabled to bridge the gap between the labor of the sexes which also, as we know it today, generates mutually alien life experiences, and relationships of domination and subordination.

To understand the essential and novel component of a democratized division of labor we must move decisively away from the limitations of our own experience, especially as regards the nature of what we now misleadingly call "free" labor markets. We probably cannot abolish the distinction between mental and material labor; however, we can attempt to turn it into a structure of opportunity for all rather than a straitjacket for the vast majority. And we must deal with the fact that in a high-technology, high-information society, some ways of doing work will inevitably convey, if not more earning power, more prestige and more immediate access to decision-making responsibilities, than will others. Merely formal equal opportunity will defeat itself: will ratify inequalities of the kind that make equal citizenship seem chimerical.

There may be many conceivable ways to turn formal opportunity into real opportunity. At this historical moment, though, we can only address our own reality, not all conceivable reality in general. Our reality—that is, the reality of advanced industrial societies, East and West—is the separation of "education", "home," and "work" from each other. It is the separation of "education" from "work," and the tracking of one into the other, together with the total separation of "home," that produces the reality of our unequal opportunities.

Again, I can think of only one way of restructuring the labor market that could fulfill the conditions both of providing roughly equal material resources for citizenship and breaking open the vicious circle of career tracking. That is, the core of any democratic division of labor in a complex economy ought[1] to be the integration of work and education, and the articulation of both in support of rather than in conflict with, the family or home.

What might this mean practically? To implement a democratic division of labor we would have to conceive of, as equivalent alternatives, either performing a socially standard job; or undergoing the training attendant on doing such a job well (if hitherto untrained for it), or doing some different, socially useful job; or undertaking an educational venture that will lead to general self-improvement (and thus to one's more competent functioning as a participating citizen); or functioning as a parent (itself an occupation devoted to, among other things, the creation of citizens) with full social support; or some combination of all of these: but in whatever case, producing initially and roughly the same socially standard reward. Those already in the work force should be guaranteed the opportunity to do any of these things as an adjunct of or alternative to their immediate work, whether their employment is in the public sector or the private sector, full-time or part-time, career oriented or transient, etc. In the normal course of events as well, all persons about to enter the work force, either not yet having been in it or having been out of it for a while for whatever reasons (including specifically their displacement by economic rationalization or their immersion in familial responsibilities) should be guaranteed the opportunity to develop their capacities in socially useful ways that have not yet been open to them. It should be spelled out here, too, that a skilled intellectual or technician learning a craft in midlife might very well be enhancing his or her satisfaction, or social utility, as much as or more than a craftsperson undertaking a liberal education. The only special advantage of the latter kind of education is that it will probably be useful to any kind of worker to enhance his or her political opportunities outside the workplace.

Two additional comments must be made here about this proposal. First, the democratic division of labor ought to inhere within the realm of education itself. In referring to education, then, I do not mean to suggest the endless round of classes, assignments, and examinations that literally becomes the stuff of nightmares for those of us who've been subjected to it in meritocratic societies. The purpose of education ought to be not to mystify, but to render social institutions and social life generally, if not transparent to our understanding, at least translucent rather than opaque. How the work of education and training might be carried on is a separate question that will require the constant attention of democrats. At the very least, though, we must assume that the underlying content of any educational endeavor in a democratic society will be to relate what can be learned to what has been or will be experienced, with the proviso that in civic life what is experienced is to be experienced equally.

In this endeavor the role of teacher must probably always be intellectually authoritative from the standpoint of the student; but if intellectual authority is bolstered (as is our practice) by administrative autocracy, its fundamental purpose in a democratic regime will be corrupted. The relationship of students to each other both as peers and as teachers of each other, and the regularized relationship of teachers to students as well, must be rooted in whatever framework will enable all people to be active and equal participants in their own socialization to political equality, rather than passive recipients of a pseudodemocratic education into which they have no input. The teaching profession, we might say, must have as a major purpose the intention of rendering its own authority translucent as well. Democratic practice can only grow out of the practice of democracy.

This is what John Dewey meant by "progressive education" in his most articulately democratic statements of that creed.[2] Of course the American public elementary school today (and probably the public elementary school anywhere) is a far cry from Dewey's conception of the school. Our schools are primarily custodial and disciplinary institutions. They are staffed by teachers and administrators of mediocre intellectual qualifications (compared to most businesspeople, or to lawyers, or engineers or academics in the realm of higher education), who receive mediocre compensation and have very limited resources to work with (again in comparison with equivalent persons in those other fields). The schools therefore give most children a minimal, mass-produced education that makes no attempt at all to develop inquiring, experimentally oriented minds. A mass public education that would instead expect and demand of students their mastery (as Dewey would have put it) of the practical world, would require the devotion of a much greater proportion of social resources and commitment; would have to be considered, perhaps, the primary productive sector.

Second, all these variations on our integration of work and life must, in a democracy, have as their common element the provision of a particular kind of leisure time, in addition to humanly required leisure time in general: regularized and normal opportunities for participating in the civic activities and decision-making processes of one's own choice and capacities. In this regard, the way we conceptualize the provision of "leisure" is a crucial aspect of the democratic division of labor.

In thinking about leisure as a good, we usually assume that the way to more leisure is through a shortened workday; Marx indeed treated the length of the workday virtually as the fundamental determinant of the quality of life. In the same way, we could reconceptualize what I have argued for here as merely a shorter average workday, at the conclusion of which citizens would be supported somehow in their efforts to do other things such as relaxing, having a good time, getting educated, raising children, participating in civic affairs, etc. If by this we simply mean, that it is our goal to diminish the amount of average social time spent doing unpleasant factory labor, that will by definition be a primary goal of equal citizens.

However, once we assume that not all socially useful labor is unpleasant, then this economistic way of looking at the question of work is clearly unsatisfactory. It simply restates the separation of work, education, and home that is our problem; and posits the maximization of opportunities for so-called "individual choice" outside of work without giving any thought as to what will be out there for individuals to choose from. The community has to spend time providing opportunities for the use of self-fulfilling or communally fulfilling leisure, unless we make the assumption that those are not real human needs. In which case, liberal capitalism will do very well to satisfy us.

Thus, we would redefine those social roles we now think of as nonemployment, as consisting of work that is essential to the way of life of democratic equals, not merely peripheral to it. And we would treat all social roles we value enough to insist on maintaining them, as though they really were of value to us: to empower each other to carry out those roles to the limits of our abilities.

It is both humanly wasteful and inherently subversive of a democratic social order, that the work we do should by itself determine what else we can do; or that what else we can do should by itself determine what work we can get to do. In either of those cases the

immediate location in the division of labor to which chance, ambition, or manifest skill have cast us becomes a permanent social role,
the possibility of achieving civic equality is destroyed, and the costs of
class conflict and envy spiral upward. In the democratic division of
labor, however, work in the sense of what we now understand as paid
labor would have to be thought of as one among several integrated
modes of using our time fruitfully. Except voluntarily, it should be no
more of that time for any one person than for another, and should be
no more for all than is required for all to maintain the decent material
standard of living they desire: else we will have replaced the enlarging
pursuit of civic well-being with the frenzied pursuit of consumption.
And if a particular kind of work is stultifying or limiting, those doing it
should have no reason to doubt that in the normal course of events
they will be able to participate in one or more of the kinds of work that
are, contrarily, considered to be fulfilling and enlarging.  Whatever a
citizen of a democracy does should always be accompanied by the
opportunity of learning how to do something different as well; and
should never be so time-consuming as to preclude participation in
rewarding adventures of life that others, of no greater moral desert,
have time to participate in.

Democratization of the division of labor, furthermore, requires that
work in general be defined and arranged so that job rotation, apprenticeship leading to mastery, and personal development within and
across all career lines, are considered to be a normal and expectable
part of every person's way of life. That means, specifically, that exposure to the training that makes it easier to engage in a life of work flex-
ibility, skill development, and active citizenship would be treated as a
*normal and expectable* part of every person's training and education, regardless of his or her place in the technical division of labor;
and regardless of his or her commitment to that kind of personal
development. Now we require people (except wealthy people) to work;
on the whole only people who want to achieve certain kinds of success are expected to procure an education for themselves. In a social
order based on the democratization of the division of labor, by contrast, to go to work, including the work of being a parent, would entail
to go to education: though not necessarily to school, which, as John
Dewey pointed out, is the narrowest possible way of conceiving and
implementing education. But however we came to define becoming
educated, that is how the labor market would empower us. Most

other ways of being in the world (most of which we now call "jobs") can be defined so that organized or informal learning, in all its varieties, is part of them. To do a job on that basis ought to be what is normal and expectable among equal citizens; to drop out of learning and into the routinization of one's work life or home life would then become the nonconforming commitment.

I emphasize the words "normal" and "expectable," moreover, in order to point out that those words can mean whatever the inhabitants of a given community want to make them mean. That is true only within natural human limits, of course, but it would be absurd to think that it is humanly natural to work, even though the work may not be of one's own choice, but humanly unnatural to learn even though that may not be of one's own choice. Every imaginable social order deprives us of some area of autonomous choice, in that from the cradle we are led to expect certain things, to think of them as normal, that we might not come to expect or think of as normal unassisted.

In a more democratic society the expectations instilled in us from the cradle would be expectations to do the sorts of things that make democracy possible. A societal commitment to an egalitarian, empowering division of labor would convey to all parents and children the assurance that any and all efforts at personal development would be truly rewarded. That should be true not just in our experience of formal schooling but in all encounters with those who are better trained and more knowledgeable: whose primary task, to repeat an oft-stated notion, should be to to render themselves redundant. (The role of trained experts in a democratic society is explored at greater length in Chapter 9.)

The pursuit of self-discovery by all would thus be structurally meaningful rather than, as now, chimerical or foolish or pointless or obviously self-deluding. Above all, given an overall commitment to the principles of constrained inequality, the democratic division of labor, and political equality, self-discovery would also be achieved, or at least pursued, in a social context that would multiply rather than diminish our opportunities for discovering ourselves through the act of working with others at cooperative, humanly useful tasks.

The political results of such a redefinition would be immense. Presumably more persons doing or acquainted with the doing of primarily material labor would take on roles of active political leadership, but that is not the main point about a democratic political order. Most people never take on such roles anyway, if for no other reason than that providing effective leadership to a group of people requires skills that no particular training can easily provide. These are the skills required to negotiate cooperation, and they are probably at least as much dependent for their development upon both aspects of personality and exposure to certain types of occupation, as on any general education or particular type of training. Involving future citizens in cooperative decision making from the inception of their primary education may attenuate those natural or developmental differences, but will probably never eliminate them.

Still, that is not a crucial problem so long as representatives and leaders are effectively related to and controlled by their constituents, as the idea of political equality in any event demands. More realistically, creating a relatively classless social order entails that even if there remains a distinction between jobs that require primarily mental and primarily material labor (as there probably must), fewer and fewer people are effectively locked into a career pattern that debars them from ever experiencing one kind of work or the other; or from participating knowledgeably and effectively in a particular work process; or, above all, from exercising some political authority outside the sphere of work regardless of their position in the technical or occupational division of labor.

A democratic division of labor defined in this fashion would make possible more rotation and devolution of complex tasks and responsible positions than has yet been thought possible in any technologically advanced society. It would also make possible the bridging of the gender gap, in a way that current proposals which limit themselves to the necessary but not sufficient institutions of shared parenting, day care, etc., never quite manage to do. It would replace that formal equal opportunity which in the sexual sphere will never overcome millennia of biological and social inertia, with an opportunity structure arranged not to compensate for the effects of sexual differentiation, but to render them irrelevant in the social sphere.

There is, further, an even more crucial potentiality in the democratic division of labor. We must assume that in any society nearly as technologically advanced as our own there will necessarily remain an extensive array of important tasks that many people are unable to master thoroughly enough to be permitted to perform them. In that context, the democratic division of labor as defined here, with its emphasis on education as an integral aspect of work, would at the very least make possible the intelligent control of experts by their clientele. Thus the intelligent participation in decision making by that clientele would also be possible, again to a much greater extent than we now deem possible. Given the principle, furthermore, that what we mean by merit ought always to relate to a person's capacity to improve general social utility rather than his or her own fortunes, a democratic society might even at the same time be more genuinely meritocratic. It would certainly squander much less useful talent, by enlarging everyone's capabilities to the fullest, and by dispensing with the system that rewards the most to those who serve the wealthy rather than the many.

Together, these decisive changes in the division of labor are the precondition of equal citizenship for all. Whatever the ultimate form taken by mental and material labor, and whatever the ultimate form of the relationship between the people who do them, democracy requires the empowerment of all citizens (except those who actively resist it) with the intellectual capability to listen to, reason with, if need be confront, and finally work with those experts who otherwise will be ruling by fiat. That is the sort of intellectual capability that is certainly possessed by all normal people. It is not necessary that everyone be a trained chemical engineer (in the morning, and a trained nuclear engineer in the afternoon, and a critical critic after dinner). It is only necessary that all those persons who are potentially affected by the organization of technical work should, as a matter of course, have experienced economic and scientific reasoning and argumentation generally, and been very seriously exposed to the relevant body of technical knowledge in particular: an experience which would also empower us as citizens beyond the narrow confines of the workplace. The democrat must share Dewey's faith in the accessibility of experimental reasoning and Marx's belief that the human nature of individuals only realizes itself in practical social activity. Without that faith and that belief, the commitment to political equality is hollow.

No doubt it would not be costless to reverse the procedure by which the relevant education and training is reserved for a privileged elite and denied to everyone else; but there is no reason that it should be unbearably expensive either. There are quite enough pointless commodities that we are spending billions of dollars on right now, and that we could easily do without. In any event, the costs of empowering that capability for those who require it, as well as the general intellectual capability requisite for full citizenship, are the kinds of costs that must be borne by all, if we want to live in a society of equal citizens.

# III

Up to this point I have made no direct mention at all of industrial democracy, or workers' control. As I have already argued, for many kinds of workers no version of industrial democracy will really be relevant to the kinds of work they do, the workplaces they inhabit, the lives they prefer to lead.[3] As much as anyone else they may desire educational opportunity, either to do a more advanced version of the kind of work they're already doing (e.g., become a master rather than a journeyman, a doctor rather than an assistant to a doctor); to enter upon an entirely new career; to engage in an occupational specialization or the private, individualized production of goods or services; or to enhance the kinds of capabilities that enable the person better to engage in civic activity at large: but not to allow them to democratize an essentially undemocratizable workplace.

For perhaps as many or even more people, the standards of industrial democracy—participation in workplace rule-making, in choosing representatives or leaders rather than submitting to bosses, etc.—will be fully relevant. As John Stuart Mill argued, industrial democracy— the devolution and equalization of workplace tasks—is itself a profound educational experience. That kind of industrial or workplace democracy, however, can only be a result, never an independent cause. We can legislate it or implement it all we want, but it will remain a chimera as long as the real social class division between material and mental laborers remains intact. On the other hand, begin to overturn that division, challenge it and undo it from the bottom up, through the reintegration of life activities that I have suggested here, and industrial democracy is inevitable.

To see this, let us imagine the same apparent chain of command in two different enterprises; a chain of command from planners through management to workers, (or from professionalized experts to laypersons). If the planners have mastered a body of knowledge which the workers themselves have never even encountered, and engaged in a kind of activity that the workers themselves have never engaged in, then the workers will be effectively excluded from the decisions that will determine the contours of their lives, except insofar as they can get to express a crude version of self-interest through their representatives. If the representatives are able to deal with management on equal intellectual terms they will have more in common with its representatives than with their own constituency, and be at heart more likely to appreciate the coherently expressed proposals of the former than the incoherent fears of the latter. In either case, the chain of command is likely to wind up necessarily distributing only commands.

On the other hand, if in a relatively egalitarian society a normal part of either general education or training on the job itself has entailed exposure to the types of general reasoning and the kinds of particular knowledge required for the planning function, then the distinction between workers and planners will not be so sharp. A good deal of job rotation will already presumably have taken place; at a minimum, a free flow of mutually informative communication among those exercising different job responsibilities will also have occurred. Some of those occupying the role of worker will have themselves been involved in planning at one time or another; or they will hope to be involved in it later, when they have accumulated more relevant experience and information. Thus they will already be internalizing the potential perspective of the planner. Conversely, most of those currently occupying the role of planner will have themselves been less authoritative workers for some amount of time or other, since training in planning skills will be attached to work rather than taking place in an educational sequence (college, graduate school) open only to those who have passed hurdles of class, status, and paper merit (tests) to get where they are. A planner, that is, will simply be a worker who is at a point in the trajectory of his or her life's work of having mastered the skills of planning sufficiently well to engage in them on behalf of others. Moreover, if the skills necessary to do intelligent planning have been made widespread enough so that a good deal of job rotation is possible even at the highest levels, most of those engaged in the task of planning will expect to be again engaged in less complex work tasks at some later point in their work lives. In either case, they in turn will perforce feel the perspective of the worker as well as of the planner.

In these circumstances, the apparently identical chain of command will now, willy-nilly, receive suggestions, and issue proposals rather than commands. All workers will not be able to substitute for those who organize and plan; but they will be able to control them. The workers will be able to participate in the key process of agenda-setting; of ruling themselves. In turn, of course, the prospect that even more among them will go on to participate in wider realms of decision making will be greatly enhanced. Experience only enlarges our abilities, and above all that is true of experience in discussion, argumentation, and the exchange of knowledge.

Real workplace democracy, in sum, can only be possible if access to the knowledge that grows out of such experience comes to be considered a normal, or essential component of the life of any citizen. The less sharp the distinction between what I know and what you know, the more tenuous will become any relationships of domination and subordination between us. That is the real meaning of the democratic division of labor.

## IV

Even though by its very conception the democratic division of labor would abolish all permanent hierarchies in the productive sphere, in one crucial respect it still remains equivocal. I have said that the democratic division of labor makes possible the bridging of the gender gap. But that will not happen automatically. Gender discriminations, unlike those which confront racial and other, similar minorities, have their origin neither in the division of labor in production, nor in invidious, exclusionary social practices; at least, not in those alone. Gender distinctions, rather, to some very significant extent, and most especially in contemporary capitalist societies, also have their root in the division of labor in reproduction.

At the same time the division of labor in production and the division of labor in reproduction seem to be conceptually and institutionally separable. Thus it has been possible for a liberal democrat such as Mill, and a radical democrat such as Rousseau, to argue that although women are not at all inferior to men—are even in important ways superior to men—it is socially dysfunctional to ignore the differences between them, especially with respect to the division of labor in reproduction. Women, in this view, contribute the most to society when they are engaging in the traditional female nurturant roles: roles which, though essential, cannot be filled as satisfactorily by men. Therefore, the division of women's labor between workplace and home ought not to be exactly the same as men's. We can see quite easily that this kind of separate-spheres argument might have even greater force in a society devoted to, as I have put it, the empowerment of citizens before the production of commodities.[4]

The separate spheres, however, cannot be kept separate; and no egalitarian theory can countenance a separate spheres argument. All our experience testifies that hierarchy within the sphere of reproduction, and within the sphere of production, replicate each other. Very simply, if much more is expected of women within the sphere of reproduction, then much less will be expected of them within the sphere of production: at which point the division of labor in production will have become "democratic," if not for whites only, for men only. Social systems are systems; it is not possible to maintain conflicting roles and expectations across institutional boundaries.[5] Whatever the logic of "separate but equal" may seem to be, we can find no historical case in which that alleged logic is not overborne by the real psychology of segregation. In no system of segregation can a foundation of belief in the moral equality of those who are in any way separated from each other be stable. The worldly logic of separate spheres leads inexorably either to the open assertion or to the concealed assurance that one of those spheres is superior, and the other inferior; so too with the identifiably distinct peoples who on the average inhabit those distinct spheres.

Moreover, there is and must be a profound organizational inequality inherent in any proposal of separate spheres for men and women. Integrate our approaches to work, education, homemaking, and civic participation without changing the division of labor in reproduction, and women will still have one obligation more than men. They will still have a double day (now a quadruple day, perhaps). Furthermore, so long as women remain typecast as domestics, whatever else they also are, they will continue to be stereotyped both by men and even by themselves as having primarily the domestic virtues. There are many kinds of work for which the domestic virtues do not seem very helpful, and women will encounter both internal and external pressures to stay away from those kinds of work. In an egalitarian society, certainly, our attitudes toward work would have to be more humane, more compatible with a democratic rather than a class-based division of labor, less tied to a kind of antihuman devotion to the work world and alienation from the world of private relationships and private joys. But none of these structural necessities of equality will militate against the pattern I have described here, as long as the division of labor in reproduction remains unchanged.

Though less so than in our own pseudodemocratic society, women might still have to be "superwomen" to function at the same level as men in certain social roles while playing a typical female part in family life as well. It is indeed illustrative of the asymmetry between men and women that such women as I am describing here are often said to "want everything," or to be "trying to have it both ways." No one ever says of a man who wants children and a career that he "wants everything." If this difference persisted, then, some women, recognizing the potential impact on them of an overall social commitment to a female-centered division of labor in reproduction, would freely make the decision for themselves to expect a secondary role in the work world when they later came to enter it, as a fair price for having had the opportunity to fulfill themselves in the world of domesticity and perhaps motherhood; they would be voluntarily recreating a dual labor market. Others, however, would discover too late that the price they'd paid for having the honor of raising citizens was higher than, as it turned out, they were willing to pay.

Yet other women, probably a minority, would make the conscious choice to avoid the whole world of children and family. While we can guess that in some cases this would truly express their innermost personal needs, we can be sure that in other cases they would be sublimating what might be their innermost needs in order to make it equally "in a man's world." Aside from the fact that that would seem to be preeminently the kind of moral choice we don't want to be determined by marketplace considerations, it is also very likely that they would not find the equality they sought, and for which they had sacrificed one of their human potentialities. For them, the superficially egalitarian division of labor would be a fundamental betrayal.

Thus the retention of any version of the traditional division of labor in reproduction, combined with the likely absence of total democratization in the division of labor in production, might very well result in the persistence of tacit discrimination against women at work. That some women might find this condition acceptable or even beneficial is irrelevant in a discussion of democratic equality, even were they to be a majority of women. No group of women can speak for all women; no one has the right to alienate someone else's rights without the latter's consent. If only ten women want absolutely equal treatment in the social world, equal consideration of their special needs at workplaces, in career lines, and so on, then in an egalitarian democracy a thousand women who are willing to trade off some of that equality to remain in the home instead cannot legitimize the denial of that right by agreeing to it. Their only legitimate option is not to take advantage of it themselves.

For some societies, we could say that those of their inhabitants who long for equality are simply being perverse, so that if they come to identify themselves as a permanent minority they have only themselves to blame: they shouldn't have had such a bizarre belief in the first place, they should have been realistic and played the game. But we will hardly be able to say of women who, in an otherwise egalitarian society, demand equality, that they are being bizarre or unrealistic; they will only be wanting to play the same game everyone else is playing. They would thus—in the circumstances I've described—be a genuine minority through no fault of their own. The ideal of democratic equality commands that no one suffer from their minority status: that no persons be deprived of effectively equal opportunity to accomplish their legitimate ends. Though the argument in favor of a gender-based division of labor in reproduction is not overtly antidemocratic, we can finally see that it must probably lead to consequences incompatible with the principles of political equality: the existence of a permanent minority within an otherwise egalitarian social formation.

We are led to the conclusion, therefore, that democratization of the division of labor in production requires, concomitantly, democratization of the division of labor in reproduction. This does not mean the abolition of the family, in some utopian (or dystopian) sense. Rather, democratization must mean at a minimum the transformation of the family: not that biological parents do not (in the normal course of events) remain responsible for the care of their children and the organization of housework, but rather that more people are engaged in the process, it takes place in more locations, and the time allocated to it is divided up differently, than is the case in the contemporary nuclear family. A democratic division of labor in reproduction requires that as a matter of course, that is of mutual expectation, men share parenting in some rough equality with women, regardless of how much time off from external employments this may require.

As between husband and wife, the conditions under which they enter, or leave and reenter, occupations and education ought to be as equal as possible. The belief that women cannot be as committed to the public world as men, along with the humanly destructive attitude that unswerving commitment to that world is what's required, will persist in the absence of a serious social commitment to shared parenting. So we will recreate the notion of career as a competitive ascent of the most ambitious, rather than as a normal train of development of all those willing to work reasonably diligently; and husbands will benefit from that conception to the comparative exclusion or subordination of their wives. In addition, any egalitarian society will have to manifest a deep commitment to making available more communal forms of childcare in the world at large, outside the private home. (It is conceivable, but surely very unlikely, that most parents would want to stay in the home with their children until the latter were at the age of readiness for institutional schooling). These could presumably take the form, variously, of community day-care centers or nursery schools organized by workers' or students' cooperatives at places of work and places of education, etc. (Centers and schools, that is, staffed always either by cooperative volunteers *or* by trained persons who are rewarded with the standard social wage: egalitarians could not countenance the creation of a servant class to take care of other people's children.) There are doubtless other ways of doing this, but we cannot reason ahead of our time to them. The clear principle, though, is that participation in the democratic division of labor (in both production and reproduction) should enable parents at one and the same time to be freed from or attached to the exigencies of childcare, when and as they desire; rather than being at the mercy of institutional arrangements that mandate their separation or attachment at other people's convenience. Just as shared parenting is necessary to make possible the equality of men and women, so communal responsibility for childcare, in some form, is required to make possible the equality of parents and nonparents, within the division of labor.

Moreover, within the structure of our civilization, the sexual division of labor seems to encourage in men a tendency toward aggression, misogyny, and violence. Conversely, however much we strive to avoid a dualism in which "male" and "female" become morally polar terms, at the same time we must acknowledge that there is recognizably such a thing as a distinctively female discourse less oriented toward norms of aggression and destruction. There is little hope not only for democratic equality but for any version of the good life, unless that discourse comes to suffuse the public sphere. This feminization of the public order is incompatible with the comparative restriction of female virtue to the private sphere of domestic labor.[6]

To be sure, a familiar and plausible argument against the coupling of programs for shared or communal parenting with the notion of "female discourse" is that the latter hardly makes male parenting seem a very attractive proposition. But this is to assume biological determinism as the source of excessive masculinization, rather than—more reasonably—a particular conjuncture of productive and reproductive structures. Thus we cannot propose shared parenting as an instrument of social change; that would be to ignore some intractable social realities. But we can speak of new parent-child relationships in the context of a transformed society. And though feminism cannot be the sole motor force in this transformation (the midwife of its history), the feminist impulse and agenda must certainly be an important element in any transformative movement.

Beyond that consideration, I know of almost no defense of the traditional nuclear family (a rather recent tradition) that acknowledges its real social context. Earlier I remarked that in the democratic division of labor the family, or home, must be articulated more closely with institutions of production and education. By "articulation" here I mean a conscious, programmatic trade-off of entry and exit opportunities, incentives and rewards, and social supports (e.g., the provision of child care) between those spheres. Even at its most extensive, however, that democratic division of labor will still be a far cry from the ideal of pure communalism, in which there might be no social division of labor at all, and thus no institutional boundaries between work, home, and education. Our reality instead will surely be the continued social and physical separation of those institutions to at least some degree, and the continued existence of an economy that, no matter how egalitarian, continues to be built around the sale of goods for money in an impersonal marketplace. In such a society the notion of a culturally or biologically natural family is wholly chimerical, for the ubiquity or universality of the family can only be demonstrated by including as "normal" instances of the family precisely the types of family that its ideological advocates decry: families in which divorce is an accepted outcome of marriage, abortion is an acceptable method of birth control, both parents work full-time away from the home, childlessness is preferred to parenthood, and so forth. When the location of both income-producing work and child rearing is problematical; when neither the real producer of a family's income nor the rightful division of that income is perfectly obvious; then the outcome of a particular set of family behaviors necessarily becomes the subject of permanent and perpetual negotiation and renegotiation, rather than a natural course of events. But family relationships that must be negotiated are political and economic relationships as well as natural ones: they are relationships of power.

Given this social milieu, the failure of all pro-family arguments in a democratic context is their failure to confront first, the extent to which families are cemented by bonds of violence; and second, the subordination of women within the economic sphere. These two aspects of male domination are related. Women who accept the asymmetry of the normal family of pro-family ideology and their consequent temporary or permanent relegation to the household, become economic dependents, compelled either to remain within the family bonds no matter how miserably their husbands treat them, or having broken loose, to enter the work world as second-class and economically straitened citizens. Concomitantly, women who do strive to realize some kind of mutuality in marriage and economic independence through work inevitably wind up doing two jobs for the price of one.

Short of a reversion to completely communal social arrangements (and most communes have been built around the subordination of women), an egalitarian regime will have to guarantee the economic independence of women. That can only happen if parenting is treated like other life activities in the division of labor: freely combined with them, equally deserving of reward and social support, and subject to similar principles of democratic equality. There is a democratic theory of the division of labor in reproduction as well as in production. Its essence is that the work of reproducing humans is not merely an uncontrollable fate visiting happiness or despair on individual women, but is also cooperative, communal work; just as much as the work of producing vital goods and services.

Of course any egalitarian must acknowledge, or even emphasize, that the biological difference between men and women is real. So too is their inevitably differential involvement in early child rearing, no matter what structures of social support for shared or communal parenting exist. For this reason, the principles of democratic equality in this context require some specific applications that would be irrelevant in the case of men; a single standard of rights is not possible across gender lines. The sexual conservative who argues both that biological differences are crucial *and* that constitutional principles ought to be gender-blind, is engaged in a self-contradiction. Given the reality of biological differentiation, it is necessary to prevent the deepening of the effects of that differentiation against the wishes of women. That is not an afterthought in democratic theory, but part of its foundation. Thus what have come to be called the reproductive rights of women, as typified in the slogan that women ought to have control of their own bodies, are not an appendage to the notion of rights; they are fundamental to it. (See chapter 10).

Admittedly, an important caveat has to be added here. It is futile to ignore the fact that in most advanced industrial societies today where the notion of reproductive rights is an issue, women are not only the strongest proponents of that notion, but often also its most fervent opponents. All the considerable leadership ability of, for example, the male Roman Catholic priesthood or the fundamentalist ministry of the "Moral Majority," would be of little moment if not for the adherence of so many millions of women to the antiabortion crusade that those men have inspired. At this point the potential egalitarian coalition ruptures before it has even begun to coalesce. It may be that at this moment in history the sexual egalitarian can say nothing to women who defend an inegalitarian family as the institution that offers them the most hope, respect, and protection: what, after all, in the midst of a male-dominated capitalist social order, can the egalitarian offer them in its place?

Perhaps we can do no more than wait for history to catch up to philosophy. It does not seem likely that traditionalist women can go on ignoring the conditions to which I have alluded above, forever. The conventional nuclear family is under increasing strain. Men are deserting it, and when they remain in it are abusing it; the disappearance of the family wage, most notably in those societies where antifeminist feeling is best organized, makes it necessary for more and more women to leave it as well. In these historical circumstances, the expectation of sexual egalitarians that eventually the family will appeal to fewer and fewer women as a solution to their dilemma, is a reasonable expectation.

At the same time, some ways of stating the issue for women are more productive than others. Especially, the slogan "women to have control of their own bodies," can be a troubling one, and not only for traditionalists. That slogan, if we are not careful how we use it, can be taken to imply an individualistic orientation toward the person equivalent to the individualistic notion of property right, and therefore to be incompatible with any communal notions of social solidarity. Undoubtedly some people have used the slogan in exactly that way, and their usage does demand criticism. That is not a necessary implication, however. The slogan can and should imply rather that women as a community ought to have control over their own bodies; and that this should be accomplished within an overall set of social definitions that have been arrived at via a political process based on not merely the equal, but in this case the predominant participation of women as a community. Much contemporary feminist theory emphasizes the bonding nature of "femaleness" at the same time that it conjoins "woman's body" with "woman's right."[7]

Thus, the critique of reproductive rights based on a presumably excessive individualism inherent in that notion is already passe. To be sure, reproductive rights is a general conception with particular policy implications that may vary. For example, now the concept of reproductive rights is inseparable from the more limited idea of abortion rights. That is a historical accident, however; in this respect at least, the form that reproductive rights take is contingent on technology. If, for example, an instant abortifacient were to be perfected, then reproductive rights would demand access to it rather than to abortions. Similarly, if as in the doomsday scenarios of certain Neomalthusians all water supplies were spiked with an antifertility ingredient so that conception could only be accomplished after taking an antidote, then reproductive rights in this area would mean that women should be in charge of the procedure for securing the antidote. At this moment in time, however, those who insist that abortion right is an essential aspect of sexual equality are quite obviously correct. To dissent from this position on moral grounds is to that extent then to dissent from the philosophy of sexual equality. Again, we cannot reason ahead of our time.

Beyond all these considerations, finally, the equality of women might also require action to limit what we can call the surplus effects of biological differentiation. In the absence of such action, unchecked biological tendencies could bring about a continuation of some extent of sex-role stereotyping even in an otherwise egalitarian society. Some mothers might, as now, accrue the kind of work experience that leads to the assignment of higher level responsibilities, at a slower rate than men or childless women. Thus, in imagining a democratic division of labor, and even a democratic division of labor within the sphere of reproduction, egalitarians should be alert to the possibility that mechanisms for compensation—some variant of what we now call "affirmative action"—might be called for in an otherwise fully egalitarian social order.

# V

Again it is necessary to offer some brief consideration of what all these reflections on the two divisions of labor might mean in practice.

Let us imagine, then, a young woman who, uncertain of her life's goals, has entered adulthood with none but the very simple skills that qualify the person to be a clerk typist, data programmer, word processor, etc. Immediately upon taking up some such task of routinized labor, she will already find herself in a quite different position from that of the similar young woman in a pseudodemocratic capitalist society. Whether she works in the manufacturing or the service sector, and no matter how confused are her ambitions, she will not be a secretary, clerk typist, etc., in the same sense as her contemporary equivalent. That is because she will not have "chosen," as a theorist of human capital would put it, to be a high-school graduate and thus a performer of other people's routines, instead of a college graduate and the follower of an intellectually skilled career. That "choice" will not be available to her unless she goes out of her way to make it. As an entry-level worker, she will be presumed also to be doing some kind of educational "work." That might be the equivalent of what we now call a "liberal arts education," which at its best teaches the intellectual curiosity and skills at communication that are the hallmark of any intelligent civic or workplace participation; or of some kind of more limited professional or vocational trainee program or internship designed to increase her opportunities within the general area of her employment. These different types of education might take place separately and consecutively, or together; but ideally, given everything we have said about democratic politics and the democratic division of labor, they will both be normally available to her. The same would hold true if she were entering upon work in a factory, or a hospital, or a school, or whatever. We cannot compare her unfavorably, as we could in capitalist society, to a male management trainee, because, that is gender aside, what she will be too.

Of course, unlike him she may and (statistically speaking) soon will become pregnant. If she is the kind of woman who finds immense joy in mothering, she may want to remove herself from the workforce for some months, even some years. That would have to be a very deliberate choice, though, because there will be a range of supportive institutions designed to make the alternative choice seem attractive. Not only would there be day care centers and nursery schools both in her neighborhood and at her place of work or education, as well as at the father's places of work or education; there would also be the general expectation that the father would share the necessarily wearying child care and housekeeping time spent at home with her. Between them they might find it easier to cut back on their commitments, perhaps for a while to engage in either schooling or laboring but not both. Whatever the case, given the social determination that the division of labor in reproduction ought to be democratic, it would be a violation of that understanding for him to suggest that only she should make that familial commitment.

If she is a single parent, undoubtedly, it will be more difficult for her, but the same principles will still apply; she will only require more social support. In any event, if we compare the situations of either her by herself or her and the child's father to that of a childless and more ambitious single man or woman who is dedicatedly moving through the role of trainee and beyond, we will discover in most fields of endeavor no more than a temporary inequality. When they return to a more full-time immersion in the public world they will have less experience and training than a childless person of the same age. If we think of life as nothing but John Locke's "joyless pursuit of joy," then they will seem to have "fallen behind." That would be a strange and sad conception of human life, though (as even Locke must have thought, given his revealing choice of words). The more advanced worker, after all, will have had to forego being a parent; and unless we think that that is a valueless, unrewarding activity, he (or she) will have incurred at least an equal loss of time—or more.

At any rate, experience at most complex tasks has a diminishing marginal utility. At the age of 30, the man who has had three or four more years worth of experience and training than the woman (or her husband) is going to have an advantage when someone has to be recruited for a position of responsibility; or when their work mates or neighbors come to choose someone to represent them in the conduct of some external civic affair. But by the age of 40 that advantage will have completely disappeared. Given the democratic principles of rotation in office and job rotation wherever technically possible, the parents will be as qualified to put their trained talents to use at one enterprise or another as the nonparents. In different kinds of enterprises or professions this general line of development would presumably take place in different ways, whether at separate educational institutions; in programs located within specific enterprises and limited to the types of skill development such enterprises find generally useful; or through the intimate personal relationship of master and apprentice. However it takes place, it will take place for everyone who wants it.

If, to return for one last time to our imaginary secretary, it turns out to be the case that like many women and men she would rather remain at one routine task throughout her work life, she will still have the opportunity to train herself for potential leadership roles within or without the workplace. She will be guaranteed rather than denied the kinds of further education, developmentally fruitful leisure time, etc., that in our division of labor are usually available only to those workers who have already had the most of them. Thus she may wind up exercising supervisory power of one kind or another, as a representative of work mates or neighbors, over colleagues who have gone on to master more complex work tasks that she chose to forego. The democratic division of labor, that is, multiplies opportunities for expansion of one's capabilities in every possible way.

I have so far, for the purposes of this comparison, been taking the viewpoint of the secretary rather than the management trainee. Just as the full force of that dichotomy disappears from the point of view of the secretary, from the position of what I've called the manage-

ment trainee the dichotomy loses its force as well. A management
trainee in a democratic society (whatever that might mean in terms of
specific organizing tasks) will be simply a secretary, or machine
operative, or data programmer, etc., who wants to learn how to be a
manager. That is to say, aside from their gender, in an egalitarian
society the secretary and the trainee will have become indistinguish-
able. All that we ought to mean by terms such as "management
trainee," or "medical student," or "engineering student," is that the
person has made the decision to learn how to be something other
than a secretary, or operative, or paramedic, as soon as the opportunity arises. The latter terms, by contrast, ought merely to denote a
group of people who have not yet made that decision, but who will be
fully supported in making it whenever they decide to. Human nature
being as variable as it is (whatever it is), some people will probably
want always to remain as secretaries, or operatives, or paramedics or
nurses, because it will be less trouble to do so. But neither gender nor
age nor previous education nor current job position ought to prevent
them from making the change, as and when they desire. And at the
very least, even the secretary who would rather remain a secretary
will, in the normal course of events, be undertaking the kind of continuing education that will render her, or him, capable of being more
of a participatory partner with the manager or doctor instead of being
forever an uninformed receptacle of, and routinized processor of
someone else's orders. That is what it means for occupation or
gender to be descriptions of our person, rather than determinants of
our fate.


# VI

However persuasive I have been to this point in positing the democratic division of labor as the core of that social equality which is the
precondition of political equality, there is still an obvious objection to
this program. It will be raised by those who think that any attempt to
democratize the division of labor must be utopian, in that left to our
own free devices we are bound to generate a serious mismatch
between individual human desire and apparent social need; and that
authoritative agencies for the allocation of unfree labor will therefore
be essential for realization of the democratic division of labor. What
will we do if all conductors want to be train drivers; if all cost accoun-

tants want to be welders or all welders want to be cost accountants; if all computer programmers would rather be computer designers; if all paramedical personnel view themselves as doctors in training? More generally, it will be said that no one will want to do any kind of material labor anymore. Given the opportunity for training and the encouragement to expand their horizons, everyone will want to do mental labor instead. We will have a society of all experts and leaders and no routine workers or followers.

There are several comments to be made on this traditional criticism of egalitarianism. The first and most important is that this objection to the egalitarian program is actually the most telling argument in favor of it. If it is true that "everyone" really wants the opportunity to do "mental labor" as I have defined it, then it's appropriate to ask how we can possibly defend the morality of a social system that consigns most people to doing what they don't want to do; in many cases without ever giving them a realistic change of proving that they could do. If capitalism's proudest boast is that it's the only safe way to frustrate human desire, then its intellectual fortress has already fallen before a shot was fired: it remains only to spread the news of the surrender.

Beyond that theoretical response, worries of this sort are based on a misapprehension. The jobs which are both socially vital and also demand continual and intense commitment by and development of the practitioner are probably very few. It is highly unlikely that everyone associated with the work arenas in which they are located, e.g., nuclear engineering or neurosurgery, is going to be yearning to practice them rather than merely be associated with them. The assertion that all people innately have the same motives and ambitions is unbelievable. If socialists and utopians have been too prone to make that assertion over the past two centuries, it has been out of a laudable desire to point out that the ways individuals behave in capitalist societies should not be taken as revelations of their natures. Of course that is correct. Such social stereotypes as the unambitious woman, the slow-moving black man, etc., are clearly formed at least as much by patterned and often coercive social expectation as by individual character. It's a wholly unwarranted deduction, though, that no one is ever lazy, slow-moving, unambitious, driven, etc. Given the most absolutely equal opportunity imaginable, therefore, and the permanent eradication of all social stereotypes, there is still no reason to believe that all people would want to work at the most demanding, most responsible, most intellectually or technically complex, or most prestigious kinds of work.

I suspect that the truth actually lies much more in the opposite direction. The problem for egalitarian institutions would probably be to find enough people to do the burdensome, anxiety-creating jobs, without instituting sharp gradations of reward that would have the effect of reintroducing the social division of labor between mental and material work. That is a danger egalitarians would cheerfully face up to, as an alternative to never having made the effort to change in the first place. If there were still, in some field, too many apprentices who wanted to be masters too quickly, then the principles of democracy would require that the practitioner not be freed from the duties of an apprentice on becoming a master. That condition in itself would function as a deterrent to those whose ambition sprang more from career-ism than from genuine interest and commitment, and organizational equilibrium would probably soon be restored.

It is no requirement of classlessness as I have defined it that every-one be equally consumed by the desire to do, and equally possess the capability for doing, the most intellectually skilled kinds of work. The variety of talents necessary to enrich our enjoyment of life is so immense that it must be a truly exceptional person who can find nothing of value to do for the community in which he or she lives. The democratic requirement is only that the treatment of people be equal, in relevant ways, no matter what kind of work they are doing; and that given generally equal opportunity only the vagaries of human per-sonality, and chance, should determine who finally gets to do what in a world where not everybody does the same thing.

## VII

From the perspective of social organization, then, we are left with only two final difficulties. First, we must consider the alleged problem of "dirty work." By that I mean work which seems to be different even from ordinary material labor, in that we cannot conceive of paying the kind of premium to get it done that we would be willing to pay to get such dangerous but socially essential jobs as mining done. It is also work that does not foster the kind of collective pride in a hazardous or essential job well done, that can substitute for monetary compensa-tion in certain situations. As I have pointed out, the answer given by the capitalist division of labor to this question is not very inspiring itself. But in any event, and more profoundly, there are probably fewer instances of such work than we think. Given equal material reward by the community, equal opportunity for one's children, and the rights of workers to organize themselves cooperatively to provide a desired public service, there are not many types of work which are likely to provide no self-esteem or satisfaction at all. In most cases where that seems to be the case, that is not because of any degradation intrinsic to the work but because the rest of us evince disdain for it. Egalitarianism ought to decrease the occurrence of that mode of judging; there will be nothing material to be gained by it and no way of imposing such work on a class (or caste) of people obviously different from oneself.[8] Still, there are some kinds of truly menial work that merely make the conditions of work or the enjoyment of leisure activities for others more pleasurable. The housekeeping of public spaces probably falls into this category. Such work, though, could be required of all people at a certain time in their lives (e.g., teenagers, students); or could be required of certain convicted criminals in place of the degrading conditions of incarceration we now so fruitlessly impose on them; or could become the purview of those who, given every genuine opportunity, would still rather drift, idle, and work only occasionally at minimal tasks for a less than standard reward. Or we simply might not be able to find ourselves willing or able to force people to do the kind of work that no one wants to do and which is too much trouble to organize as a collective task. In the end, if no one really wants the job, let alone the "career," of being a janitor, then we should all be sweeping our own floors. If that will make productive organizations less efficient at the production of goods for distribution, less efficient at the production of goods for distribution is precisely what they ought to be.

Second, the work force of organizations and enterprises constructed not only to produce goods and services but also to implement the egalitarian program, would likely manifest very fluid career trajectories. Superficially that might seem to promise to cause difficulty. In our terms, that would be a very transient work force, shuttling between what we consider work and nonwork activities, and consisting both of workers who are committed to a particular enterprise and those who are using the educational opportunities offered by it as a springboard to a new career somewhere else. It would also seem to be an overstaffed work force, requiring more people to get the same amount of actual production done, in comparison with an enterprise that could rely on everybody to work seven and a half hours a day for five days a week.

That only looks like a difficulty on paper, though. In any society, no matter how we slice up work time in relation to other uses of time, everyone has to be supported somehow. The difference in an egalitarian society would be that more of that support would be funneled through agencies of public or communal employment, rather than through individual family income flows and government grants, as is now the case. That is ultimately only a bookkeeping difference, based on a difference in public political philosophy about how equal opportunity ought to be made real; the difference is not material in any profound sense. Of course the result might be spreading out the work, with more people putting in some time at the production of commodities, but no one or few people putting in what we now consider a full working day. That might be a less-efficient production process, in our sense; in might also be a much more enjoyable one, leading to a generally more fulfilling life for more people. It might also be more socially productive since, with the sharing out of work, the unemployed as a class of those who produce and earn nothing at all, but require immense social supports, would disappear. How to decide where the tradeoff ought to be made is something that no one but the people involved could decide, via the processes of political equality. This is not really a revolutionary proposal; only its egalitarian goal is revolutionary. In Switzerland, for example, "military service is subsidized by industry in various ways. A soldier in a refresher course . . . is being paid as usual by his civilian company, and the government's reimbursement to the company is only seventy [sic] percent—and, of course, the lost work is irrecoverable . . . The higher a man rises in the army, the more of his time—by a very large factor—his company gives, for army time in no way invades vacation time."[9]

Doubtless only a utopian fantasist, a Fourier, could hope to say how other organizations or communities might go about allocating time to the various types of legitimate, rewarded social behavior that equal citizens might be engaged in. What we can say here is that every social order develops norms about what constitutes, in the largest sense, "a fair day's work for a fair day's pay." To say that in a democratic society both "work" and "pay" ought to be defined differently than as we define them now, is in no way to imply that such common understandings could not be reached among the citizens of a democracy. By the same token, every community develops norms about what constitutes the kind of commitment to it that ought to be rewarded with an equal say in the conduct of its affairs. That kind of determination too could be made by democratic citizens. That comparatively footloose workers might have to seek their say in public affairs elsewhere than at the workplace would strike no one as unreasonable, since all are capable of understanding that every way of life has its own costs. I have no desire to substitute my own mythology of the empowering labor market for existing mythologies of the free labor market. Life will always contain restrictions and limitations imposed by those among whom we live. The question is not whether there are restrictions, but who is authorized to impose them, and on what grounds.

In sum, a person's growth through the life and work cycle ought to be mediated by his or her desires and capabilities, and by the community's overall resources, but not by the restrictions of a tracking system into which the individual has fallen, or been recruited. At present, the allocation of men and women to their work, and usually, through that, to their place in the social order, is made at a kind of social crossroads where the impersonal marketplace for labor, the burdens of class and caste, and the psychosocial history of the individual meet in uneasy conjunction. Typically, the first two of those forces dominate the third, which is to say that most of us have no part and never will have any part in establishing the social understandings to which we will be subject. Our choice is limited to one of several available predefined modes of arranging work, education, leisure, and family structure that will best mesh with our personal needs. In a democratic society the determinations of the labor market and of class and caste—that is, determinations by the powerful for the powerless—would have to be replaced by the determinations of conscious discussion, experiment, and cooperative decision making.

I began this essay by insisting that all theories of economic democracy must confront the issue of where people who fill the roles of workers and women have come from, and how and why they got to be workers or housewives. The purpose of the preceding discussion, then, has been to answer that question from a distinctly egalitarian perspective: to answer it in a way that makes of the democratic division of labor a distinctly different social formation, rather than the familiar undemocratic division of labor. That answer has been that people limited to doing primarily types of work we now consider "working class" or "women's work", will be men and women who are doing what they do because it is what they truly want to do. They will be men and women who, having been encouraged by the entire arrangement of social structure to explore the kinds of training and experience that lead either to intellectually complex labor or to participation in planning responsibilities on one hand; or to less intellectually complex labor or freedom from managerial responsibilities on the other hand, have discovered that they prefer the latter way of life and want as little to do with the former as possible. The democratic division of labor is neither more nor less than that.

# Notes

[1] Some readers will surely be wondering at this point, what is the source of this "ought" that appears here, and that recurs, scattered here and there, throughout these pages. Is this "ought" given by history (as for Marx); or is it a utilitarian "ought;" or does some latent, unexpressed general ethical principle lurk within this essay? In a sense, the answer is "all of the above." I assume an historically expressed demand for democratic equality, without which my own philosophizing would be meaningless. On the other hand, democratic theory as I postulate it here requires that that demand be expressed by a majority of real people, not imputed to any universal class or other reified historical force; in that sense this "ought" is utilitarian. Finally, I assume an ethical logic of democratic equality that has ("ought") to be applied whenever we are trying to decide what general policy democracy would require; in that sense, I insist on a normative principle of ethical consistency: an insistence validated by nothing more than the normal expectations of human discourse.

[2] John Dewey, *The Public and Its Problems* (Denver: Alan Swallow, 1927).

[3] For an excellent discussion of this point, see Carmen Sirianni's "Production and Power in a Classless Society," cited in footnote 2 to chapter 4; see also Ellen Turkish Comisso, *Worker's Control Under Plan and Market* (New Haven: Yale University Press, 1980).

[4] John Stuart Mill and Harriet Taylor Mill, *Essays on Sex Equality,* ed. by Alice S. Rossi (Chicago: University of Chicago Press, 1970), pp. 178–79; and Jean-Jacques Rousseau, *Emile*, trans. by Allan Bloom (New York: Basic Books, 1979), Book V.

[5] What I call the "division of labor in reproduction" is roughly similar to what is called the "sex gender system" by Gayle Rubin, "The Traffic in Women," in *Toward an Anthropology of Women,* ed. by Rayna Reiter (New York: Monthly Review Press, 1976), pp. 157–210. I have also been greatly influenced by Ann Ferguson's notion of a "dual gender system," of which the "sex/affective system" is the element corresponding to the division of labor in reproduction; see her "Women as a New Revolutionary Class," in Pat Walker ed. *Between Labor and Capital*, (Boston: South End Press, 1979), pp 279–309. However, my use of the language of a dualistic division of labor is a matter of convenience only. I do not mean to endorse dual-systems theory, which treats the two spheres of the division of labor as analytically separate—

one being a manifestation of capitalism, the other of patriarchy. My references to two different divisions of labor are not meant to suggest that different principles operate in the different spheres; a strong argument can be made that the division of labor in production is a division of labor by gender as well as by class. See Iris Young, "Socialist Feminism and the Limits of Dual Systems Theory," *Socialist Review*, No. 50–51, vol. 10 no. 2/3 (March-June 1980), pp. 169–188; and "Beyond the Unhappy Marriage: A Critique of the Dual Systems Theory," in Lydia Sargent, ed., *Women and Revolution* (Boston: South End Press, 1980). Interestingly, some of the best description of women's work in the man's world of production has been written by dual systems theorists, and their own analyses tend to bear out Young's claim that the division of labor by gender is crucially important in the sphere of production. See, e.g., Heidi Hartmann, "Capitalism, Patriarchy, and Job Segregation by Sex," in Zillah R. Eisenstein, ed., *Capitalist Patriarchy and the Case for Socialist Feminism* (New York: Monthly Review Press, 1979), pp. 206–47; and Batya Weinbaum, *Pictures of Patriarchy* (Boston: South End Press, 1982). See also Louise Kapp Howe, *Pink Collar Workers* (New York: G.P. Putnam, 1977); Barbara Garson, *All the Livelong Day* (New York: Doubleday, 1975); Carol Adams and Rae Laurikietis, *The Gender Trap, A Closer Look at Sex Roles, Book 1: Education and Work* (London: Virago, 1976); and Diana Leonard Barker and Sheila Allen, eds., *Dependénce and Exploitation in Work and Marriage* (London: Longman, 1976). The most compelling recent attempt to construct a theory of the relationship between the two spheres, beyond a critique of dual-systems theory, is Johanna Brenner and Maria Ramas, "Rethinking Women's Oppression," *New Left Review*, No. 144 (March-April 1984), pp. 33–71. Their argument, developed with great subtlety and attention to historical nuance, is that "historically developed capitalist class relations of production, *in combination with the biological facts of reproduction* [my emphasis], set up a powerful dynamic toward the family-household system, assuring women's continued subordination to men and their exaggerated vulnerability to capitalist exploitation . . . Thus, gender divisions are not so much embedded in the capitalist division of labor or relations of production, as produced by a complex balance of forces at a given point in the history of capitalism. Most crucial among these are the development of the forces of production, the organization of the working class, the self-organization of women, the state of the economy . . ." (p. 71).

[6] For fuller, though sociologically inadequate, analyses of the psychosocial dynamics of gender differentiation within the family, see Nancy Chodorow, *The Reproduction of Mothering* (Berkeley: University of California, 1978); and Dorothy Dinnerstein, *The Mermaid and the Minotaur* (New York: Harper and Row, 1976). Despite severe methodological limitations and her tendency toward a genteel version of sexual Manicheanism, Carol Gilligan's *In a Different Voice* (Cambridge: Harvard University Press, 1982), has deservedly become the most influential contemporary statement about the reality of "female discourse." See also Kathy Ferguson, *The Feminist Case Against Bureaucracy* (Philadelphia: Temple University Press, 1984).

[7] Linda Gordon, *Woman's Body, Woman's Right* (New York: The Viking Press, 1976).

[8] Cf., Herbert Gans on "The Uses of Poverty," in his *More Equality* (New York: Vintage Books, 1974). Even within a capitalist social formation we can find, for example, an instance of garbage collectors organizing a cooperative, worker-controlled service, and thereby providing themselves with a degree of self-esteem and job satisfaction that is usually denied sanitation workers in the U.S. See Stewart E. Perry, *San Francisco Scavengers; Dirty Work and the Pride of Ownership* (Berkeley: University of California Press, 1978).

[9] See John McPhee, "A Reporter At Large," *The New Yorker*, vol. LIX, no. 37 (October 31, 1983), p. 95.

# 6

# SOCIALIZATION OF THE MEANS OF PRODUCTION

## I

The democratic division of labor, then, is founded in those institutions that help us to abolish the reserve army of labor and to bridge the class gap between mental and material labor and between the labor of the sexes: constrained inequality; the guarantee of socially valued activity for all; the integration of the demands of work, education, and home; and, underlying all of these, the social agreement that the empowerment of citizens is the highest social priority.

As I have pointed out earlier, however, none of this can be accomplished in the slightest without the transformation of the relations of production from an autocratic to a democratic form. Despite the so-called "knowledge revolution," the division of labor between those who own productive property and thereby do not have to work for a living, and those who must work for wages for a living, still remains the most decisive and far-reaching in its effects. A democratic, egalitarian approach to attenuating the class distinctions, and thus the unequal political relationships, among managers and operatives, white-collar and blue-collar workers, the knowledge class and the working class, etc., cannot even be framed coherently until we have realized the social relations that I call, "equal access to the means of production."

The principle of equal access to, or democratic organization of, the means of production, poses two inescapable requirements that seem incompatible with each other by traditional socialist standards, but are inextricably linked for the political egalitarian. The first require-ment is for a public sector of production (as distinct from education and training, or parenting) within which the socially standard reward is available to those who seek it. Since the standard reward must be precisely standard in order to maintain the regime of relative class-lessness, the public sector must be significant and even dominant within the political economy of democracy; it must encompass the sphere within which the sustenance of equal citizenship primarily takes place. In that respect relations of production that we ought to call socialist are precedent to the attainment of political equality. What exactly we might want to mean by that word, though, is a com-plex question.

We can begin by saying, that the traditional socialist model of a centralized, command economy, is unsatisfactory for egalitarians. If for no other reason, that is because it is communities rather than the State that must have the minimal resources necessary to support their own members in the luxury of participating in the common life, or of representing the community in its transactions with others (else political life will quickly become as pseudodemocratic as it is among us). In order to avoid direct confrontation with and ultimate depen-dence on the national state or its equivalent, citizens require intermed-iary and immediately accessible sources of well-being under their own control. Every citizen must have some kind of direct link to the carry-ing on of a society's basic material activity. This fundamental principle—in the absence of which democratic socialism would inevit-ably become authoritarian socialism—tells us that however legal jur-isdictions are defined, however the narrow question of the legal own-ership of the means of production is settled, and whatever means of central oversight and planning are created, direct control of the bulk of productive capital must be in decentralized hands. Otherwise it will not be possible to sustain political equality, for the centralized state no more than the market is capable of distributing the material resources of citizenship. Communities must normally form the basic social units within which the citizenship needs of their inhabitants are met. The Marxist tradition of wishing away the problem of conflicting interest, and the need for group self-protection by imagining ''the proletariat'' to be the universal class, has proved to be a sure step on the road to the totally unresponsive and impermeable state monopolies of Soviet-style Communism. Clearly, then, some version of community ownership and control of some productive economic institutions is essential. By itself, though, that is not enough.

## II

Essentially there are two alternative methods for organizing public ownership of the means of production. (From here on my use of that term also comprehends financial institutions that contribute to production, the means of production of organized social services, and of land that produces agricultural or other goods primarily for the market.) The first is ownership by "the public" which, through boards of managers, becomes what Marx called "the universal capitalist." This would seem to be the logical method of public ownership for a centralized economy. As is clear from Marx's terminology, it raises troubling questions as to how a wage earner for the universal capitalist is different from a wage earner for General Motors. The second method is cooperative ownership by all those who work as part of a given enterprise; this method too poses problems for democratic theory.

Decentralized cooperative ownership has the immediately recognizable virtue that it seems to do away with the notion of a detached, distant, managerial elite that is really in control of the enterprise's destiny. Presumably whoever manages a cooperative enterprise is there as a delegate of the cooperating workers, or perhaps also of a local community in which their work and their nonwork lives are embedded. Thus, workplace cooperation checks both workplace autocracy and the expansion of the national state at the same time.

However, even though communal life can be built quite happily on material bases that are quite divergent from each other, regional disparities in certain fundamentally requisite resources, natural transportation facilities, etc., will probably always require reallocations that can only fairly be accomplished by some supracommunal, national, or international body that might as well be called the State. It is difficult to imagine the disappearance of large-scale centralized authority of some kind, as long as the human universe consists of something more than wholly independent communities; as long as interdependency rather than self-sufficiency is the rule of life. Unless all versions or functional equivalents of the state form are to be abolished completely, and unless the competitive anarchy of the capitalist marketplace is to be reproduced in the guise of thoroughgoing, unmitigated decentralization, the need for public oversight will recreate some variant of detached managerialism somewhere in the body politic. Wherever it reappears we will say that "politics" on the large scale is taking place. Completely communalist visions of social life are consistent within themselves, but they all share the defect that in the absence of the complete self-sufficiency of a commune, problems of political order and commodity pricing are reintroduced as questions of foreign policy. We will therefore need to develop principles of political representation that will be no different from the principles of representation by which "the public" would attempt to control nationalized industries in the traditional sense.

Thus the notion of "equal access to the means of production" poses a dilemma that is no more simply resolved by intonation of the phrase, "community control" than by that older incantation, "the socialization of industry." There would undoubtedly be more direct involvement of workers in a local cooperative enterprise than in a nationalized one; yet it is not beyond the bounds of likelihood that local workers' cooperatives might only get to be involved in the making of very marginal decisions, the others being made in some central "political" location: regardless of how carefully we have attempted to abolish "the State." That might be true as well even of municipal or regional (even of national!) enterprises.

Furthermore, like formal public ownership, the notion of cooperative ownership also raises troubling questions: about how a person gets to be an owner (shareholder), or to stop being one; how shares are transferred; what a share actually entitles a person to; etc. In addition, small-scale cooperative enterprises are likely to limit their ownership only to those immediately involved with them in some way or other; whereas the nationalization of productive industry makes it possible to distribute ownership shares (in the form of bonds) and thus claims on either authority or income, to the entire public.

To ask "what form of public ownership?," then, is to ask the wrong question. Rather, we want to know the political conditions of public ownership, however it takes place. The principle of political equality commands that the relationship of workers to their work ought to take on as democratic a form as possible in a society of political equals; neither local nor general public "owners" ought to be able to override it to further potentially contrary views of how an enterprise might be more "efficiently" conducted. But conversely, those who are affected by the work that is carried on around them, and upon which they depend for their immediate well-being, must have some kind of say in the crucial decisions about the disposition of the products and services, as well as the external costs, it creates. Nor does it matter that we, as philosophical observers distant in time and space, might be able to make a sophisticated methodological argument that it's impossible to distinguish between "what affects me" and "what doesn't affect me." Having an equal say about "what affects me" will be the substance of what a good deal of their politics will be about. Where citizens think they need an equal say they will demand it; and where they demand it, the principles of political equality will suggest to everyone that maybe they ought to have it. Thus we might imagine an emblematic dialogue between say a chemical worker and a teacher living near the chemical plant. The former says, "You don't try to tell me how hard to work every day, and I won't try to tell you where our chemical wastes are going to be disposed of"; the latter replies, "You don't try to tell me that I have to put up with whatever waste disposal methods you find easier, and I won't try to tell you how hard you have to work." That is a dialogue for a nonutopian but genuinely democratic society in which there are truly conflicting interests. Politics—the public negotiation of what it is that can be reasonably said to "affect me" and what it is that can be reasonably said to constitute "my say"—will not disappear in any egalitarian but nonutopian social order; and thus, no resolution of the question of ownership of the means of production should be thought of as obviating the need for continuous free political dialogue.

Thus, in some important sense democratic control of an economy entails socialization of ownership (whether by way of nationalization, regionalization, or municipalization), *and* cooperative workers' self-management, *and* community control or oversight of enterprises that impinge on it significantly. The exact form that social ownership and control takes does not really matter; it will probably depend more on local or regional or national traditions than on anything else. Ownership might devolve on citizens through their receiving shares as actual workers in an enterprise, or by their individual purchase of small shares (such as the Liberty Bonds of World War II in the U.S.), through the activities of pension funds in which they have a share, or

of local or communal corporations that would invest in a local enterprise on behalf of all their members. Whatever the methods, their
common purpose would be twofold. There would be a democratic
procedure for raising the equivalent of investment capital, and for
insuring all citizens who directly or indirectly contributed of a direct
and equal link to society's material base, and thus to the public
management of capital (on the one person one vote rather than one
dollar one vote principle). At the same time, no one would become
an owner of corporate enterprises in the traditional capitalist sense.
That is crucial. The essential purpose of public ownership is not to
convey the traditional powers of ownership to people who once
lacked them. Those traditional powers of ownership shouldn't be possessed by anyone in a society of political equals.

That is, all relationships at work, or among workplaces and communities, are going to have to be negotiated among equals in an egalitarian regime. Political equality in this respect consists simply of
abolishing as a class that special class of persons with whom such
negotiations can never be on equal terms. How precisely that abolition occurs is of much less importance, as long as it does not consist
of substituting a new class of dominant owners (now known as "the
State") for the old; and as long as it is undertaken by a majority intent
on the creation of democratic industrial *and* political relationships.
Generally, I should think that in a large nation conventional nationalization decreases the chances for public control, and some kind of
municipalization combined with a workers' cooperative regime
increases them. But the greatest productive entitites may at first only
be controllable through the tool of nationalization; and it may be
unacceptably costly to truly decentralize them. In any event, the public ownership of business is only a tool, the end being democratic
control however realized. The democratic majority itself will always
have to decide which version of the tool is most appropriately chosen.

# III

Given these considerations, how far should the principle of abolishing
private ownership of the means of production be taken, in order to
ensure equal access to the means of production without reconstitut-
ing the tyrannies of economic centralization? As a first approximation
it might seem that democrats should say, only those who employ the

labor of others should be expropriated, and only those enterprises in which the labor of others must be employed should be socialized. But that formula, designed to preserve the world of individual enterprise amidst a dominating realm of public enterprise, is an evasion. It is astonishing how few people in the occupational structure of a modern economy neither work for nor employ others.[1] If our principle is that those enterprises in which some people are employed by other people should be socialized, we will wind up with an entire economy under public ownership.

Why, it might conceivably be asked, should we reject this prospect out of hand? Though nationalization of an entire economy is associated so far in our historical experience only with tyranny, some democratic socialists might argue that as long as the public control of enterprise is predominantly local or communal, and monopolistic behavior is regulated, then the likelihood of tyranny recedes, democratic relationships are enhanced, and the perversions of the free market can best be eliminated.

There are both prudential and principled reasons for rejecting this vision. Questions of political power aside, the centralized public economy is hardly a satisfactory alternative to the illusory free market. The free-market argument against monopoly may be anachronistic, but that does not mean it is incorrect. In the absence of constraining competition, centralized decision making (whether by governments or by giant corporations) can be very inefficient, rigid, and unresponsive, in addition to its political drawbacks. Whether planners and decision makers in an enterprise are actually bureaucrats under illusory controls from below, or genuine delegates of their comrade workers, in a noncompetitive economy they will be limited in their perception of the meaning of their actions by either their own or their comrades' knowledge and intelligence. Among the great virtues of competition, on the other hand, is that in dealing with its demands we must deal with facts of life that force us to accumulate knowledge about the world beyond our own limited visions of our own interests. In the long run, even a dominated but competitive market makes parochialism unlikely. Conversely, even the most thoughtful, democratized, central or local planning does not overcome narrowness in professional or interest-group outlook, if it can be undertaken by a self-selected clique of like-minded persons or neighbors. Within limits, therefore, democrats will find it desirable to foster competition for access to markets and to goods, and limitations on anticompetitive pricing and other enterprise behavior, among a mixture of public and private enterprises.

Moreover, even decentralized community ownership could cause similar difficulties. The search for a democracy rooted in the community could very easily lead to the installation of a series of localized monopolies. That community-owned enterprises need not be giants does not insure that they would not be monopolies. Some would serve the community exactly as intended, but others would offer benefits only to some, while potentially harming the interests of others (outsiders, rebels, would-be innovative entrepeneurs). Nor is it an answer to this complaint to echo the Rousseauian or populist version of Marxian apologetics; to assert that independent entrepreneurs or smallscale communities seeking competitive terms for their behavior as producers or consumers would be part of the collectivity, as the individual, according to Rousseau, may be part of the general will. To assume away the problem of conflicting interests in the good society, by conjuring up "the people" as an alleged reality, is to accomplish no more than to invent a proletariat to which everyone belongs.

In addition, and more crucially, many kinds of goods and services are apparently best delivered by the independent small businessperson, and are going to continue to be delivered in that form (if only via a black market) no matter how stringently socialist legislation attempts to abolish that social role. Surely egalitarianism must have an important place for those who love the entrepeneurial way of life: not in the exploitativeness which is only essential to it in certain social formations, but in its creativity and independence. In the loosest sense of the term—attempting, perhaps impossibly, to free it from any linkage with particular social formations such as liberal capitalism—the private sphere is the sphere in which we learn to resist and escape from the kinds of social expectations that really amount to social control. A society that is all social expectation, and no individual resistance will be a tyranny.

At the same time, and seemingly conversely (but it may actually be the same point) there are also undoubtedly many people who crave subordination, nonresponsibility, and simple routine. That is a kind of independence and resistance too. To act as though such people are inauthentically human, or suffering from a false consciousness, is to make indefensible assumptions about what is natural in human economic behavior. We cannot assume that everyone will be satisfied by the chance to participate in cooperative, democratically organized economic activity; or that the way in which goods or services are produced through such activity will satisfy all consumers equally. Given human diversity, to insist on a purely public productive base would be to subject those who prefer a different kind of participation in economic life to a version of majority tyranny. That would be to make democratic equality and individual rights contradict each other. If they really do, there is no hope for either.

Perhaps Marx's most signal failure as a social analyst, in addition to his general treatment of mid-nineteenth-century social classes as fundamental social essences, was his particular treatment of the petty bourgeoisie (and the agricultural population) as nothing but a remnant being gradually ground between the upper and nether millstones of capital and labor. That failure has plagued socialism of all varieties (even social democracy) ever since. The proliferating world of retailers, farmers, independent contractors, artists and craftspersons, purveyors of personal services and public entertainment, and the like, is not a hangover from precapitalism or early capitalism but is actually part of the essence of advanced capitalism itself. Bigness is not easy to organize without a well-developed network of supporting institutions. Bureaucratic controls become more inefficient the wider their net is cast; small scale enterprise provides many services for large scale enterprise at better quality and more cheaply than the latter could provide for itself.

In addition, the role of different kinds of enterprises in technological innovation and invention is crucial. Though cooperative workers might well be as good as or even better than entrepreneurs or managers at organizing their own labor, we do not really expect a committee of workers, however well-educated and active in the roles of citizenship, to sit around a table inventing microchips or the cathode tube together. And suppose someone does exactly that. Would we expect them, even in utopia, to drop everything until a cooperative factory in which they will have no more say than any other individual can be established somewhere? And at any rate, given full employment, how are they to get workers to do this, except through the whole paraphernalia of political bargaining and the negotiation of trade-offs which, as can be attested by both Communist and capitalist societies, is sure to stifle initiative and development? Of course, we know that public policy can encourage innovation, and we should be able to hope that it would be as progressive as possible within the limits of what it would be trying to accomplish (the "production" of citizens). Still, on these grounds alone it seems that the sphere of private enterprise should be protected.[2]

Thus, for all these reasons the independent sector has not been abolished (and will not be) by monopoly capital, but has grown along with it. Even though it now employs a much smaller proportion of the population than it once did, it must continue to grow, or at least remain in place, no matter the extent to which capital itself is nationalized or otherwise made a public resource. The millions of businesspeople and independent professionals in the advanced capitalist societies who refuse to see themselves as either labor or capital constitute a genuine social grouping in their own right.

At the same time we should resist any romanticization of the small business sector. The ideal of a society composed wholly of small, independent, competitive producers is a utopian dream. It is impossible to re-create the world that many American critics seem to have in their minds as an alternative to monopoly capitalism: an early capitalist society of simple commodity producers trading directly with each other, at the marketplace equivalent of a New England town meeting. This kind of capitalism, it is often implied by these criticisms, has been deformed in the age of the giants. But that is a misunderstanding. Advanced capitalism is not centralized and regulated and cartelized because it is monopoly capitalism, but just because it is capitalism. Capitalism is centralized not by historical accident, but by its nature. The greater the proportion of the market they control, the more secure and extensive are the capitalists' profits, and they will no more fail to seek concentrated market power than flowing water will fail to seek to reach the low ground. Return to that world, and we would just be starting all over again.

Moreover, no democratic movement can be based primarily on the interests and ideology of the petty bourgeois sector, and for good reasons. A political mobilization based on small property holders and small businesspeople would be warring not only on large capital but also on organized labor. Workers, after all, are well-aware that no matter how many small businesses there are in the free market utopia, most of them are unlikely to own one. Nor is it the experience of workers that independent businesses in the truly competitive sector are less authoritarian and more solicitous of human need than the monopolistic and oligopolistic giants; often, as in the revealing case of Japanese capitalism, the contrary is true.[3]

Thus, it is often suggested that, independent of its effects on consumers large-scale enterprise is also necessarily more exploitative of workers, and of accidental consumers of its output (e.g., of pollutants). But the evidence is at best indecisive for the critic of bigness. The "mom and pop" grocery store is often an autocracy; family farms exploit migrant labor mercilessly; there are "hip" restaurants catering to liberal arts college students in which the waiters and waitresses are treated like transient dirt. Some factories, such as those of Volvo in Sweden are, contrarily, models of employee participation, decentralized group initiative, the encouragement of teamwork, humane working conditions, and so on. Our experience worldwide is that any man or woman who intends to make a career of a particular kind of work that is organized both as big business and in small local units; who wants the protections of unionization, supervised working conditions, and up-to-date facilities; and who yearns for job security, might be well advised to choose the large-scale over the small. In a socialized economy this means the public over the private.

That contrast comports with some of our intuitions, too. We automatically think of the small grocery store or the small restaurant as belonging to a person, who has a personal human stake in the enterprise, often works harder and longer at it than his or her transient employees, and thus is likely to have a low tolerance for their efforts to relax on the job. Even for those who believe in unionization or workplace democracy as matters of principle, to talk of them in the context of, say, Joe's Pizzeria, often seems as troubling as it seems to talk about due process and civil rights in the family: an image of human community, however anachronistic or romantic or simply false, is being violated.

On the other hand, large-scale enterprise seems the natural home of workplace democracy precisely because it is a community of citizens, who have both the solidarity with and the social distance from each other that the notion of citizenship entails. No one owns a corporation; individuals who hold either public or private shares in it but do not actually work for it have no personal relationship to it such as would be violated by its, and their, subjection to the rules of formal democracy. In this respect, the notion of "human scale," though real enough, is not necessarily compatible with political equality, and perhaps even incompatible with it. The human realm, however fervently we try to reject the notion of the family or of face-to-face community as a realm of natural inequality between the sexes, will always be a realm of natural inequality among the generations; and that kind of inequality easily becomes a model for employer-employee relations.

Thus, it is not surprising that historically, the petty bourgeoisie (for that is the social class that primarily dreams of the precapitalist utopia) more easily makes alliances with giant capital against labor than vice versa, no matter how populistic its rhetoric may be at its inception. On one hand a mass movement of small property cannot be democratic in the context of advanced capitalism; on the other hand, any would-be democratic movement will condemn itself to impotence if it pretends those persons do not exist, or that they belong to one of the social classes they refuse to belong to. That is the contradiction of democratic political economy with which all egalitarians must grapple.

## IV

Although I have not answered the question, how far public ownership of the means of production should extend, this discussion should have clarified it. What we see is that some seemingly obvious, simple answers to that question are not in fact really very helpful for the reason that the traditional antinomies in this discussion—big vs. small, private vs. public, monopolistic vs. competitive, market vs. nonmarket—are all equally misleading or false. For the egalitarian, the issue is not what mode of political economy is most efficient, or most decentralized, or even most humane, but how power is distributed.

Thus, the egalitarian critique of capitalism is based on an analysis (see chapter 3) of the structural power of big business: a structural power that gives members of the capitalist class their inordinate political influence and power. Small capitalists are also capitalists, but even as a class in capitalist society they do not shape the contours of our existence. (Teachers or social workers or skilled craftspersons reading this book, for example, should ask themselves if they feel politically subordinate to the man or woman who owns the shop downtown that sells exotic varieties of candles; or to the local independent bookseller.) The small capitalist is often at least as much a victim of corporate capital as he or she is an exploiter of labor, and indeed only has the chance to exploit labor because when labor as a class confronts capital as a class, and that is the primary social confrontation, the two kinds of capital become temporary allies.

But what of small capital in a social formation no longer marked by that primary confrontation; in which the central engagements of capital are for the most part undertaken by representatives of the citizenry rather than by the capitalist class?

Suppose, for example, we imagine the contemporary life style of present-day Americans suddenly transposed to a realm of political equality. We could well say about that realm that the existence of a sufficient supply of ''instant on'' energy, at a price low enough to be afforded by the average person, would be an ordinary part of the way we would then live, would make our lives more enjoyable, and would be intimately and naturally related to the rather frightening intemperance of what is oddly called North America's ''temperate climate.'' Private monopoly or oligopoly, in the supply of that energy, extorting above-average or simply immense profits from consumers without giving them some compensating benefit, would be intolerable to democrats; as it ought to be now to would-be democrats. The same is true of food and housing, which in our society now return monopoly profits to middlemen who monopolize the means of distribution.

On the other hand, to take an extreme counter-example, luxurious oceangoing yachts will never be a mass consumer product, and neither their availability nor their nonavailability nor their price has the slightest effect on an estimation of the pleasures that are a part of the way we live now. The most absolute and unresponsive private monopoly in the production of such yachts, therefore, would be completely trivial. The private yacht entrepreneur who escaped from the strictures of public control (with respect to the disposition and deployment of his capital) would harm no one. In fact, it would be a conspicuous and total waste of public energies and resources to try to control his economic activities, in any way. Further, since his product would be socially irrelevant, he could not possibly accrue any political power from being the only available source of supply for it (except in a community of the wealthy, and if any such existed, we would surely not worry about the democratization of their public lives).

## V

Is it the implication of this argument, then, that workplace democracy or any form of public control is a matter of indifference in the organization of small private business? Do I have a right to purchase my own independence at the price of the coerced dependence on me of those who work for me?

To a certain extent we can defend an approach to equality that frees small private business from some of the rules of the democratic division of labor, if a majority so chooses. That can be, however, only on the understanding that we have already implemented the crucial and unassailable institution of guaranteed full employment. In any discussion of the meaning of equality, one ethical principle has to be inviolate: that no one can be presumed to have chosen freely who has not had the freedom to choose. If one group of people must, by virtue of their position in a social order, comply with another group that, by virtue of its position in that same structure, need not comply with them, then the two groups form separate and unequal classes. From this perspective then, we can say that the small, owner-operated firm or retail establishment or service agency which employs casual or even (potentially) permanent, subordinated labor, does not necessarily create or participate in a system of cumulative inequalities that amount to the persistence of unequal social classes.

Even at their worst, in capitalist societies, the labor relations of the small business or agricultural world are implicated in an inegalitarian class structure only to the extent that such firms form part of a more complex system of dual labor markets, in which the secondary labor market serves the function of maintaining a reserve army of labor and depressing average wages. In capitalist societies a secondary labor market is indeed a restrictive device charged, in part, with that purpose among others. Collusion between job- and income-protective labor unions and profit- or stability-maximizing managements tends to exclude from the primary labor market those who are defined as "nonproductive" workers. These workers are doomed to migrate between the insecure, unstable, ill-paid, chaotic secondary market, and the reserve army of the unemployed. Doubtless, some workers make a truly temporary and voluntary commitment to the secondary labor market (college students, would-be artists, etc.) but most who work within that realm are locked into a less rewarding and more isolating job structure through no choice of their own. Involuntarily trapped in the secondary sector they are denied political equality, for they are frozen by no choice of their own into a way of life that precludes effective organization and economic pressure, and usually lacks social respect as well. For them, it is truly almost as much a disaster to have work as to not have it.

However, there will always be both workers and entrepreneurs who, even at a considerable material cost to themselves, will prefer the more independent, individualistic, and casual style of the small parochial enterprise, and, thus, there will always be a peripheral sector and secondary labor market. The critical condition that alone could make the continued existence of a dual labor market compatible with the demands of political equality, it follows, is the existence of the basic full employment guarantee in the primary labor market.

Put most simply, private enterprises at the periphery of the economy, employing labor according to hierarchical principles and paying it less than the standard wage, do not interfere with the search for a democratic division of labor and political equality as long as the provision of jobs, or retraining, or general education for all who want it, takes precedence over marginal productivity of labor as the principle of employment at the democratically controlled core. Political equality is as indifferent to the quality of genuinely voluntary relationships among employers and workers as among suppliers and consumers. Secondary labor markets, or for that matter institutions for the private provision of services on a differential basis (e.g., private schools, little theaters) are only a trap if you can't escape from them. If instead they are a locus in which some people can voluntarily lead lives of privatization, or face-to-face but paternalistic intimacy, or casual irresponsibility, then there is no legitimate objection to them.

Nor, as I have suggested in discussing the principle of constrained inequality, is it a compelling objection to a pluralistic economy that a private entrepeneur might be in a position to have a more commodious, after-tax standard of living, as long as that standard of living cannot be converted into political privilege, or unequal power over the lives of others. The ethos of democratic equality is consistent with any economic behavior, certainly with any economically progressive behavior that does not become self-perpetuating in the form of manipulative consumerism; without entrepreneurialism becoming the ideological tail wagging the cultural dog.

## VI

Keeping in mind these general principles about the democratic division of labor and ownership of the means of production, we can now sum up what we ought to say about the relationship between the public and private spheres in a democratic, egalitarian social order.

1. A democratic political economy must be a pluralist political economy. Both because people have different needs and personalities and diverse interests and motives, and because efficiency takes on different faces in different circumstances, openness to change and diversity has to be central to the democratic experience.

At the same time, however, there are aspects of the democratic division of labor that can only be implemented in a public arena. Thus there must be a significant public sphere in a democracy, and it must be significantly democratic. Primarily, we should think of it as the collection of enterprises or services for which the socially standard reward is paid, and in which labor is neither freely hired nor freely fired: the sphere of employment which people enter at will, and within which their self-improvement and civic improvement are understood as goods the cost of which is to be borne and benefits to be distributed by and to all, and from which they can be removed only for cause.

In our social order, everyone must make constant choices between work and education, and those whose differential needs or self-definitions compel the former choice become a working class. As well, in the liberal capitalist version of equal opportunity most women must also make constant choices between home and work, and those who make the former choice consistently—a choice urged on them by most cultural institutions—become a gender caste.

The conjoining of work, education, and home, contrarily, requires that there be widespread institutions and loci of social activity that are neither productive nor educational, neither productive nor reproductive, but ordinarily both (or for biological or surrogate parents all three) at once. It must be the case that to enter upon one or another of the institutions that we now think of separately as workplace, school, or home, is to make a claim on the community, within the limits of its resources, that it provide varieties of experience as a matter of course. The contemporary saying that "home is where they have to take you in when there's no place else for you to go" expresses the folk wisdom of capitalist society; of a society in which there literally is no place else to go for many people (and often even no home to go to). The public sphere in a democracy can be thought of as the place where they not only have to take you in but as a matter of common understanding provide you with the wherewithal for your civic well-being as well as your material satisfaction.

2. In an egalitarian regime, the public sphere must also be the realm in which the managers of enterprises or industries are representatives of the workplace community to which *·· ·ey belong, and the community in which they live, rather than the    ief hierarchs at the top of a pyramid of authority. That limitation is necessary not only to keep the division between mental and material labor from reintroducing itself to a threatening extent; it also expresses the main force of the abolition of the distinction between the owners and the nonowners of capital. In addition, this understanding of the public sphere enables us to stress, once again, that neither the market nor the State but rather communities, sustaining and governing themselves within boundaries set by the perceived need for integrative planning of a broader scope than they themselves can provide, are the fundamental constituent units of genuine democracy.

3. In an egalitarian regime, the public sphere is also the realm within which the cooperative owners, or workers, or managers of an enterprise are not free not to plan for the future under some general public constraint; are not free to curtail production of a socially desired good, merely because its market price or its publicly controlled price is less than they would like it to be. Nor could they be any freer than private entrepreneurs to pass on external costs to consumers or neighbors, or to move their physical or financial capital around as they would. That is, in common with the private sector public enterprises would not be free on their own initiatives to engage in any behavior which would contradict the goal of maximizing democratic equality. The anarchy of the free market is not objectionable because it is anarchy, but because it replaces personal cooperation with impersonal competition precisely where the latter is most destructive and the former most necessary. Calling that free market "decentralization," and even allowing it to operate only under cooperative or communal auspices, may somewhat lessen the destructive force of the competitive marketplace but certainly will not eliminate it. To be either blackmailed or despoiled by those who con-

trol a vital resource is not more pleasurable merely because they are cooperating together.

In sum, for that significant realm of enterprise we will have to call the public sphere the free labor market, the right of owners or their nominees to set conditions of labor, individual authority over the ultimate disposition of capital and the right to pass on external costs to consumers or neighbors must be suspended. Thus, this summation of the rights of productive enterprise in a democratic social order casts a revealing light on the contention of some liberal or social democrats, that ownership of the means of production is a secondary issue in the discussion of political equality; that public regulation is perhaps to be preferred to public ownership.[4]

In posing the question in this way, liberals and social democrats hope to avoid confronting the issue of coercive expropriation. It cannot be avoided, however. I have just asserted, after all, that in the public sphere certain conditions of economic authority must be suspended if political equality and the democratic division of labor are to be made manifest. But those conditions are the very fundamental conditions of individual ownership of the means of production itself. To establish the counter-conditions of equality is to expropriate the owners of any previously existing entity within which they are established, regardless, for it is to overturn the existing legal and social relations of corporate capitalism. Precisely how this aspect of expropriation should take place must be a matter of political tactics and national histories. But political equality and the democratic division of labor cannot exist until it takes place; until, that is, we abolish those legal relations which legitimize the private ownership and disposition of large agglomerations of capital, and which entail the economic and political division of labor by classes.

To put this point another way, democratization necessarily entails the abolition of private ownership of large-scale means of production in the sense of what we traditionally mean by ownership, whether one has willed it or not. How does anyone in a capitalist society benefit from the capitalist relations of production, from being a private owner or a management nominee of private owners, except by having power over the workplace, the industry, and perhaps the greater environment as well? Deprive their possessors of those powers and they are no longer capitalists: they are only high-level hired hands. Who then will want to do the job: who would be a private manager of private capital if the only substantial reward were to be hounded by works committees, citizen groups, and so forth? Who would invest their money in owning if their ownership entitled them to nothing but the rewards earned by someone else over whom they have no control? These questions are not answerable in a capitalist society, that is, a society in which private persons own the means of production. As long as the prerogatives of ownership are its very purpose, owners may tolerate incursions on those prerogatives (as in social democratic societies) but not their elimination. However ownership and management of the public sphere in a democracy are thought best to be arranged, as long as the public sphere exists to serve the purposes and carry out the principles outlined above, rather than merely disciplining the excesses of profit-seeking behavior, then those who used to be the private owners of its constituent parts will have been effectively expropriated: no matter what the disposition of their capital. Expropriation of the prerogatives of control effectively expropriates the prerogatives of ownership as well. And for this expropriation no compensation is possible. In a society of political equals the right to give orders to others may be conferred by them, or negotiated with them. It cannot be earned by investing money in their labor, for the essence of democratic theory is that no one can earn power over another without that other's consent.

4. At this point, then, we are in a position to take up the final remaining question about the public sphere in a democracy: how extensive ought it to be?

The general principle of an egalitarian commitment would seem to be that most daily human interchange (of which economic production and trade is but one example) ought to be carried on freely, by morally autonomous individuals or communities; but within the precedent constraint of an universal commitment to maximize shared, public well-being. The definition of education and child-rearing as activities that are deserving of the same kind of social reward and structural support as working, because they are seen as essential to the future of equal citizenship, is itself a guarantee that the public realm will be broad, and public spirit encouraged, even before a single firm is socialized. But as I have also just insisted we cannot do without socialization of some of the means of production. Which, then, and how many?

The simple answer to this question is that we do not need to answer it, any more than we answered the question of whether socialized enterprises should be local or national, centralized or decentralized; or whether housing or clothing or bicycles should be distributed by the market or public agency. The only thing we can say for sure is this. First, the public sphere has to be extensive enough at any moment to make the full employment guarantee viable; that is absolutely essential. Second, the public sphere has to be extensive enough to make cooperation rather than competition, civic rather than private activity, the morally normative experience of individual self-development. How many people would actually have to be receiving the guaranteed standard wage to leave the rest secure in the knowledge that they could have it if they wanted it, and how many people would have to be in the public sphere at any one time for everyone to share in that moral experience, are questions about subjective consciousness that we cannot answer a priori.

That imponderable consideration aside, there is no need for a theorist of democracy to go about drawing up lists of which industries ought to be under public control and which not, for that list too can only be drawn up by the democratically constituted majority once it has become convinced of the rightness of democratizing the division of labor.

No doubt, there are certain kinds of enterprise that it would be odd for a public engaged in the creation of political equality *not* to attempt to control definitively. It is probably the case, for example, that no program for the socialization of productive property can succeed unless it is accompanied by the nationalization of banking. Otherwise the banking sector will assist those in the corporate sector who are about to be expropriated in transferring their liquid assets abroad, thus weakening the international trading position of the egalitarian society. For reasons given above, currency controls on individuals ought to be avoided in a democracy; corporate wealth is another matter entirely. In fact, the beginning of real international monetary controls will probably have to precede the successfully democratic public control of enterprise in any one country.

In general, if at any given historical moment a debate is joined (as it has been in France and Great Britain) about the extent to which proposed socialization of business ought to proceed, egalitarians ought to enter that debate on the basis of current understandings of the productive world. But that list will be passé while this book is still being read. The point is that what appropriately belongs within the public sphere will become evident to people as they try democratically to control their own lives. As with the conception of what goods and services ought to be withdrawn from market provision and provided publicly, it's impossible to announce beforehand what are the basic industries from an ahistorical, abstract, theoretical stance. Beyond that, we need say nothing further about ownership of the means of production.

## Notes

[1] See Erik Olin Wright, *Class, Crisis, and the State* (New York: Schocken Books, 1978), p. 56, Table 1.

[2] John Jewkes, David Sawers, and Richard Stillerman argued in their seminal *The Sources of Invention* (London: Macmillan, 1958), that technological advance depends primarily on the efforts of individual researchers and inventors rather than large-scale corporate enterprises. Today their conclusion might have to be modified somewhat, especially as regards the leading role of government-sponsored team research; but their argument certainly still contains enough truth to make us uneasy about the continued spread of "bigness," private or public.

[3] See the special issue of *The Nation,* "The Selling of Japan," vol. 234, no. 6 (February 13, 1982), for an unsentimentalized view of Japan's political economy.

[4] See for example Robert Dahl, "In Rebuttal," in Irving Howe, ed., *Beyond the Welfare State* (New York: Schocken Books, 1982), p. 93. And see John Rawls, Chapter V of *A Theory of Justice;* (Cambridge: Harvard University Press, 1971) and C.A.R. Crosland, *The Future of Socialism*, rev. ed. (New York: Macmillan, 1963).

# 7

# PLANNING AND ACCUMULATION

## I

To describe a system of equal access to the means of production is one thing; to suggest how that system might work in practice quite another. To paraphrase Hotspur's oft-paraphrased question, we can summon democracy from the vasty deep: but will it come when called? In effect, the democratic egalitarian must argue that some variant of public agency can be an effective adjudicator of the conflict for resources between present and future. At the moment, government in both capitalist and state socialist societies has a bad reputation, for self-evident reasons.

At one level of course, the egalitarian can point out that government freed from the burdens of maintaining the reserve army of labor, and of supporting the perennially escalating demands of insecure sectors in a competitive but dominated economy, ought to be less rather than more ubiquitous and distasteful in an egalitarian regime than it is among us.

There is a more fundamental point to be made. In order to make it, however, we have to move beyond the restrictive conceptual framework within which most contemporary discussions of the role of government take place; to rid ourselves of certain preconceptions about what it is that government is, and does.

The most crucial of these preconceptions is that aspect of liberal political theory that enshrines the separation of politics and economics as the very definition of society. Disputes usually arise, in this understanding, over conflicting economic behaviors; public agencies are then created or used to settle those disputes authoritatively. Necessarily then, government or the state is antagonistic. If we private persons, whoever we are, could have struck a deal, reached a settlement, been satisfied with our exchange, government intervention would not have been necessary and presumably we would both be happy. Instead, at least one of us is unhappy, and government can only either confirm that unhappiness, or assuage it, thereby worsening the situation of the other party to the exchange. Either way, government intervenes when there is antagonism and, most often, resolves the antagonism by force majeure, without actually mitigating it. It should not be surprising that as viewed by people who have been brought up in the liberal tradition to be economic actors, government should develop a reputation largely for being unpleasant. Resolving conflict, government actually confirms it; that is especially true of class and group conflict.

There is another way of looking at government, however. Rather than seeing government as merely a coercive policeman, we can also think of government as the locus for resolving disputes which we have within ourselves.

In my own person, I have no idea how much to spend, how much to save; how much to wrap myself in a blanket of material security, how much to leave myself open to innovation and change; how much to devote myself to private or public satisfactions; how much to cooperate with others, and how much to compete with them because cooperation has become exploitative or untrustworthy. Government is among other things but perhaps most importantly of all, the agency through which I can potentially become a whole rather than a divided person. Neither I nor most other people can make these decisions for ourselves without feeling deeply uncertain and uneasy, and thus without being tempted constantly and irrationally to undo them. Through the agencies of government we can aggregate our uncertainties into one certainty: a certainty not because it is right but because we have agreed beforehand that it will be authoritative.

Among other things, government is the agency by means of which we authoritatively resolve our uncertainties about how to divide the social product (at any moment) between the present and the future. That governments levy taxes and decide how to expend them is from this perspective irrelevant. So too all profit makers who receive returns beyond the amount necessary to support their own standard of living are also levying taxes, and deciding how to expend them. If there were no government at all (beyond the fundamental police power), then private profit-makers would even have to provide the social welfare and infrastructure functions that governments now provide. They would be governments, each of them; and if the richest and most powerful among them chose representatives to meet together and plan in an orderly fashion, they would be a Government. Basic structural planning is going to take place somehow; if public agencies don't oversee it or carry it out themselves, it will still be done; but not democratically.

Looking at the question of public agency from this perspective, we see that democratic egalitarians face not merely one but two difficult challenges. The first, and more traditional one, is whether public agency can be as effective as the market. It is perhaps even more troubling, though, to have to ask the opposite question: to inquire whether democratic, pluralistic planning, which seems to be entailed by any commitment to community control of business enterprise and self-government at the workplace, can do more than re-create the self-interested and antisocial irrationalism of the free market itself on one hand; or fall prey to some form of overarching planning that stifles local, communal, or individual initiative, on the other hand. Short of modes of centralized coercion that must be unacceptable among political equals, what powers can planners hope to have at their command, to overcome whatever parochial short-sightedness may arise and threaten the achievement of necessary provision for the future?[1]

## II

Let us approach this second challenge by imagining a crisis, in a productive sector central enough to the well being of our society as to require major efforts to restructure or redeploy the capital invested in it. By a crisis we mean that the cost of producing this particular good or this combination of goods has gone up decisively for whatever reasons, relative to the costs of other social goods; or, we might mean that for exogenous reasons demand for this good or goods has fallen sharply. In either case, to retain the same amount and value of labor or labor time as had been involved in its production before the crisis,

must bring about a massive diversion of resources from other potentially more productive sectors. Either an overproduction of goods or
an underutilization of labor will result; the workers or their resource
suppliers would ultimately have to be subsidized from the public
purse if their standard of living were not to fall.

The so-called free-market solution to this crisis is clear enough.
What the free market is really meant to be free of is the ability of workers to protect themselves against the efforts of the powerful to control
and restructure it. The supply side is to be resupplied with cheaper
labor. This has been made clear by both the Reagan and Thatcher
governments. The underlying logic of this solution is that if the marginal cost of subsidized labor exceeds its marginal product, then since
by definition it is inefficient to employ marginally unproductive labor,
the noncompetitive sectors of the economy must be "wrung out."

This is the logic of the classical business cycle of capitalism, that
Joseph Schumpeter, in a much quoted phrase, referred to as
"creative destruction".[2] It is a very selective creative destruction,
though. Economists, managers, and capitalists do the creating, but
with rare exceptions suffer no "destruction." The working class, especially its most marginal members, and marginal producers and small
distributors are asked to pay the painful price for the successful
implementation of riches through poverty. The class that implements
the strategy pays much less or not at all.[3]

It is not as yet clear whether the working class in any advanced
capitalist society will accept this strategy, and give it enough time to
work. It is plain from both the American and the British experiences
that if they do so, it will only be because no one seems able to present
a coherent, viable alternative solution to the crisis. We must understand the political significance of this prospect. What we are contemplating is the voluntary resignation from political activism—through
some combination of apathy, passive hopefulness, and fear—of large
segments of the population.

The free-market solution demands the demobilization of democratic citizenship, whether voluntarily or with the help of a very
unlaissez-faire state. Almost certainly it also demands bellicosity and
adventurism abroad, or serious repression at home or both. The
working class cannot for long be asked to accept its naked suppression unless offered the quid pro quo of national unity against some
available scapegoats who can be treated even more wretchedly. Ultimately, down this road lies barbarism.

## III

How, contrastingly, does corporatist social democracy or Keynesian liberalism as it exists today, propose to deal with the same contingencies? The short answer is that social democratic corporatism faces a serious dilemma. The corporatist solution is to negotiate a compromise between the interests of that fraction of the working class that must be dispossessed to allow capital restructuring to take place, and the interests of all other citizens in their roles as consumers and taxpayers. Through the supportive programs of the welfare state, social democratic governments attempt to flatten out the fury of the business cycle while still being able to give special support to those making innovative and efficient attempts to become more productive. For a period of 20 years in Western Europe this strategy seemed to work, but under the pressure of events it is looking only marginally superior, if at all, to the free-market strategy. Keynesian policy, as John Kenneth Galbraith pointed out 30 years ago, does not work well in an inflationary economy; when the nature of the crisis is such as to build inflation into economic structures, Keynesianism therefore begins to lose its appeal.[4] Especially given the pressures of international competition within an international capitalist framework, social democratic corporatism has the intrinsic limitation that the preservation of national capital's international competitiveness in a world capitalist market remains the overriding priority in all crisis planning, no matter how formally cooperative the relationship between capital and labor may be.

Thus, in the absence of a sharp break with capitalist pseudodemocracy, the costs of restructuring must follow predictable class lines; the class compromise that produced social democratic corporatism must be abandoned. All the while a frustrating commitment to the continued expansion of commodity consumption—the essential ethos of capitalism—is maintained and even cultivated further, as the promise of future betterment that makes involuntary sacrifice in the present worthwhile. Even a mild program of austerity remains popularly unpalatable. And in the end, if this relatively benign version of class conflict doesn't work, earlier versions of authoritarian corporatism, based on the outright suppression of organized labor, lurk in the wings: just as with supply-sideism or monetarism.

The only alternative denouement would be for a popularly mobilizing government to lead a cooperative effort in, on one hand, creating new arenas of internationally competitive production based on public planning and the reemployment of excess labor; and on the other hand, finding new ways to constrict rather than expand the sphere of commodity production as the road to happiness. Such a mobilization, of course, would also have to follow the principle of proportionate sacrifice. Absent any effort of this kind, social democracy must make fatal compromises with capital. We should not for a second forget or underestimate the potential human misery that social democracy eliminated or alleviated during the period of its success. As well, the struggle for working-class representation within corporatist political institutions has been of tremendous importance in raising the level of expectations in the working class, and among the citizens of the liberal capitalist societies generally, as to what the democratic principle may come to mean. At the moment, however, social democracy looks more like a way station between either free market economy, or some kind of full-scale social control of capital than a permanent solution. The social democratic solution too, as long as it fails to move in the direction of democratic planning and informed popular participation in decision making, and as long as commoditization remains its standard of well-being, demands the partial demobilization or deactivation of the working class, even if less fully so than the free market approach.[5]

# IV

Finally, then, how might a democracy, a regime of political and social equality, respond to a similar crisis?

In a democratic social order, calculations of the rational response to a crisis would be made differently. To begin with, it would be recognized among equals that to create a group of social dependents at a minimal level of support is to create an inferior social class or caste. Dependency would thus have to be at roughly the standard guaranteed wage. Given that principle we would then perceive, as we do not perceive in capitalist societies, that it might be more efficient to subsidize marginally unproductive workers on the job than to subsidize them through some kind of dependent's minimal social wage.

We can see this contrast clearly by way of an example. In a capitalist enterprise, even in a social democratic milieu, if a worker's wage is $10,000, and her marginal product is estimated at $8,000, there will be pressure to discharge her so that her employer does not have to incur a loss of $2,000. If, however, the cost to society of supporting the unemployed worker is $5,000, then society as a whole will be taking a loss of $3,000 above what would have been the case had the worker been left on the job. Assuming that she was producing a socially useful good, it would actually be more cost-effective for society as a whole to leave her on the job. Private employers, though, will never make such calculations, nor act on them; they would rather the worker and taxpayers take a bigger loss than that they themselves take a smaller one. If the firm were socially owned instead, in an egalitarian democracy, it would be recognized by all that one way or another we were going to have to incur a social loss of $2,000 to support that worker: that we could not as a community avoid doing this.[6]

How that would best be done would depend on circumstances. If the structural crisis were simply one of disappearing demand for labor, that could be taken as an excuse for redistributing—and ultimately lightening—the average workload. In our society, if there were suddenly little or no more need for automobiles, that would appear as an economic disaster. What would happen to the millions of unemployed auto workers and those other workers whose jobs are dependent on a healthy auto industry? For us citizenship does not entail the right to work, indeed forbids it in the sense that we forbid ourselves to interfere too deeply with the free labor market. Therefore, there is no way to reintegrate so many displaced persons into the economy except as socially expensive charity cases or by the long, complex task of restructuring industry and creating new jobs. An egalitarian, democratic society, on the contrary, might welcome genuine obsolescence by allowing workers to move elsewhere, sharing out labor, and shifting the net amount of labor away from application to the means of production and toward continuing education, pure leisure, civic participation, or greater devotion to the work of reproduction, with whatever new opportunities those activities might bring in their wake. This might mean that the average wage would fall, but so what? It would fall because there were less things that needed to be bought; the average standard of living would not fall at all. For us technological progress, even when its benefits are much greater than its side-effects, is not only a blessing but is also for many a curse. For a society of equals, if truly progressive, it would only be a blessing.

However, real structural crises are possible in an egalitarian society as well as any other. The demand for or value of an industry's product might be falling, not because of our own technological progress, but because someone elsewhere was producing the same good more cheaply. At that point democratic planners would want to use the various price data available to them to analyze the source of that comparative disadvantage. Unlike capitalist decision makers though, democrats, if they discovered that the source of the discrepancy was the existence of cheaper labor costs elsewhere, would not take that information as a signal to engage in the cheapening of their own labor; or to start the process of capital flight. Equal citizens will not tolerate the cheapening of their own labor, or the export of badly needed capital, in order to make profits for someone else, or even to make them for the more fortunately placed among themselves. People never voluntarily do that; only employers over whom they have no control do it to them. Moreover, there would be no reason for our presently typical response of regional or sectoral economic warfare, resulting in what seems to us to be irrational local protectionism. The principle of a guaranteed standard reward, allowing only of marginal distinctions, would prevent that outcome by making it pointless. Rather, equal citizens would conclude that workers elsewhere led comparatively less satisfying lives, or were oppressed by their employers or state. It would be seen as appropriate then first, to try to aid workers in the poorer or more oppressive society to improve their lot; or, failing that, to protect our own workers, in both the public and the private sectors, rather than force them to compete with a less fortunate working class. Only at the point where the paying out of subsidies to noncompetitive industries lowered the average standard wage toward that of the supposedly oppressed workers elsewhere would we be forced to conclude instead that we were overvaluing our own labor, and must agree together to live more austerely.

Even at that, if sector after sector of the democratic economy found itself noncompetitive, a reasonable interpretation of that course of events might be, contrarily, that an egalitarian island cannot survive in a sea of inequality: that the wages of self-governing workers will inevitably be dragged down through competition with the lower wages of a much greater number of exploited workers. The citizens of an egalitarian polity, therefore, might consider themselves to be confronted with a choice between autarchy or imperialism on one hand, or an extension of the egalitarian impulse to nonegalitarian societies on the other. As autarchy and imperialism almost certainly require severely coercive restrictions on economic behavior, they are likely to result in authoritarianism. An egalitarian foreign policy would therefore recommend itself instead, if analysis seemed to bear out the suspicion that the oppression of labor abroad, rather than a shortage of resources or of a willingness to work hard were the root cause of domestic economic decline. Moral consistency will usually be a virtue for egalitarians, even in realms that are traditionally thought of as being properly subject to quite different principles of correct behavior. In the long run Marx was right: there is no such thing as a purely national democratic society; and the national interest of an egalitarian democracy is inseparable from the moral commitment to egalitarianism itself.

Alternatively, analysis might demonstrate that diminishing resources or technological lag, not just cheaper labor costs elsewhere, really were responsible for the democratic economy's comparative disadvantage. Every industry that grows also eventually declines: a law of life from which there is probably no escape. People will always become complacent about any mode of accomplishment that has worked well for long enough; they will not revitalize their accustomed way of doing things in time to meet the competition from some new mode of activity that produces the same goods or services better, or more cheaply, or with a more efficient use of resource or technological inputs. Thus, there will always be circumstances in which it will be necessary to persuade some workers to retool their physical plant, and to support them in one way or another while they are doing so; or to transfer economic activity from a declining industry or sector to a more technologically advanced arena of production; or perhaps to transfer resources from richer geographical regions within the democratic community to poorer ones that were being priced out of national or international markets. In any case the chief result would have to be to get some among ourselves to train for or transfer to a new kind of work or, if the conversion process would not work out in any other way, a new place of work. So we return to our original question. Workers in capitalist societies object when, in the name of a one-sided efficiency, that kind of transfer is arranged via a free market over which they have no control. And taxpayers often object to subsidizing others when they themselves are not in immediate need of any subsidy. Could all this be done instead by democratic agreement, without unacceptable

incursions on individual choice such as would amount to replacing a
free labor market with a coercive rather than open labor market; and
in a spirit of social solidarity rather than regional or sectoral envy and
disdain?

It is not implausible, I hope, to suggest that if further education,
retraining, etc. are the normal activities of a social order, no particular
instance of them will seem to constitute an exceptional subsidy such
as produces envy or bitterness in our own society. As for the more
basic question, the relevant principle of democratic equality is that no
class or group should be able to slough off the costs of restructuring
the accumulation process on another. That requirement would preclude either unreviewable planning by an insulated public bureaucracy, or even simple majority decision by a legislature. Instead,
democratic decision making would require the submission of suggested guidelines to the affected parties, for discussion with their
authorized representatives and renegotiation with the central public
authorities where necessary. The principle of political equality and
the democratic division of labor would require that in the end any
major structural change in the condition of labor would have to take
place according to rules—about who should leave, who should stay,
how should work time be divided up, where should new plants be
located, what kind of retraining should take place and where, how
should outmoded plants be revitalized, etc.—finally chosen by the
workers themselves (and perhaps by small businesspeople in the
private sector as well). To maintain their standard of living during this
process would mean to subsidize them by transfers from everyone
else, thus lowering everyone's after-tax wages. To engage in this kind
of capital restructuring, therefore, would necessitate one kind of sacrifice by the affected workers, and another kind of sacrifice by the
citizenry at large; but the two kinds of sacrifice would be equal in
scale. Alternatively, if the answer to undesirable economic stagnation
seemed to lie in a reinforced or revitalized private sector, or in decentralized, small-scale community-operated enterprises that required
infusions of capital but could initially mobilize workers at rewards
lower than the social standard, then again the social standard overall
would have to be at least temporarily lowered to provide the necessary supports. This would be a democratic supply-side policy.

In either case, to engage in capital restructuring would necessitate
a central social mechanism to explain to citizens that the changeover

was necessary, and to recommend a requisite level of sacrifice. It is hard to think of any reason inherent either in the nature of humans or of social organization, that should make any of this particularly difficult to accomplish, given the constitutionally internalized prescription that everyone must sacrifice with a rough equality; and given the realization that citizens themselves were responsible for the future. If a reasonable, secure alternative exists, there is no reason why anyone should want to go on producing a good that they know no one else wants. In capitalist societies, contrarily, that is invariably the defensive, thoroughly rational, and quite costly response of organized workers in any declining industry: having no responsibility for the social future, why should they take care for it?

Of course some crises in a democratic society might be real crises of human desire. If free citizens were simply unwilling to work at certain kinds of labor, no matter what price they were offered, because of the danger or other forms of unpleasantness entailed by that work, then by our standards their refusal would presage a fall in the overall standard of living: a decline in general social utility. But egalitarians would think of that kind of resistance to central planning or labor market requirements as a gain, not a loss: as an indication that political equality and the democratic division of labor were making our lives richer. Some plans, even when desired by the majority, ought to be unrealizable. In such a circumstance, everyone would have to participate in the costs of retooling for those who refused to work at the tasks heretofore assigned to them. That would be the expected cost of living among equals, however; and we can reasonably assume that no one would engage in that kind of absolute refusal lightly, since the consequences of anyone being able to refuse work that was merely mildly unpleasant would be obvious to everyone.

## V

At this point, however, we must return to the original challenge to egalitarianism. In effect, my argument so far has been that the distribution of claims on the present, in the form of the allocation of sacrifice, can be handled democratically; that whatever conflicts might arise are at least in principle manageable so as not to destroy the regime of political equality. But rational planning requires more than agreement on the distribution of claims to consumption in the present; it requires not merely a cooperative but an intelligent assessment of the claims of the future. How can equal citizens, or their representatives provide this? How can they possibly know and measure what is needed except by adopting those methods for capital provision and for discounting the future, that make citizens into nothing more than the bearers of exchange value: into the ultimate fetishized commodity?

To answer this question, let us think of what we now call "profit" as the surplus earned by capital for future use: as all returns on capital that remain available for reinvestment after the claims of the present, in the form of current incomes, have been met. (As I've pointed out in Chapter 3, this would be a wildly inaccurate picture of what actually happens in capitalist societies, since so much of profit is spent as the excess consumption of the capitalist class and its servants.) How should it be decided which of those claims must take priority, and to what extent, at a given moment? In capitalist society in its ideal form, all such decisions are made by the owners of capital acting independently—Adam Smith's "invisible hand." In the real world of capitalism, those decisions are made by owners and managers after a bargain has been struck (in some cases) with organized labor, but a bargain in which capital almost always has the upper hand. Government intervention and planning may affect the process as well: usually only marginally, but sometimes decisively in the case of, for example, Swedish social democracy, or Japanese export-oriented corporatism, or French indicative planning. These are often called "mixed economies." They are not mixed, however, in a manner that can be satisfactory to democrats who desire that both the level of disposable surplus and the nature of its disposition, be regulated by the principles and practices of democratic equality. In them the rules that govern efficiency in the production of goods continue to take precedence over the rules that govern the empowerment of equal citizens. What would it mean instead to make equal citizenship the primary purpose of social behavior?

The short answer is that the organization of productive life ought primarily to be aimed at the preservation of the democratic division of labor and relative classlessness, for these are the foundations of political equality in a democratic regime.

What would that entail were the average rate of profit to fall due to exogenous increases in the cost of some necessary raw material or desired goods manufactured elsewhere, or the foreign currencies necessary to pay for those goods? Clearly, the first activity to suffer must be the consumption of commodities. Beyond that, if the production of a social surplus for reinvestment must also be cut back, then reinvestment for the preservation of human welfare, maintenance of the infrastructure of democracy, and the continued production of necessities in the future, would all have to take precedence over the unrestrained expansion or even preservation of whatever sectors could coincidentally succeed best in the short-term international marketplace.

From the standpoint of democratic equality, therefore, a mixed economy would be something quite different from what we usually think of when we hear that term. It would be an economy in which marketplace calculations and activities conveyed information about the real costs and benefits of productive activities, just as in welfare capitalist or market socialist economies; but in which the maintenance of political classlessness, and thus the preservation of social equality and a democratic division of labor rather than the pursuit of growth, was internalized by all citizens as immeasurably the most valuable benefit of economic activity.

In our society, the price of all commodities is calculated on the basis of their being sold in some kind of marketplace, rather than being given away to the first comer; offered as spoils to the victors in battle; distributed on an absolutely equal basis to all inhabitants; or burnt (in part) to propitiate the gods. All of those would be perfectly rational methods for distributing commodities. If we found it morally necessary to adopt one of them, we would find ourselves still able to calculate prices well enough to satisfy any economist, but the prices of some goods would be quite different from the prices we now pay for them. For example, if the gods demanded a burnt offering of 10 percent of all produced commodities, then automobiles would rise in price relative to toiletries, which can be destroyed almost freely. Or, if professional services were all to be distributed purely on the basis of need, their value would drop sharply relative to what it is in our society, but it would still be calculable. Even if goods were given away, and had only shadow prices used to assign hours of work to all adults, we would still be able to calculate those prices and the necessary hours of work.

The point of these examples, some of which apparently are bizarre, is to call attention to how we do in fact price goods—a method which from some moral perspectives might be considered equally bizarre. In capitalist societies we measure well-being by the amount of commoditization that takes place. The kind of valuation that takes place, however, embodies many concealed costs. Today, every time a commodity is sold in the United States, the cost of selling it includes the costs of maintaining all the conditions of a free (that is, oligopolistically regulated) market in the sale of commodities. These range from the very peculiar and expensive sales and distribution networks that are the concommitant of oligopolistic mass production, to the massive costs of advertising and other side-effects of the pseudocompetition that goes on among national and international economic giants; or the even more massive costs (via taxes) of enforcing those laws that prevent people from doing what the ethos of capitalism leads them to want to do: simply walking into warehouses and picking out whatever they want. These are what economists call distribution and transaction costs. We do not usually see or feel them as such, especially transaction costs. Yet they are immense costs, and they look even more immense when we consider that we must add to them all the wasteful costs of a division of labor based on class barriers. These are transactions costs too. They include, to refer back to the discussion of chapter 3, the costs of supporting the servant class of capital and catering to its luxury tastes as well as those of the capitalist class itself; of duplicating complicated administrative systems in the expensive format most useful to and generalized by the dominant economic giants; and of maintaining an extensive educational system most of which is divorced from any practical relationship to productive behavior, but does serve the dual purpose of reproducing social class divisions and restraining the development of overall social intelligence. These costs also include the costs of containing class conflict: overmanagment and other expensive forms of maintaining discipline amongst an antagonistic work force; strikes, sabotage, slowdowns, absenteeism, and the workers' other traditional forms of nonrevolutionary resistance to that discipline; the environmental disruption, human dislocation, and immense amounts of lost work time due to illness and injury, all of which are multiplied by capital's inattention to the well-being of its workforce and their life spaces; and the welfare and penological bills that are the inevitable price of supporting a reserve army of labor, an underclass of potentially productive citizens whose potentialities, far from being utilized, instead become a drag on social progress.

Even though we perceive them mostly as background noise, these are real costs just the same, and our overall prices reflect them. We could call them the associated costs of our moral choices about the correct way to live; except that most of us never participated in any way in making that moral choice, nor were we able to contemplate just how expensive our division of labor would prove to be. More correctly, these are the costs of reproducing capitalism as a way of life. What makes them so immense is the tremendous amount of effort that has to go into persuading people, in so many different ways, that it's all right for some of their fellows to be living a life stupendously more gratifying than their own; all right to put up with an outrageous hierarchy of reward that will also be a ladder of opportunity for only a small minority: all right, or at any rate not worth the trouble of rebelling against.

Just so, it would be possible for the prices of goods and services to absorb and reflect instead the costs of reproducing a different way of life: of education for citizenship, equal economic security for all, and the treatment of children as though their needs were central rather than peripheral to the enterprise of social existence. Those are real costs that would have to be quantified or somehow reflected so that we would know what was entailed by our commitment to the maintenance of equality. Surely they could be, since they would be felt in the same manner as we now feel their equivalents in a capitalist regime.

In any event, it is not as though we now have available to us some more real method of quantification of value that we would be forsaking if we deserted the capitalist way of life. The advocate of the market is always free to assert about capitalist society that everything has precisely the value given it in market exchange and no other value. To assert that, however, is to be so morally perverse that it is never necessary to respond to such assertions; once their import has been made clear, their authors can only be embarrassed by having made them. Moreover, the market itself is so visibly a realm of domination and subordination, of gross inequality in the ability to express, vivify, and implement one's own share of human demand, or one's individual appreciation of the value of technological progress, that to assign it that role is to exemplify the inadequacy of market valuation better than any critic possibly can. In an egalitarian society, then, we could not assume that the value of a good or activity was given solely by the amount of labor that must go into the immediate act of its creation; and certainly not by its price on the market for goods and services. We might often find it convenient to behave as though value had been constituted exactly by those two inputs and nothing more. But we could not assume that about our most fundamental social goods and certainly not about the good or value of maintaining the conditions of democracy itself. However, democratic theory tells us how to express and weigh such fundamental values: through the operation, in whatever way we may find to arrange it, of majority decision making. The value of our democratic institutions will be the value allocated to them by the democratic majority, expressed in its willingness to allocate scarce labor and other resources to them, control or subsidize the price of their outputs, etc. If we in the United States, for example, can quantify and pay for the costs of an immense military sector producing goods and services, most of which are never purchased on any market (free or otherwise), we can certainly do the same for the costs of the democratic sector. (This was the political intention of the labor theory of value for Marx: to understand "value" as a function of the inputs of associated free workers was, for him, to understand it democratically.)[7]

By the same token, unquantified benefits (the other side of the coin) are not marginal to, but are at the heart of our own way of doing business. The chief of these is the promise of continued increase in the production of commodities and services to be consumed. Nothing in the rules of cost accounting proclaims that more is better than less, or even that more is more efficient than less. It would be possible, contrarily, for us to measure our wellbeing by the extent to which we are freed from onerous labor, or from having to obey the commands of others; or by the extent to which we participate freely and equally in the definition and creation of shared values; or some combination of all of these. At present we do not. We rank our capacity to consume higher than our capacity to act constructively; to participate in creating a common life.

That this collective social apathy is by now deeply embedded in our culture certainly demonstrates its historical force; perhaps its historical inevitability. There is no guarantee that a majority will not always demonstrate this preference. Still, the historically inevitable is not inevitable forever. To the extent that a majority of us become disaffected by the unfulfilled promises of our disinvolvement we may begin to look for an alternative way of life, in which the good life will be consciously sought rather than passively accepted in the form of the accidental fallout of consumerism. If and when we do that, the only available alternative will be the creation of core social institutions that have as their guiding principle the desirability of finding ways to enhance our individual and collective powers. If that kind of benefit can't be quantified, neither can the kind of benefit we seek now. We only commoditize all our values ostensibly. We pretend that we can objectively measure the benefits of consumerism by charting the rises and falls of our personal incomes, but everyone except the truly poor is by now aware how fruitless if not fraudulent is that exercise. Where is the bookkeeping ledger that accounts for the secret terrors of economic insecurity and uncontrolled mobility, the consolations of religion, the fears of crime or of a carcinogenic environment, the hunger of unappeased sexuality and the fear of its release? These, at least as much as average individual yearly income figures, are the reality of public and private discourse in any capitalist society. The joys and consolations of citizenship are neither more nor less measurable. I doubt whether it is any more difficult to know that one has improved or maintained one's ability to cope with technology or with public decisions, than it is to know that one has improved one's standard of living.

# VI

To say all this is to assert that democratic citizens could value the future by their own lights, as much as the citizens of capitalist societies now value it as though it were nothing but a collection of consumable commodities. Would they want to, though? The doctrine of capitalism proposes harnessing greed, not altruism, by linking the investment process to the profit motive in order to further accumulation: precisely because the proponents of capitalism believe that greed is the most effective incentive of all to progressive economic behavior. What motivation, or conjuncture of motivations, can egalitarians suggest as an alternative? Among a democratic citizenry what will replace the incentive of greed, or greed combined with insecurity, as a disciplining orientation toward material life? What would happen if the members of a community of equals were just not willing to work hard enough to generate the wherewithal to meet what they thought of as their needs; to accumulate enough capital to ensure a stable future? As one skeptic puts it:

> . . . the essence of democratic politics is a gigantic celebration of the fact that you *can* get something for nothing, or at least that *you*—the individual voter—can get something for nothing . . . for government, with its legalized powers of coercion, can award benefits here while it charges costs there . . .[8]

In this regard, the inegalitarian will appropriately ask, do we have any good reasons for thinking that the citizens of truly democratic societies might behave as rationally as or more rationally than do the pseudocitizens of our own pseudodemocratic social order?

The purpose or end of democracy, as I have said, is to empower citizens. In the moral education given children in schools, churches, families, child-care communities, and via whatever media of impersonal mass communications might exist, that would presumably be the primary message. Let us suppose, for example, that we spent as much time in front of television sets as we do now: but for every advertisement for consumer products that now appears before us, there was instead an advertisement for training programs, work-study programs, institutions of liberal education, public discussion groups, town meetings or other local collectivities, research and development agencies, and the like. Children in that society would grow up thinking that rational social institutions produce that kind of wellbeing; and the odd eccentric who tried to tell them that efficiency really means less civic or self-improvement and more commodities for the same investment would be considered perverse or unpatriotic by them. I hasten to add that I do not offer this vision as an actual herald of the future, for any system of cultural communication, no matter how well-intentioned, as unrelentingly manipulative and invasive as the one to which we now subject ourselves is utterly incompatible with even the faintest pretense of democratic self-government. Rather this exercise of the imagination is only meant to remind us how much there is in our own or any culture that goes beyond individual acts of consumer choice, and how deeply and unconsciously we have internalized some very arbitrary versions of value in the name of rationality, instrumentalism, and utility. A different way may be difficult to conceive of; but it would hardly be unnatural or irrational compared to what we do now.

Thus, the injunction to be, and the consequent expectation of being primarily an equal citizen rather than a competitive consumer, would be bound to have effects at deep levels of character development.

Specifically, accumulation for its own sake could not possibly be the primary orientation of a social order based on the democratic division of labor. The engine of competitive, relentless growth would, surely, be fundamentally restrained by a public sphere based on the principles of the democratic division of labor. If it were not so restrained, indeed, democracy could hardly have come into existence to begin with. Reciprocity rather than competitiveness would necessarily be the moral norm of an egalitarian society. The institutions of gift giving, of nonpecuniary incentives to do difficult work, of the free exchange of labor among people with complementary skills, and of volunteerism as a general way of life rather than as the special province of underemployed housewives, must all surely be maximized in a society of equals (at least as compared to our own society of envious pseudoequals.). All of these are modes of behavior that cut against the grain of a single-minded, unappeasable devotion to immediate material betterment.

Under the sway of materially productive capitalism, of a culture devoted to mindless accumulation, we have lost sight of many nonmaterial ways of living well. Some of these—participation in social solidarity, in the creation of a satisfying cultural milieu, in a community of mutual respect—stand at a morally higher level than mere material wellbeing. That is because maintaining political equality is dependent on our internalizing the expectation that when we are in economically straitened circumstances the first thing to go must be not investment for the future, nor investment in the essential institutional arrangements of democracy, but our current consumption of commodities. Equal sacrifice only would, only could be the willingness of equal citizens to put material consumption—the consumption of fetishized commodities—last. There is no inalterable reason why that should not be possible. Inflation based on an unexpected scarcity of supply can happen to anyone; but demand-led inflation is purely the creation of the demand-generating structures of capitalism itself. The obsession that more is better than less and faster is better than slower may be our nature; there's no evidence that it's "human nature."

At the same time, I do not want to define democratic equality as though it were the absolute enemy of fleshly pleasures. Regardless of how intensely we think of equal citizenship as an essential part of the good life, the good life must still begin with the production and repro-duction of our material existences. All other forms of joy or self-fulfillment are grounded in our first having satisfied our basic material needs: ". . . Men must be in a position to live in order to be able to 'make history.' "[9] Furthermore, what we mean by "being in a posi-tion to live" is very much culturally determined, and no one can judge what it ought to mean for someone else.

In saying that, admittedly, we explicitly reject, in the name of demo-cratic egalitarianism, all forms of philosophical or religious dualism that denigrate the joys of the flesh and elevate the achievement of spiritual oneness or well-being or a right relationship with nature to the position of ultimate end. In general, it is obvious that I have neglected the relationship between religion and democracy. That is simply because I do not believe that there is any. No religious movement has ever had a consistent political program. The Church gives us libera-tion theology and apologies for capitalism. Judaism gives us Jews who think their historical role is to be witnesses to injustice, and Jews who think their historical role is to reconquer all the Biblical lands. Protestant individualism helps explain American liberalism; yet it also helps explain the rise of Nazism in Germany. Those thinkers who tell us that there cannot be social change without some religious revival may be correct, but have the causal cart before the horse. Social and political change may be accompanied, explained, and justified by reli-gious revivalism, but will not be caused by it. Religious millenialism and political revolutionism (to take the most frequently cited compari-son) may have much in common emotionally, but have little in com-mon intellectually. Religious discourse and political discourse are ultimately alien languages, and one can neither substitute for nor encapsulate the other; spirituality is not a politics.[10]

In principle I have rejected as well the notion that there is a simpler, less technological, less urban, more self-sufficient life to be recap-tured (though, like many of us who make no real attempt to live up to it I honor that notion in the breach). Nostalgia is not a politics either. Doubtless these acts of rejection testify only to my own limited under-standing and experience of life. However, I fail to see how either the spiritual mystic or the single-minded apostle of the polis could possibly be interested in a democratic theory or an egalitarianism that can be available to most people; or can have any comment to make on any likely variant of democracy other than to note its failure to attain some narrowly defined version of the good life. This essay, for better or worse, is really not addressed to people who think that material life and all its epiphenomena, such as organized productive and political institutions, are irrelevant to human endeavor.

The political independence that egalitarians would insist on certainly entails the possibility, for which we must be cheerfully prepared, of having to forego material pleasures in order to maintain civic satisfactions. But it does not entail being morally committed to avoiding material pleasures in the first place. In our civilization at least, a democracy that is the enemy of productiveness, variety, and progress in the satisfaction of human wants and needs, is a democracy that will never be implemented by a majority—and thus won't be a democracy either.

Modern capitalism feeds an insatiable appetite for growth, upon which its continuation is dependent, by first creating new needs and then seducing its pseudocitizens into becoming consumers. The sense of moral and esthetic revulsion that ought to follow from recognition of this condition is fundamental. But we must not allow ourselves to leap from that sense of revulsion to the unwarranted conclusion that what becomes the dominant form of consciousness under capitalism is nothing more than a false consciousness, such as would totally disappear were only capitalist institutions to be replaced with more morally correct or esthetically pleasing ones. No evidence at all exists for the proposition that the sensibility of those who reject or are revulsed by the life of consumerism is more truly "human" than that of those who to some extent accept or enjoy it. The most we can claim is that to move toward the regime of democratic equality is to move away from the regime of unalloyed accumulation.

## VII

This reflection leads many critics of egalitarianism to doubt that people will freely choose to work as hard as they have to work to maintain a decent life under whatever resource constraints we face. In the pregnant formulation of its opponents, equalizing, we therefore suspect, necessarily means equalizing down. Given the option, it is always implied that a majority of people will choose to work less hard even when they ought (need) to work harder; they will attempt to free ride. Thus, democratic societies are doomed, finally, to the stale greyness of a static or declining economy.

The truth, of course, is that the followers of every way of life, without exception, pay a price, usually a terrible price, in foregone goods that they cannot produce because the method for producing those goods is incompatible with the organizing principles of their way of life. We should remember that that is most decisively true of our own inegalitarian political economy, which exacts an immense toll in the form of wasted lives and talents and thus productive potentialities; alienated public spirit; useless or even destructive trash being produced in the place of socially essential goods (e.g., bridges that won't fall down); the despicable treatment of social victims; and a distance between class and caste-defined life styles so immense that our society is quite openly a psychic war of all against all. For all of that we receive in trade the possibility of unlimited wealth for some and the free pursuit of variety by many. As a side-effect we also receive the political right to be let alone in our private lives, in return for ceding to a governing elite the real power to participate effectively in public life. The benefits of the overall trade are far from trivial, and as I have acknowledged a majority of people, for whatever reasons, are apparently made reasonably happy by them much of the time. Nor do I mention them here in order to dismiss them, but simply to remind us that the flowering of the private spirit has its costs as well as its gains.

That much having been said, it's reasonable to draw attention to what democratic equality as a way of life might imply positively for the spirit of innovation: for the production of need-fulfilling goods or services beyond those with which we are familiar.

Both materially and morally, a democratic society would offer certain positive incentives to material progress. For example, the Japanese experience with the effects of lifetime guaranteed employment have made us aware of some unexpected consequences of an emphasis on job security. Knowing that they cannot raise profits by the simple expedient of economizing on labor, Japanese managers (in the guaranteed-employment sector) have been forced to look to continual technological improvement as the price of competitive survival. In a related manner, the same incentive to improvement of the means of production ought to exist in a democratic society. Self-managing workers might instinctively gravitate toward torpor, but there would be powerful pressures on them not to. They would know that they could not dispose of each other (except via the normal processes of retirement), and that conditions elsewhere in the social order might even compel them to take on more workers (or nonworkers) seeking job security or self-improvement in the public sector. They might feel no need to better themselves materially; democratic society might already be producing enough. But once the threat was recognized that too much slackness was actually running down essential productive plant—and there would always be someone in a position of planning responsibility to be on guard against that possibility—democratic workers would know that only by increasing their own productivity could they maintain their standard of living at the same or less expense of labor. There is no earthly reason why under such circumstances people should not want, in effect, to make work easier for themselves by improving the technological or organizational apparatus attached to it: as long as they know that they will be the beneficiaries of the process.

In capitalist societies, the fat are never in a morally secure position from which to ask the thin to tighten their belts; to undergo an austere present on behalf of a more abundant future. The gales of Schumpeter's creative destruction blow too unevenly; though many are blown away, some benefit quite nicely indeed from the storm. Thus capitalist societies lurch from one crisis in the realization of profits to another. Rarely are their leaders able to mount a definitively successful campaign for the necessary restructuring of production without the aid of massive coercion of labor; or without, alternatively, undergoing the incredibly self-destructive birth pangs of depression or war. Everyone always wants more because someone else always has so much more than they do. Cooperative self-restraint is never on the agenda in peacetime.

In an egalitarian society—that is, one marked by constrained income inequality, the abolition or weakening of class and caste barriers, the centrality of cooperatively organized labor, real turnover among and genuine linkage of rulers and ruled—the program of austerity that capital restructuring or the development of new methods of accumulation always requires, could, if it were really necessary, be a rational program for all. A sacrifice that everyone makes does not feel like a sacrifice, but rather like participation in a common activity. Hard work done in the expectation of a reciprocal contribution by others is not nearly so hard. Sharing is still the most fundamental human activity. Invidious competition, and suffering passed down from the powerful to the powerless through an impervious and hierarchical chain of command, are only invitations to open or covert civil disorder. The promise of democratic equality is to make manifest to all citizens a single standard of social efficiency, rather than a meretricious standard built around all our inequalities, discriminations, and misappropriations of the social product.

So we confront a contradiction that, we have some right to hope, will not prove to be entirely a contradiction. Political equality, we may say, requires a civic temperament that accepts austerity and collective sacrifice among rough equals when they are essential to the accomplishment of our ultimate goals; without at the same time necessarily being grounded in the kind of morality of austerity and sacrifice that proclaims the enjoyment of goods to be a false human consciousness.

Nor should we forget what enjoyment really means. The consumption of commodities is merely the means to an end. The end is the enjoyment of life. There is nothing intrinsically more enjoyable about commodities produced for exchange in comparison with other forms of self-actuation. The various civic and individual uses of leisure time, and participation in individual and communal development by means of improving one's own capacities, are also potentially sources of immense satisfaction (as all children know before they have been fatally socialized into the contrary pleasures of privatization and competition).

Moreover, even within the sphere of material consumption itself, the nature of that consumption in no way must necessarily be the same as it is among us now. Consumption is not just the totality of goods and services we desire and obtain; it is also a structure itself. A given structure of consumption enlarges some possibilities and diminishes others, without at all necessarily changing the actual total or mix of our satisfactions. The structure of consumption that has triumphed so thoroughly in all capitalist societies entails (except with respect to certain welfare- state services) the individual enjoyment of individualized goods or services that have been purchased by individuals on a market that sells to individuals.[11] Thus, for example, as access to transportation comes to mean owning a car, the serviceability of alternative modes of mass public transportation diminishes. That is a commonplace observation, but the real heart of the matter actually lies much deeper. A "car" is defined as something that individuals own (unless it is a taxi or limousine), so that in most circumstances to be thrown back on auto use is also and ineluctably to be thrown back on individual auto ownership. Furthermore, joint ownership of cars is an unhelpful concept because we all tend to be employed, and thus to live, on fairly rigid and almost identical schedules, which are fixed by someone else rather than by ourselves in mutual cooperation. The structure of consumption of this particular good, in other words, is tightly articulated with the structure of production. It is even more tightly articulated with the inegalitarian structure of reproduction, since most childrearing is done individually and in relative isolation. Thus the seemingly inexorable requirement that access to transportation be immediately accessible to our own individual, private hands, is strengthened on every side and in every way.

The entire preceding analysis, however, has to do only with the social meaning of automobiles; nothing in it is given by their technology or their operational principles. An individualized mode of transportation is needed because we live largely as separated individuals. The automobile naturally serves that purpose better than the train or the bus, but the automobile serves that purpose so exclusively only because that is the purpose we are trying to have served.

We cannot tell how we would want to behave were more of our time spent in, and valued behavior associated with, public rather than private spaces; and civic or cooperative rather than alienated and isolated activities. (It's interesting to contemplate, perhaps, that few people drive to mass political demonstrations in private automobiles.) What would be the effect, if on the average we felt less insecure materially as individuals than we do now; or if our major units of commodity production were not competing with each other to see which could sell the most goods to the greatest number of consumers, but were merely trying to satisfy expressed demands? Perhaps it would make little difference. In some respects, certainly, cultural traditions and geographical realities underlie aspects of particular consumption structures in ways that cannot be explained by mere descriptions of the capitalist marketplace, accounts of mass media manipulation, and so forth. Americans, compared to say the Dutch, will always value modes of transportation that get us to and through wide-open spaces with a reasonable degree of speed. To put it even more crudely and yet quite appropriately: we cannot imagine any variant of egalitarianism taking root in France unless it is so defined as to be compatible with the continued provision at least occasionally of haute cuisine for those who wish to devote some of their income to consuming it. Yet in the end, there is no reason why we should not be able to enjoy these, or their cultural equivalents without sacrificing democracy to the continued frenzy of "the joyless pursuit of joy." The billions of dollars of annual expenditures that it takes today to persuade us to go on living the life of uninhibited consumerism is testimony enough about the equivocal nature of our dedication to that life.

Why should a society of equals or near-equals want to put any effort into persuading each other that they all need more and more material satisfactions; that everyone must run faster and faster just to stay in the same place? Given nothing more than our continued ability to produce the means of material satisfaction at the overall level (though presumably not in the same mix) to which the middle class citizens of the advanced capitalist societies are accustomed, there is no reason to believe that the institutions of equality would of necessity create a society of "blue ants;" of regimentation without variety or innovation.[12] Equality is not similarity; a democratically constituted society of equals should produce more diversity, and more self and mutual fulfillment in diversity, than do the paradoxically levelling hierarchies of consumer capitalism.

# VIII

In sum, I have made no claims that democratic planning would work. I have claimed only that it is in principle workable: that rational decision making is possible among people who are committed to treating each other as equals. It is perfectly likely that a people might become impatient with the necessity for continual mutual deference to each other's needs and interests; and that they might decide to surrender their equal participation in self-governance to a managerial elite that they allowed to grow up among themselves. They would then be no worse off than we are now: and a lot better off if the democratic way of life could, instead, sustain itself. The potential failure of a democratic planning procedure that has never as yet been tried, hardly seems so inexorable as to make it foolish to contemplate the attempt.

# Notes

[1]  The best recent discussions of public planning and its accomplishments in capitalist societies are those of Andrew Zimbalist and Howard Sherman, *Comparing Economic Systems: A Political-Economic Approach* (New York: Academic Press, 1984), Part II; and Adam Przeworski and Michael Wallerstein, "Democratic Capitalism at the Crossroads," *democracy*, vol. 2 no. 3 (July 1982), pp. 52–68. See also Carnoy and Shearer, *Economic Democracy*, especially ch. 7; and Ira Magaziner and Robert Reich, *Minding America's Business* (New York: Harcourt, Brace, Jovanovich, 1982). There is no point in seriously considering the allegation by such free-market ideologues as Milton Friedman that public planning is counterproductive. That allegation is simply false, and its appeal lies rather in the realm of fantasized wish-fulfillment than of respect for the facts. See in this regard Lester Thurow, *The Zero-Sum Society* (New York: Basic Books, 1980), chs. 1 and 6, as well as his *Dangerous Currents* (New York: Random House, 1983); Robert Heilbroner's review of Friedman's *Free to Choose* in *The New York Review of Books*, vol. 27 no. 6 (April 17, 1980), pp. 4–5; and Gus Tyler's "The Friedman Inventions," *Dissent*, 27 (Summer 1980), pp. 279–90. As for the strengths and weaknesses, and also the variety of planning in state socialist economies, see Zimbalist and Sherman, Parts III-V.

[2]  In his *Capitalism, Socialism, and Democracy* (New York: Harper and Row, Publishers, Inc., 1950), ch. 7.

[3]  See Robert Lekachman, *Greed Is Not Enough: Reaganomics* (New York: Pantheon, 1982); and Frank Ackerman, *Reaganomics: Rhetoric vs. Reality* (Boston: South End Press, 1982). But the most devastating account of "Reaganomics" is probably the *Economic Report of the President* (Washington, D.C.: U.S. Gov. Printing Office) for 1982, in which the bizarrely contradictory amalgam of supply-side economics and monetarism shoots itself carefully and visibly in the foot.

[4]  John Kenneth Galbraith, *American Capitalism: The Concept of Countervailing Power* (Boston: Houghton-Mifflin, 1956).

[5]  See Robert Heilbroner, "The Swedish Promise," *The New York Review of Books*, vol. 27 no. 19 (December 4, 1980), pp. 33–6; John Stephens, "Impasse and Breakthrough in Sweden: After the Contradictions of Social Democratic Policy," *Dissent*, vol. 28 no. 3 (summer 1981), pp. 308–318; and Walter Korpi, *The Working Class in Welfare Capitalism* (London: Routledge and Kegan Paul, 1978). On Austria, see the *New York Times* of January 28, 1982. For more general discussions, in addition to Leo Panitch, "Trade Unions and the Capitalist State," cited in note 5 to Chapter 2, see Alan Wolfe, "Has Social Democracy A Future?," *Comparative Politics*, vol. 11 no. 1 (October 1978), pp. 100–25; Gosta Esping-Andersen, "The Political Limits of Social Democracy: State Policy and Party Decomposition in Denmark and Sweden," in Maurice Zeitlin, ed., *Classes, Conflict, and the State* (Cambridge, Mass.: Winthrop Publishers, 1980), pp. 257–75.; and Francis Castles, *The Social Democratic Image of Society: A Study of the Achievements and Origins of Scandinavian Social Democracy in a Comparative Perspective* (London: Routledge and Kegan Paul, 1978). Whatever their assessment of its future, most commentators do not think that the Swedish "middle way" travels easily, for both cultural and historical reasons.

[6]  This example is suggested by Dan Luria and Jack Russell, "Rebuilding Detroit: A Rational Reindustrialization Strategy," *Socialist Review* No. 63–64, vol. 12 nos. 3–4, (May-August 1982), pp. 163–84. For a more detailed consideration of their notion of "social cost accounting," see Chapter 11.

[7]  My interpretation of the labor theory of value is that by it Marx primarily intended both to characterize and to criticize the social relations of production under capitalism, rather than to demonstrate the transformation of price into value (although he may have thought that that was possible). Among the many exponents of the labor theory

of value who have argued this interpretation, the one whose discussion I find most persuasive, and most clarifying of my own reading of *Capital*, is E. K. Hunt, "Marx's Concept of Human Nature and the Labor Theory of Value," *Review of Radical Political Economics*, vol. 14 no. 2 (Summer 1982), pp. 7–26.

[8] Peter Jay, "Englanditis," in R. Emmett Tyrrell, Jr., *The Future That Doesn't Work: Social Democracy's Failures in Britain*, (Garden City, N.Y.: Doubleday and Company, Inc., 1977) pp. 169, 171.

[9] Karl Marx and Frederick Engels, *The German Ideology*, Parts I and III, ed. and tr. by R. Pascal, 3rd ed. (New York: International Publishers, 1963), p. 16.

[10] Thus Ivan Illich is a sometimes inspiring, often challenging, and always radical thinker. But he is not a radical democrat. See for example his reflections in "Peace vs. Development," *democracy*, vol. 2 no. 1 (January 1982), pp. 53–60.

[11] Many aspects of this cursory discussion of the social structure of consumption are expanded on in the fuller analyses of Stuart and Elizabeth Ewen, *Channels of Desire: Mass Images and the Shaping of American Consciousness* (New York: McGraw-Hill, 1982); Fred Hirsch, *Social Limits to Growth*; William E. Connolly, "The Politics of Reindustrialization," *democracy*, vol. 1 no. 3 (July 1981), pp. 9–21; and Connolly and Michael Best, *The Politicized Economy*, rev. ed. (Lexington, Mass.: D.C. Heath). For a more historical perspective, see Rosalind Williams, *Dreamworlds: Mass Consumption in Late Nineteenth Century France* (Berkeley: University of California Press, 1982).

[12] Thus Robert Heilbroner's vision of the future Sparta, *The Human Prospect* (New York: W.W. Norton, 1974), applies at least as tellingly to liberal capitalist societies as to any conceivable egalitarian alternative.

# Part 3

## *Political Equality*

# 8

# WHAT IS POLITICAL EQUALITY?

What I have tried to do so far is point to some logical outcomes of the popular demand for more democracy, while at the same time describing a good society rather than a mere collection of rules for individual political behavior. At this point then I must try to answer the question, what is political equality? What fundamental principle lies at the heart of these prescriptions about social relations, choice, and access?

To approach an answer to that question we must first ask, what is the fundamental problem of political life, from the standpoint of the democrat? We can be sure that is the right question because both liberal democrats and radical democrats have consistently approached their theoretical task by asking it, and—more to the point—have consistently given the identical answer. From the standpoint of the democrat of any persuasion, the fundamental problem of political life is how we are to be certain that the nature of our social and political institutions, at any historical moment, comports with the wishes of the people as to what those institutions ought to be like; and how the people can empower themselves to change those institutions.

The problem having been stated in this way, the liberal democrat always proceeds by stressing the realization of individual capacities, individual preferences, and individual participation. The difficulty with this position lies in its failure to come to grips, finally, with questions of class and caste. As long as capital accumulation is the province of a privileged class or a privileged elite, then the rights of individuals or communities to this or that entitlement can never be fully realized.

In a democracy, it ought to be the case that the people can vary the mix of their institutions of sustenance and accumulation as their desires change (and as the natural facts of life permit), without incurring the prohibitive social costs that attach to major social change in a stratified social order. It is not enough that individuals have the capacities to express their preferences. If a democracy is what we are after, we want to live in an institutional framework that is responsive to individual preferences in an egalitarian manner. In thinking about political equality we must attribute capacities not only to individuals but also to the social order itself. If we must have definitions, then to begin with democratic political equality is the condition of individuals and voluntary associations in which they are (roughly) equally able to express their preferences coherently; together with the condition of society in which individual and communal preferences are equally capable of being realized.

Thus, in discussing the social structure and political economy of democracy, I have attempted to describe a kind of social order in which structured social inequality does not inexorably lead to political inequality: a social order of which the egalitarian can confidently assert that it makes political equality attainable. This is a social order in which the fundamental contradictions of class vs. class, race vs. race, and gender vs. gender, have been eliminated or resolved: in which there is no definable group of people whose relationship to the whole is such that as an individual each member of the group is comparatively unlikely ever to get the chance to participate in politics. Social equality in this sense means that we are never able to say of anyone: he or she is statistically unlikely to ever exercise public responsibility merely because of the possession of some social attribute: being poor or a factory worker or a member of a racial or ethnic subculture, or a female, etc. It is in this way that we should understand the link between social equality and political equality.

However, these are not the only kinds of contradictions that undermine democratic equality. Nor are they the only fundamental contradictions inherent in our own kind of society, in the sense that if they are resolved, social justice and equal citizenship will emerge without further ado. To eliminate or attenuate these structural contradictions is only to take a necessary first step.

What we should think of as the primary political contradiction is equally real and equally fundamental.[1] In confronting it, we are necessarily led to specify more fully what we mean by "democratic political equality."

That everybody should count for one and nobody for more than one is a compelling sentiment, but not a description of a political order. Clearly enough, it commands us to the institution of majority rule, which, in one way or another, will have to be the bedrock decision-making process of political equality. But majority rule by itself, that is, fairness and equality in voting procedures, does not produce political equality: or produces it, but only trivially.

The principle behind majority rule—one person one vote—is not really to give everyone equal influence over decision-making. In any jurisdiction larger than a very small town, considerations of time and numbers will ensure that at any given moment all the people cannot govern directly; they can only vote either for leaders or for policies, the majority choice to govern. But that is to say that any single individual has virtually no impact on a given decision, for his or her vote will be only a thousandth or a millionth or a billionth of the total. The true ideal of majority rule, in other words, is not that everyone has equal influence, but that no one has any influence! The moral and symbolic purpose of majority rule is to give all persons the sense that the governing choice has nothing to do with the desires either of themselves or of any other definable individuals: the governing choice governs only because it is the choice of the greatest number among those choosing, whoever they may be.

The problem for egalitarians, of course, is that this is not a description of how policies can ever actually be made and chosen. The liberal individualist approach to political equality falsifies the reality of social life. We necessarily exist in and realize ourselves through organized communities, and these communities, except on the smallest scale, have a complex life that we cannot fully grasp as isolated individuals. Thus, in and of itself the conventional liberal prescription, that one has an equal right to be heard and represented, is a prescription for powerlessness—for alienated politics—just as the abstracted, individualistic liberalism behind the notion that we should all have an equal right to sell our labor power freely on the labor market is a prescription for alienated labor. In each case, the kind of freedom which is exercisable only as an atom—an isolated individual unit in a world whose major contours are determined by powerful collectives and their leaders—is the freedom not to be taken into account really while one is being taken into account formally. That is why the history of capitalism is a history of the struggle of real people (rather than formal individuals) against the institution of the free labor market; and for the intrusions on individual freedom of such collective enterprises as trade unionism and government intervention.

The struggle over equal political participation cannot and should not be a struggle against the vote in the same sense that the working class has struggled against the market, since the vote is properly believed by almost everyone to be a necessary condition of whatever we are going to call democracy. But the struggle for political equality has to be a struggle for more than the vote; for more than the mere right to have one's preferences "taken into account." It has to be a struggle for the right to unalienated political life. In the kind of political community we live in, the mere equal right to speak and to vote can mean nothing more to most people than the chance to write a letter to a representative, or to an organized lobbying group, etc. Such communications are made, in actuality, only by people whose opinions already have been hopelessly devalued (how many people ever, for example, receive a personal reply to a communication to their representative?). Conversely, the people who really do get to "insert their preferred alternatives" where and when it counts don't have to write; they are usually consulted without having expressed any specific desire to be consulted. That social reality must always overcome any formal rule for equalizing the expression of and attention to "preferences."[2]

As opposed to divisions among classes and castes, then, the political division is between the people as a whole and the governing elite or elites. All our attempts to eliminate or attenuate class and caste divisions will come to nothing, at least from the standpoint of democratic political equality, if governing institutions remain so constructed as to facilitate the development of elites that are wholly or partially unconstrained by the citizenry on whose behalf they are supposed to govern. The example of planning, as we have just seen, highlights this possibility, and forces us to grapple directly with problems in managing the people/elite contradiction. But public economic planning is not the only potential locus of that contradiction; it may inhere everywhere that the expert confronts the layperson, or the authoritative insider confronts the outsider. As long as there is any division of labor at all, any significant physical or intellectual or geographical distance between people in one social location and those in another, the crucial question for any design of democratic political institutions will be how to control elites. Or, more accurately, how can we manage to benefit from the development of special abilities of one kind or another, in some citizens as compared with other citizens, without at the same time permitting the possessors of those abilities to become an elite: an opposed political class? Liberal democratic thought has traditionally focussed in an unhelpful manner on the intellectual capabilities of abstract individuals to participate equally in some ill-defined or minimal manner. But often what we require instead is to know when and whether we are being truly represented, and how to continue in that condition. We must focus on the relationships that obtain between those with less and those with more politically relevant knowledge and skills. Like the social division of labor, the political division of labor must be, in some sense, classless and genderless.

These considerations, taken together, give us the sense of what we ought to mean further by political equality: "ought" to mean, in order to accomplish what most people are really desiring when they desire to count as much as anyone else in political life. There are three crucial aspects to this strong notion of democratic political equality.

1. Since many if not most of the important contours of our lives are determined publicly and collectively, our equal participation in that determination will require the exercise of educated capacities utilized to their utmost. This aspect of political equality is comprehended within the democratic division of labor (see Chapter 4), and we need say nothing further about it here.

2. Since even the most participatory variant of majority rule imaginable cannot eliminate the function of those who set agendas, select authoritative policies from among contradictory suggestions, implement plans, and conduct discussions, political equality requires institutional methods for insuring both that representatives do not become an opposed class; and that there are other meaningful modes of participation available to those who are not, for whatever reasons, able to fill any representative function.

3. Since the rule of political equality is everybody to count for one, nobody for more than one, political equality cannot exist when there are permanent or long-term minorities in the polity. Any group of persons whose capabilities or desires or opinions are regularly devalued,

though their behavior does no tangible harm to others, have been effectively deprived of their right of equal participation in the polity. A minority must be nothing more than a random collection of people who lost the last vote; if that proviso does not generally hold true, then we have not political equality but majority tyranny. It was Rousseau above all others who understood this last requirement, and his entire discussion of the concept of the general will may be read as an attempt to explain the distinction between legitimate majority rule and illegitimate majority tyranny. The notion of a general will has been subjected to criticism on grounds ranging from its alleged utopianism to its alleged tendencies toward totalitarianism, but most of these criticisms miss Rousseau's point: he was describing the condition of legitimacy of a democratic society. In a theocratic society, decisions will only be perceived as legitimate if they seem to emanate from genuine deputies of a genuine god; in a hereditary monarchy decisions will only be perceived as legitimate if they seem genuinely to emanate from the monarch, rather than from private persons who have some kind of sway over the monarch. Just so, in a democracy decisions will only be perceived as legitimate by all citizens if they seem to emanate from the people as a whole: if the choice of policies seems finally to be a disinterested process, regardless of the passion that may have gone into the making of the choice.

Thus the guarantee of meaningful participation and democratic representation for all, on one hand, and of the rights of minorities on the other hand, is the necessary subject matter of any discourse about political equality: the political life of democracy.

## Notes

[1] This point has been argued at greater length by Ernesto Laclau, in his *Politics and Ideology in Marxist Theory* (London: New Left Books, 1977); Bob Jessop, "The Political Indeterminacy of Democracy," in Allen Hunt, ed., *Marxism and Democracy* (New Jersey: Humanities Press, 1980), pp. 55-80; and in a different but related vein, E.P. Thompson, "Notes on Exterminism, the Last Stage of Civilization," *New Left Review*, No. 21 (May-June 1980).

[2] The language in quotation marks is from Robert Dahl, "On Removing Certain Impediments to Democracy in the United States," in *Beyond the Welfare State*, pp. 71-98. This article originally appeared in *Political Science Quarterly* vol. 92 no. 1 (Spring 1977), pp. 1-20; and was reprinted in *Dissent*, 25 (Summer 1978), pp. 320-24. It has since been expanded into a book, *Dilemmas of Pluralist Democracy* (New Haven: Yale University Press, 1982).

# 9

# PARTICIPATION AND REPRESENTATION

## I

In a democratic polity, the social function of experts must be either to carry out socially necessary tasks on behalf of larger numbers of citizens who cannot carry out those tasks as a nonhierarchical collectivity; or to help individuals and small groups fulfill personal needs that they are unable to fulfill unaided: preferably in such a manner that they will no longer need the assistance of elites to fulfill those needs for themselves. The primary democratic institution is therefore representation.[1] To invent (or reinvent) democratic, egalitarian representation we have to break with the existing paradigmatic understanding of what constitutes representation, and refashion our understandings of participation, authority, and political equality.

We do live in a real world of representation. It governs our lives, and usually we are the better off for this: "My attorney will take care of that"; "our spokesperson has a statement for you"; "she represents our neighborhood on the school board." But we also live in a shadow world, the world of alienated political life and pseudorepresentation. Just as the fetishism of commodities conceals the truth of our economic subjection by rendering it invisible, so the fetishism of the pseudodemocratic state conceals our subjection by rendering it invisible, in the guise of pseudorepresentation. Our pseudorepresentative world is populated, as by movie actors on the giant silver screen, by presidents, senators, congressmen, mayors, agency heads, union delegates, holders of proxy shares, etc., who flicker by us, larger than life, and then are gone. Even those representatives who ought to be closer to us, such as state representatives or city councillors, are usually little more than spokespersons for a particular clique among several cliques, the others going largely unrepresented.

That shadow world is the product of our collective choice to live in milieux of size, distance, and complexity, and as long as we do that it is probably inescapable. Its importance is less than we like to believe. Most of the time, especially, if there were no American president, or European prime minister, at all, our lives would not be one whit worse—and sometimes much better. Still, only an independent legislative body can make general rules for millions of people living in a web of finely articulated but endlessly confusing social and economic relationships; only impersonal bureaucracies can enforce those rules; and often even only a president, or someone like a president, can make effective policy on behalf of those millions when our interests seem to conflict with the interests of some other millions. The problem for democrats, therefore, is not to totally abolish that shadow world, of alienated politics; at least not unless we have first abolished our existing way of life in virtually all its detail. Our problem, rather, is to contain its metastasis; and gradually to reverse the inverted process by which the shadow world has come to dominate our existences, and the real world has become an arena devoted to usually futile defense of small bits of turf.

At any level of political life, it is *representation* that we must think about. We certainly want to extend institutions of collective, participatory decision making as far as we possibly can, but they cannot be the whole of a democratic decision-making process. Town meeting democracy—direct democracy—is not a form through which great numbers of people can govern themselves, or even cooperate together consensually when that is what they actually want to do. And in fact, the most interesting aspect of direct democracy is that far from its being the antinomy of representative government, the two are profoundly linked.[2]

For what happens at a town meeting, after all? A decision is reached, after discussion, by the assembled citizens, and some official—the town engineer, the town manager, the town counsel, etc.—is then authorized to carry out that decision. Town meeting democracy, in other words, results in the empowering of authorized representatives by citizens. This makes town meeting democracy decisively different from our own pseudorepresentative system; for the meeting authorizes its agents to do *something*, whereas we authorize our representatives to do *anything*. And the citizens of the town have participated in something close to the full sense of the term during the authorization process; whereas in the pseudorepresentative system we cast only abstract, alienated votes. However, town-meeting democracy without a representative system of some kind to receive its democratically made decisions would be radically incomplete.

The same is true of the various modes of mass democracy such as the referendum. Unless it provides carefully crafted and seriously supported forums for public discussion in small groups, mass democracy can only ape the worst features of pseudodemocracy without even having the one real virtue of even the most spuriously representative government: the virtue of providing a forum for informed and educative public debate. Otherwise we reduce democratic choice to its closest American equivalent: deciding whether to watch the American Conference football game on NBC-TV or the National Conference game on CBS-TV. Given the existence of approximate forums for debate and discussion, either policy-makers or groups of citizens acting independently might use initiative and referendum processes not to make policy but to demonstrate the existing state of public opinion, as in the various nuclear freeze proposals that were on ballots around the United States in 1982. But neither mass democracy nor town meeting democracy eliminates our need for a democratic theory and practice of representation; of "adversary democracy."

## II

The best way to begin to think about democratic representation is to take as a point of departure the pseudorepresentative system we inhabit. The most striking aspect of this system is that political elites and their deputies lead lives grossly different from those of ordinary persons. Transportation policies are made by people who fly in (subsidized) private planes, are driven by chauffeurs, and generally travel first class in every possible way. Safety legislation is voted on by people most of whom have never worked in a factory or a mine.

The administrators of national health services never wait in a doctor's waitingroom. Housing codes for public housing are drafted by people who will never live in public housing. Education policy is set by people who send their children to private schools. Cities are governed and administered by people who live in suburbs, or in special enclaves away from the high-crime, high-poverty districts. Agricultural policy is made by people who have never tried to keep a family farm going. Obviously there are exceptions in all nations to these generalizations, and also differences among nations: the small proprietor is probably better represented in the French Parliament than in the American Congress, for example. But the generalizations hold as such.

Especially, since legislators and high-level public servants in all democratic nations are paid considerably more than the national average wage, the rounds of periodic belt-tightening they engage in, to combat inflation by increasing unemployment and lowering living standards, create a pinch which most of them along with other members of their class will never feel themselves. One could multiply such examples endlessly; perhaps we should conclude this catalogue with the note that ex-President Eisenhower, who continually threw the weight of his office against proposals for a national health insurance program in the U.S. on the grounds that it's bad for people's character not to pay for their own medical care, never paid a cent of his own medical bills from the age of 18 to his death. The tears of the political elite in the pseudodemocracies are almost always crocodile tears.

In addition, not only are political elites of a different effective social class from the bulk of their constituents, they are also professionals at governing and managing. Both in legislatures and bureaucracies a large proportion of the governing class stay in the realms of power all their adult lives, barring wholesale political upsets. Even as governments change, the number of persons who return to ordinary community life, away from the new world of influence created by their political and business contacts, is small, and usually consists of young persons who were close winners in marginal constituencies in elections to a lower house. Otherwise the professional member of the governing class, even the middle-rung administrator, usually moves in a heady and permanent world of favors and contacts.

Governing elites in the pseudorepresentative system themselves lack the essential quality of citizenship. They know how to rule, but they don't know how to be ruled. Whatever the extent of party competition here or there, politicians and administrators form, in effect, a separate governing class, removed from contact with most citizens, and, whether in legislatures or public bureaucracies, fundamentally out of their control.

What is nondemocratic about all forms of pseudorepresentative government—whether unitary or federalist, whether based on central-ized or fragmented political parties, and no matter what social and material circumstances it encounters—is that it turns political access and influence into an episodic and occasional or even nonexistent event in the lives of most people. It makes experts at political action of people who have had something visibly important to gain or to pro-tect from that action, and apathetic incompetents of the rest.

## III

We can then contrastingly define democratic representation by rea-soning not from the top down but from the bottom up: first to define what it ought to look like; then to estimate the constituency size for which it might be feasible; and finally to look for ways of building up from the resulting basic unit of literally democratic representation to whatever less concrete bonds of obligation may be necessary for effective decision making at higher levels. And we should do this without departing from the spirit in which we have begun.

A representative is someone chosen by a group of people to represent them on some matters which they consider ought to be the agenda for action at a forthcoming legislative meeting or administra-tive hearing, or on any other matters which they have reason to believe will be placed on that agenda by the representatives of other groups. That is the basic act of representation. Every self-defined group, whether their community is defined by the geography of their residences or their places of work or their minds, must be represented in this way for self-government to be a reality.

The most important thing to note about this prescription, is that it offers a model of representation for a society of equals. Thus, it ought not to be subject to the complaint, correctly levelled against group theory in a pseudodemocratic setting, or vanguardism in Leninist theory, that all members of an interest group or a class do not neces-sarily have the same interest; and that active leaders may misrepresent apathetic or alienated followers. The point about a society of social equals is that the occurrence of apathy should be randomized, a mere function of that mysterious entity we think of as personality, rather than correlating with class or caste membership.

There is, in fact, nothing new about this version of representation; it goes on all around us all the time. Only its contemporary theorization is new (or reconstructed). There is nothing utopian about it either, for here and there it is practiced all the time. Some people get together and draw up a manifesto, a commentary on some existing proposals, an agenda for some kind of action, etc. They circulate it to friends and neighbors, coworkers, etc., with whom they hope to join in a group, for their consideration, comments, amendments, and ultimately signatures. The final group of signatories then meets to approve the "agreement of the people" and to choose one or more spokespersons. Out of a given group of say 100 signatories there might be one candidate for that position, or 50, but that is a matter of absolute indifference. There is no question of the losers in the election going unrepresented, as in existing winner-take-all elections everywhere. There is no question of some candidates being more or less remote from, unknown to, and unrepresentative of their constituents on actual issues. There is no question of candidates selling themselves like soap to constituents who by purchasing them give them the effective power to make their own agenda for action with little or no reference to their electors, as in most existing electoral systems. Whoever is chosen is an equal member of a solidary group, no more so nor more less so than anyone else in the group. That is the group's true representative.

These are the basic building blocks of democratic self-government. As to what their size should be, that (to follow Rousseau) must obviously vary from one political community to another, depending on the intensity with which a given people adhere to common moral guidelines in their thinking and to neighborliness in their daily lives. The maximum feasible size would doubtless, for example, be greater in a Parisian arrondissement than in a neighborhood of equal population in New York City; would be greater in a factory, among people performing a common task, than among the residents of any diverse, geographically defined neighborhood. My own thinking circles around numbers in the hundreds, but that is really beside the point. The sole purpose of radical democratic theory today is to inspire people to struggle for a vision of self-government; if it succeeds in any

way, it will be the real historical nature of the struggle that will determine the way people relate to each other politically, not off-the-cuff
observations by political theorists. What is important is only that we
recognize the need for limits on the size of constituencies, or else we
will wind up recreating the impersonal oligarchic polity founded in
coalitions of notables; of pseudorepresentatives. In that respect the
traditional concentration of democratic theorists on size has always
been correct.

It is not just to ensure real personal contact, and preclude impersonal salesmanship from above as the source of political action, however, that we have to emphasize formal limitation on the size of constituencies. The strongest criticism of pseudorepresentation is that it
destroys the foundations of real citizenship. Any substitute that does
not instead maintain those foundations is no substitute at all. If for the
most part we cannot have universal citizen participation in actual
governance in complex modern societies, we can at least have it in
the choice of those who will do the governing. In a sense Joseph
Schumpeter and Walter Lippmann were right when, in criticism of
Rousseau, they said that the only thing "the people" could really do
was to choose their leaders; but they were fatally wrong to consider
pulling a lever for a fantasized leader figure as an expression of either
choice or participation.[3] (For this reason political science courses in
"participation" that focus on voting behavior should be seen as no
more than exercises in public relations for the pseudorepresentative
system, even though that may in no way be the intention of those
who teach them.)

If being involved in the choice of leaders is to be a major component of effective citizenship, the involvement must be intense,
educational—in a word, *participatory*. What is intended by the
aforementioned phrase beginning "Some people get together" is that
groups of citizens feel empowered to choose representatives for each
and every separate arena of public business that they wish to attend
to, or feel threatened by. In a society where the business of control-
ling, authorizing, and implementing actions taken in the name of a
national, regional, or local public interest were defined as broadly as I
have suggested it should be, it could well be that everyone from some
group of like-minded people might wind up being a representative to
some function or another, elective, supervisory, administrative, productive, or whatever. Participation and representation are not antithet-

ical; on the contrary, they demand and strengthen each other. Even among those who, for whatever reasons, never serve but are only served, being represented properly will almost certainly demand, and potentially receive, a self-enhancing amount of civic commitment and energy. Simply to negotiate unanimous agreement on some group need or demand or action will involve every member of the group in active political life: in participatory democracy.

A democratic as opposed to a pseudodemocratic polity will be one in which legitimate public policy at whatever level will be made by representatives who have the kinds of ties to their constituents that are described above; and who, if they must form governing coalitions in order to govern, will be authorized to form them, accountable to those who have given the authorization, and subject to recall if they violate the terms of their authorization, through those same kinds of ties. A mass democratic party (such as the Swedish Social Democratic party) will not generate policies that eventuate in political equality unless it is mobilized by constituencies to which its leaders are directly accountable. And political equality will not subsist for long unless these acts of what we might call reverse mobilization, continue to be the fundamentally defining acts of citizen sovereignty. It is indicative, indeed, that I feel compelled here to refer to the process of mobilization from below as "reverse mobilization." That is not because I agree that this is the opposite of the more real kind of mobilization, namely mobilization from above; but rather because social scientists have so overwhelmingly agreed that mobilization is something leaders do to (or for) followers. Democracy can only take place when that consensus is overthrown.

# IV

All the same, a national or regional legislature or executive, and perhaps even that of a large city as well, clearly cannot be constituted by representatives chosen in this fashion. If the people cannot be the sole sovereign in any real sense: if actors in the shadow world must initiate or oversee some of the most important public business, then we must find a way to prevent the shadow world from dominating the real world of representation as it does now. What can prevent this predictable inversion of democracy? A successful answer to this question has several crucial aspects.

First, it is in this context cf democratizing representation that political decentralization—shorn of its existing association with the competitive scramble for, and surrender to, the centralized determinations of private capital—becomes crucial. Procedurally, what we should mean by decentralization is the provision of rules for legitimate decision making distinct from the simple aggregation of a society-wide mass. To be effective, decentralization implies a requirement for consensual decision making (with the understanding that "consensual" here refers to *any* requirement for more than a simple voting majority). A federation of democratically constituted communities would multiply such requirements, as well as particularized veto powers: else its inhabitants would all be reduced to being abstract citizens. "Community" would then become a dead concept, and with it, the basic constituency building blocks. The fundamental political activity of a society of equals ought to be bargaining: bargaining by representatives with each other on behalf of their various constituents, and with their constituents in order to secure the terms of their authorization. Only a process which combines both bargaining and dialogue will be truly educational and truly civil.

Second, though this kind of representation would certainly be irritating and inefficient, it would almost as certainly be very educational in the long run, for individuals, groups, and society as a whole. If we don't believe that participation in the making of complex, public decisions increases people's understandings of their own possibilities and limitations, then we have no business being egalitarians. Just how far this principle of devolution ought to extend is a question that can never be settled constitutionally, but only in practice: trying to settle what is fundamentally local by definition is about as useful as applying the same exercise to "interstate commerce." The practice of settling such questions would be the practice of listening to local representatives asking for, or demanding, a veto power. The quid pro quo they would have to offer would be their support for other local representatives demanding their own veto power over some unrelated matter. We might think offhand, for example, that the duly ascertained majority of any community ought to have an absolute right to prevent the burying of nuclear wastes on or near the territory they inhabit; or the transportation of liquid natural gas through it; etc. But what absolute veto powers might be demanded in return by those who found it useful and legitimate to produce and distribute such materials?

Society as a whole would thus have to ultimately constitute itself
dialectically, first as the legitimate framework within which bargains
about power were struck; and second as the outcome of the sum
total of those bargains. And that is exactly how a society of democratic equals ought to constitute itself, for neither pole of the dialectic
is satisfactory without the other. This kind of full-scale constituency
representation, then, no matter how cumbersome, is the real cement
of equal self-government.

At the same time, however, the outcome of many public representations in a complex social order would be neither the negotiation of
mutual veto powers, nor the achievement of a more-than-majoritarian
consensus, but rather the simple, traditional summing of diverse
representations into an authoritative majority vote. In saying that we
implicitly raise the apparently difficult question of how votes would be
cast in a forum where representatives of strikingly different numbers
of constituents are present. The obvious way to conduct decision
making by representatives in a democratic society is to allocate casting votes per a given number of constituents. The allocation in a
given case would have to depend on the presumed size of the
interested population, the presumed extent of its divisions, etc. All
that sounds difficult, but again technology comes to our rescue: neither allocating blocs of votes, nor summing up fractions of them, is
of any difficulty in the age of the computer. The monomaniac casting
the tiniest fraction of a vote can be given his say for the same limited
length of time as anyone else; as Mill suggested, he might sometimes
be right.

At the same time, decision-making procedures are empty without
some specification of what the decisions are to be about. Where
everything important is done at the center, and everything secondary
or derivative at the decentralized peripheries, then political effect will
be withdrawn from them. Voter turnout will be light in local elections;
Rousseau's sovereign will be the apathetic sovereign of a trivial jurisdiction. But given the easily observable intensity, even fierceness, of
parochial attachments among the most modernized of peoples, we
ought to feel safe in concluding that that disparity is a consequence
of over-centralization, not its cause. If a system of representation is to
have meaning to people, then its avatars have to have something of
consequence to do; and not just to do, but to do within the boundaries of an agenda that they themselves have largely set. Thus, criti-

cisms of existing participatory decision-making bodies such as community controlled school boards, investment boards, and other bodies designed to bypass "existing democratic institutions" (in the words of one critic) assert that voter turnout for all such special boards is invariably much lower than it is for ordinary elections. The implication is that these supposedly participatory institutions are thus really elitist rather than democratic. The assertion is correct, but the implication misses the point. For example, though voter turnout in the 1969 school board elections in Ocean-Hill Brownsville was originally lower than the turnout in ordinary elections, the school fight was a first, and necessary step in an historical development which has finally eventuated in increased voter turnout among black people in many jurisdictions, and in black majority victories on behalf of community leaders who were originally partisans in that struggle. Furthermore, such elections have always been defined precisely as special. They do not take place on the same election day to which the voters are otherwise habituated; mass media do not pay the same amounts of attention to them; and so forth. Before we accept such arguments, let us see what happens when the election of a local governing board is held on the same day as a presidential election; and receives the same amount of coverage from newspapers and television.[4]

In other words, the representatives of constituencies have not only to bargain for their constituents, but they have to bargain about important, publicly recognized matters, or else the process will gradually obsolesce. Tasks such as establishing and regulating communal enterprise, establishing variations in income, preventing the despoliation of the local environment by external forces, allocating labor time and time for other publicly recognized activities, underwriting the costs of representation and other forms of civic activity, guaranteeing support to dependents, and negotiating differences among those who consume them, are all examples of the kinds of particularized applications of general policy or constitutional principle that might be performed locally or regionally in an egalitarian social order. Some of those tasks, moreover, will necessarily convey veto powers on local communities. Thus, the people who carry them out will be, in a limited but important sense, a sovereign people. Egalitarians would want to limit national legislatures to inscribing overall social goals that have somehow been made the subject of general and genuine citizen agreement; mandating the procedures of economic planning; setting levels of national taxation and rules for the disbursement of its proceeds; legitimizing the conduct of centralized public enterprise; regulating the aims and conduct of affairs with other jurisdictions; and in general declaring the consensual moral and social purpose of the citizenry in the only forum for debate and discussion that can be equally attended to by all citizens.

Negatively, on the other hand, in addition to our finding a proper balance between centralization and decentralization, in a democracy there ought also to be constitutional mechanisms designed to prevent the growth of caesarism, or of any political relationships that are essentially exploitative or manipulative. The representative system in some trade unions or labor movements accomplishes this directly in the Madisonian manner: workers elect shop stewards, who in turn elect delegates, etc. This is the ideal model for how layers of authorized representation can be built from the bottom up. However, not all kinds of social life, as I've remarked, have the communality of the workplace; and in any event, no society of any reasonable size—that is, where the political process is intended to sum the desires of millions of people—will be able to dispense with the mass electoral process for at least some levels of representation and leadership.[5] Moreover, no matter how savagely we criticize the shadow world of political life, we must understand that civic liberty is likely to flourish only in the space between the world of impersonal, abstract representation and the world of immediate, neighborly political life. It is true that without layers of truly direct democracy at the base, we will be subject to familiar forms of elective autocracy; but it is equally true that absent the checks and balances of impersonal, supracommunal politics, local democracy is sure to turn into a stifling parochialism. It is no accident that society-wide universal suffrage is what the working class, the women's movement, and popular forces generally have fought for. Egalitarians can hope to add more fully democratic institutions to that historical incarnation of democracy; but should neither hope nor want simply to replace it.

If that were not the case, I could be content merely to repeat Marx's description of the Paris Commune's sketch for a nationwide Communal organization:

> The rural communes of every district were to administer their common affairs by an assembly of delegates in the central town, and these district assemblies were again to send deputies to the National Delegation in Paris, each delegate to be at any time revocable and bound by the *mandat*

*imperatif* (formal instructions) of his constituents. The few but important functions which still would remain for a central government were not to be suppressed, as has been intentionally mis-stated, but were to be discharged by Communal, and therefore strictly responsible agents.

Just as the Commune itself, with its majority (according to Marx), of "acknowledged members of the working class," presumes a transparency to the social division of labor that we now know to be unattainable, so the plan for the National Commune makes a similarly oversimplified assumption about "the division of labor between city and country." No matter from what perspective on social organization we approach the matter, some kind of genuinely centralized policy making is inevitable. (However, for the general idea of constituency building blocks suggested here I am, as ought to be obvious, indebted to Marx's evocation of the Commune; as well as to Hannah Arendt's loving description of wards and councils in *On Revolution*.)[6]

However, that centralized policy making is necessary does not mean that its scope must be as unlimited as it is among us. In a democracy, as opposed to a pseudodemocracy, central executives ought to be limited to implementing those mandates, as well as conducting negotiations between regions or localities that can't find any other legitimate authority, superior to both in jurisdiction, that they are willing to listen to. No democratic constitution ought to provide an executive with explicit emergency powers. (It is sobering to reflect on how few emergencies have actually existed in the recent history of even so imperial a power as the United States, if we discount those of its own making—i.e., flights of geese erroneously identified as incoming missile attacks, etc.) When emergencies do arise, they will be met anyhow. To prepare for them beforehand in the structure of government is to insure that wielders of a routinized emergency power will aggrandize every power potentially within their grasp, great or small, as an allegedly necessary component of that power. In general, an egalitarian community will have to be dedicated to being pacific except in clear self-defense, for powers of self-government can never outlast the insatiable demands of national security, once the latter's military aspect is accepted as being uppermost. Renunciation of international power is the very first requirement of democracy.

On the other hand, it's utopian to assume that the role of armed force can be renounced by a people merely because they are equals among themselves. Thus, no discussion of executive power is complete without discussion of the relationship between democracy and the military; as well as their domestic arm, the police.

Absent civilian control of the military, democracy is not just unlikely but impossible; history attests to that very authoritatively. And civilian control will never be achieved if military leaders are permitted to become a socially hermetic and self-selecting caste. As for the police, their two most important domestic functions in contemporary industrial societies, are to prevent members of the underclass from disturbing whatever version of social peace is built around their subordination; and to enforce existing legal class relations between workers and employers. The former function ought to disappear when the reserve army of labor (along with all the execrescences of racism and other forms of discrimination that are everywhere attached to it) is abolished. The latter function ought to disappear, at least in large part, when the managers of productive operations, on whose behalf the police maintain order, are the workers, or the workers and their neighbors, themselves. Whatever remaining kind of police force might be necessary in a democracy, its leaders ought to be civilians; and a good many of its remaining functions ought probably to be performed by civilians as well. And a national secret police, we should add, is incompatible with democratic equality. A state with a secret police is a police state, however attenuated.

These constitutional considerations are not by themselves sufficient. Assertions about what representatives ought to be permitted to do, and which representatives ought to be authorized to do what, still leave unexplored the problem of authorizing representatives in such a way that they do not become, as do pseudorepresentatives, dominating, manipulative, and exploitive.

The simplest and probably most effective way to ensure that representatives function as responsible and responsive agents is to enforce very strictly the traditional principle of rotation in office. Whether by election, lot, or appointment—and the most appropriate method depends on the office to be filled—rotation is as important for preventing the development of a separate political class with a separate way of life as it is for preventing the development of a separate social class of experts within the division of labor.

Again, it is less important that everyone hold office than that no one who holds office think of it as a permanent career, with its own lines of advancement and group consciousness. The idea of rotation must therefore be taken seriously and literally. Parties and other elite political groups develop their own reward and punishment systems. They make their own attempts to secure a monopoly on definitions of the public good, a private version of their insitutional well-being, and a well-kept distance from all those of their constituents or would-be constituents who are not inner-group activists.

In a different way, the same thing is true of those more professional administrative offices that are not disposed of by party or electoral fiat. Those too become spoils, though the victor who claims them does so not by winning elections but by winning credentials. The difference is often trivial. And although Europeans more than Americans have always thought that administration demands more measurable expert skills than does politics, it is hard to find evidence for that belief. The senior French civil service, for example, is the envy of technocrats everywhere: almost all of its members are graduates of the technocratic Ecole Nationale d'Administration. But nothing on the record demonstrates that the French government in its administrative functions has been either more or less effective an instrument of public good than any other—no matter what standard of good one uses. Generally speaking the most favorable testimony to the merit of permanent civil servants who have passed through special training programs is offered by themselves; and although democrats can sympathize with the recognizable human impulse that prompts it, there's no reason for us to take it seriously.

# V

How can rotation in office best be implemented? The basic principle should be that of a limited, nonrenewable term on all offices. Already, for example, the Green Party in the German Federal Republic has instituted this rule for its officeholders and officials. All democratic grass-roots organizations in the United States and elsewhere ought to begin to do the same; to whatever extent—with respect to officeholders—is constitutionally permissible.

One of the more painful and embarrassing, yet also angering sights of pseudorepresentative politics is the sight of an 80-year-old man who has monopolized a parliamentary or congressional seat for 30 years, fighting tooth and nail against the efforts of constituents to remove him from office long after the time at which his own legislation compels them to retire from their jobs; and then breaking out in tears when he has finally suffered his tragic loss. Certainly any term of office should not be so short as to prevent the holder of office from developing a sense of accountability to constituents. Still, the most important battle in what will always be an unending war between democracy and oligarchy is the battle to keep officeholders from developing precisely this sense of proprietorship over their offices, this sense of oneness with the job, and a feeling of comradeship not with the people whose good they are supposed to serve but rather with their fellow officeholders. The appropriate length of term for a given position will doubtless always be found to vary, since the development of job-related knowledge and skills (conjoined with the imparting of them to successors) does not follow a set pattern everywhere that public goods and services are produced. The simple rule is, if it is so long as to allow the creation of a self-conscious officeholding caste of men and women who forget even what it means to be a citizen, then it is too long.

From what has been said so far, it must be obvious that the various institutions of rotation in office ought hardly to be limited to elected officials, but must apply to all offices, elective or appointive, legislative or administrative, directly representative or purely policy making. Whoever makes policy of any kind for the public, ought to be institutionally responsible to that public, or to one or more of its various components. The public planner, the chief of police, the person chosen by the workers in some firm or industry to speak for them before the planner, the overseer of plant safety regulations or productive efficiency on the shop floor, and the engineer the town sends into the plant to see that public safety as well is being preserved, are all representatives; only the first of those cannot be a direct constituency representative. All should be subject to the general rule I have described here.

At the same time, though, we must recognize that the principle of rotation in office is a defensive, negative principle. By implementing it we protect ourselves against the monopolization or corruption of office; but why should a society of civic equals assume the normality of monopolization and corruption in the first place? In the first instance, that is, it is much more important for us to discuss the ways in which officeholding itself can be reconceptualized so as to be appropriate to the philosophy of political equality.

Beyond rotation in office, then, civic equals would surely require that any candidate for a high-level elective office must have already performed some agreed-upon amount of service as one kind or another of constituency representative. In this way, and probably in this way only, could we implement the requirement that when national legislatures reach an agreement on general rules, they do so with an inspiration that has come to them from the basic democratic constituencies. (Here and elsewhere in this chapter I use the word "national," to mean any jurisdiction that is too large to be governed solely by the consensus of representatives from local communities; and yet is recognized by the inhabitants of those communities as somehow politically legitimate.) We could hope that those whose experience of representation has been solely the experience of an instructed delegate from solidary communities, will not easily throw over the cast of mind that such an experience ought to induce.

In our own pseudodemocracy that requirement might not seem to imply anything especially positive about the outcome of representation. But in the egalitarian political and social milieux of democracy the experience of service ought to have a different meaning and a different effect.

The idea of politics as an independent career dedicated to the search for power and glory is probably inescapable. Some people simply have more talent at being aggressively self-seeking than others do. In any event the motivations for public service are emotionally and intellectually inseparable from desires for personal success. People possessed of a burning drive to fulfill a personal moral vision by entering public life, might well find more support than they do now, if they lived in a social order infused with a deeper appreciation of communal ties than is common among us (even though they would find less support for naked personal ambition). Moreover, representation at the most generalized levels of policy making will always entail some freedom from constituency discipline; even the direct constituency delegate in the style of the Levellers, armed with remonstrances from the people, will often have to negotiate in a constituency's interest without being able to engage in constant referral for further instructions. Representation is an institution that to some extent always inescapably transcends the purely mechanical amalgamation of crudely individual interests. The kind of representation I am describing here should accomplish that transcendence as often as is necessary to generate collectively ethical behavior; but not so often as to subordinate individual and group needs to the actions of an uncontrolled elite. Even our ideals of the legislator as romantic hero or heroine, on the model of James Stewart in *Mr. Smith Goes to Washington* is not necessarily repudiated by the democratic demand that representatives be truly representative. We have only to think of that Leveller spokesman, a regimental agitator at the Putney Debates, who when asked not to "make a public disturbance upon a private prejudice," replied, "Concerning my making rents and divisions in this way. As a particular, if I were but so, I could lie down and be trodden there; [but] truly I am sent by a regiment, [and] if I should not speak, guilt shall lie upon me, and I [should] think I were a covenant-breaker." There is as much heroism and glory, potentially, in fulfilling obligations as in escaping from them.[7]

In addition, even the discipline of experience as a democratic representative will only take hold if it is preceded and accompanied by the more fundamental experience of living in a community that manifests democratic relationships in its core commitments. Assuming that the expert-amateur distinction must continue to be real, that at any historical juncture some people will be expert at very important types of production or reasoning, and others will not, then experts must be of and by rather than merely for communities. Specifically, all our notions of the training of experts ought to be turned around. An understanding of the ideals of service and representation ought to replace the acquisition of technique as the first skill demanded of the trained professional; and the first of these ideals would be, as I have already indicated, that the highest accomplishment of the trained person is to render his or her own skills obsolete by finding ways to convert them to general usage. Beyond that simple statement, if such an ideal is to become a social reality, it will only be because we have come to conceive of the opportunity for training itself as something both desired by individuals and given to them, as a token of their citizenship in a democracy, by communities. It should not be, as now among us, the product of almost nothing but the drive to advance a privatized version of self-interest, paid for either by individual resources or by public financing so remote from any intimate connection with its beneficiaries that it carries no weight of moral dedication to public service with it.

I do not mean by these remarks to conjure up the unsettling vision of a rooted rather than rootless society, in which children are little more than the putative indentured servants of their elders and neighbors; or, for that matter, in which those who engage in scientific inquiry are nothing but the dependent hired hands of those who, publicly or privately, employ them. On grounds of social utility alone, the intellectual independence of inquiry is absolutely essential; and democratic socialists are probably as capable of mistaking that requirement as are profit-seeking capitalists. The point is not that people learning to do important tasks expertly in a democracy ought to learn to be public servants; it is enough that they think of themselves as public persons. Given that initial motivation, equal citizens would be able to rely on a kind of commitment that is now often mythic and wholly unreliable: the commitment of those doing scientific or intellectual work to police each other dispassionately, from a standpoint of fidelity to the work itself. It is perfectly reasonable that communities seeking to maximize their own well-being generate the tasks that experts will be rewarded for undertaking; what is unreasonable is for those who ask for expert help to specify how it ought to proceed, and what the findings of expert inquiry ought to be. That distinction has to be an integral aspect of the collective morality of a democratic social order, if equality is not to overwhelm the pursuit of knowledge; or the pursuit of knowledge to subvert equality.[8]

Thus, what democracy requires is that all communities treat what we now call professional training as a social resource, to be cultivated for the benefit of all as consciously as we now cultivate arable land or wasting energy sources. If that is accomplished, then the market process of exchange among equals and adjustment for marginal inequalities (see Chapter 4) will provide those communities each with a roughly equal supply of public-spirited "human capital." An expert can fill many and varied social roles. But in a society of equals one of the most primary roles of the expert must always be that of representative.

Contrarily, if in this respect Rousseau is right and Madison wrong— if it is a contradiction in terms to posit the cultivation of a larger public spirit based on a sense of obligation learned among immediate kin and neighbors—then almost everything I have said up to now is futile. The prospects for democracy except among testamentary small-scale collectives must be very dim. This seems to me to be a question that, almost above all others, history leaves open to our own actions and their future consequences. How democratic equality is struggled for and created will determine where and how it is rooted; we know of no law of human nature or social organization to tell us what is or is not possible in this respect.

That caveat aside, this discussion of recruitment to office and the nature of training for responsible public service in a democracy, is still incomplete. For even were all citizens trained to be capable of some high-level expert work, it would still have to be decided who should do what, when, and where.

The basic requirement in an egalitarian social system ought to be the same regardless of the exact method followed. Recruitment for planning, administration, and other nonelective public service, ought to be by outsiders ultimately drawn from the basic constituencies, or from recommendations by the basic constituencies or their representatives, rather than by agency-oriented insiders. Directing boards containing both kinds of persons would also be perfectly feasible, so long as the outsiders—that is, the representatives of affected communities—would have some kind of determination of or veto power over the final composition of public agencies. It is a safe Benthamite generalization that if ever there is a principled clash between clientele and professionals about the former's needs, the customers are always right. That generalization should apply to all administrative positions, moreover, no matter how lowly. Excessive rudeness to a medical patient is as surely grounds for reprimand as is excessive obsequiousness to an international energy cartel.

On the other hand, jobs for the boys is hardly a satisfactory substitute as a principle. The most offensive aspect of the philosophy of jobs for the boys is not that it breeds corruption (which may turn out to be endemic to social life, and is anyhow often somewhat less than intolerable). What is worse about the system of patronage, rather, is that it necessarily carries with it a strong element of coercive monopoly, and monopoly in whatever guise it appears is the natural enemy of equality.

There is probably only one way to eliminate patronage in a public job-appointment system without reverting to the other extreme of government by examination-based civil service elitism on the French model. That is to adopt as extensively as may be feasible the system

of appointment that both Aristotle and Rousseau thought the democratic method par excellence: the system of appointment by lot.

No doubt, an age of scientific and industrial complexity seems to
demand a method of selecting policy makers and enforcers more
responsive to the requirements of training and knowledgeability than
that of simply picking names out of a hat. For highly trained persons
performing extremely specialized tasks, recruitment through community boards, some rotation in office, and the ultimate and realistic
threat of recall for breaches of public trust are the only possible controls on appointment to and continuation in office. But thousands or
even millions of jobs with an important social impact, though said to
have the requisite of exclusivistic technical expertise by the spokespersons for those professions with a monopoly on staffing them, are in
small or large part actually political (based on the negotiation among
or manipulation of conflicting groups); or service oriented (existing to
fill the needs of a self-defining clientele).

As to such jobs, which are the great bulk of public service jobs, the
point is not to advocate pulling names out of a hat. The point is to
ascertain how relevant names get into the recruitment hat in the first
place. The idea of choosing public servants by taking a random sam-
ple of the total population is obviously absurd. But it is only slightly
more absurd, if more obviously so, than the alternative method of
using educational attainments, examination results, and interviews to
give an implicit rank ordering of that same total population for every
single skilled task. The point that democrats must insist on, in confrontation with meritocratic arguments, is that the defenders of the
merit principle and everything it has come to imply in the way of non-
responsive expert bureaucracies, fail to understand what capability
and talent really are in the realm of public services.[9]

What after all do we mean by the merit of a person? Nothing more,
surely, than that person's ability to do an assigned task in the most
appropriate manner. In the case of the kinds of tasks about which we
are talking here, the most appropriate manner is that which best ful-
fills the needs of those on whose behalf the task is being done. How
are we best to know those needs then becomes the crucial question
in any discussion of merit, democracy, and public service. The proponents of recruitment and promotion by competitive examination
and civil service standards, indeed, have never added anything to the
Platonic conception that a pilot must be an expert navigator, a doctor

an expert surgeon, a chef an expert cook, and so on; nor have they got beyond the simplistic exposition by Thrasymachus of the medical analogy: a physician is a physician only if he treats his patients correctly, and a ruler is a ruler only if he rules correctly. To Cleitophon's interjection, toward the beginning of Plato's *Republic*, that right is what people believe to be in their interest rather than what actually is in their interest, Thrasymachus, having argued that justice is "that which is advantageous to the stronger," scornfully replies "Do you suppose I should speak of a man as 'stronger' or 'superior' at the very moment when he is *making a mistake*?" [My emphasis][10]

None of Socrates' companions in that dialogue, that is, could move beyond a philosophical framework in which somewhere there are true interests to be located, and what is right must ultimately be palpable and knowable to an objective, well-trained observer. Therefore they never (Cleitophon momentarily excepted) appreciate the democratic perspective that what is right is exactly what the people believe to be right, or in their own interests. Although the utility of free and independent inquiry cannot be overvalued, the socially relevant conclusions that ought to be drawn from that inquiry is a completely separate matter. The meritocrats among us are able to attach elitist conclusions to the principle of free inquiry only because our way of life, which they fail to interrogate, does not comprehend as one of its sustaining components, the principle that full public education and discussion is the only necessary and sufficient precondition to democratic decision making. If we make no attempt to educate our palates then, to be sure, we will not be able to judge the feast.

The premise of a society dedicated to the education of all palates is essential, therefore, if we are to adopt the position of Aristotle in his reply to Socrates and Thrasymachus, that the user of a house will judge it better than the builder, and the diner be the best judge of the feast, or even of a good government. There are only houses, feasts and governments thought to be good by those who inhabit, consume, or participate in them; and thus the more educated are our judgements, the better our houses, feasts, and governments will be.

A democratic society, then, is not one in which the leaders, policymakers, administrators and their subordinates are the best men, but rather one in which they are representative of well-trained men and women. Nor do we turn our backs, with that epigraph, on Aristotle's parenthetical comment that positions requiring "some practical experience or professional skill'' should be exempted from the operation of appointment by lot. Where such positions are exempted from that method of recruitment, representation is still achieved so long as it remains to the constituencies to decide what they want to mean by those wholly equivocal phrases. The crucial thing for the achievement of democracy in action is that citizens come to appreciate that they are almost always equally as capable of making judgments about relevant qualifications as anyone else; and often, when their needs are directly at stake, most capable of all.

The merit of a public employee is twofold. He or she knows how a particular service or good can be produced or distributed, and what kinds of services or goods their prospective users prefer. If a society consists of a multiplicity of interests, therefore, its employees must generally be from a multiplicity of backgrounds (to which they feel some kinship). Where a particular producer of a good or service has one or two particular collections of interests as his or her primary prospective clients, then policies concerning that product must be made, at least in major part, by people sharing the same interests or backgrounds, or else by those who have their seal of approval.

That needs are best appreciated when they are shared, in other words, is one of the things we must understand when we talk about capability and talent in a democratic society. Among the chief merits of a city planner is that he or she lives with an ordinary income in a representative area of the city to be planned; of a policymaker in an energy agency, that he or she know what it means to face debt or frost as permanent alternatives; of the public member of an oil indus-try advisory board, that he or she has no friends in the industry and no faith in the veracity of its spokespersons when they report on their proven reserves, their profits, or their international relations. The role of public servants in a democacy is to be representative, and the role of a representative is to represent; to do otherwise is to be ultra vires, to be incompetent.

The relevant skill pools for public services in a democracy consist therefore of candidates for office or position who are believed to be sufficiently competent by the people themselves, from whatever per-spective the people themselves believe to be most appropriate. By "the people themselves" I do not mean the pseudodemocratic mass but rather the fundamental constituency units. Appointment not only by lot but even by administrative co-option to any public job ought to be appointment for a term, drawn at random from lists submitted at the democratic grass roots. And as I have indicated before, what determines whether a job is public in that sense is nothing more than the will of some group of affected constituents to have it treated in that way.

Thus for example, men might go on desiring to command the dominant positions in fields of medical practice that serve mostly women, but not many constituency groups would be found to waste their precious energies and powers on trying to get male doctors to be the administrators of such services. On the other hand, in the absence of a spontaneous movement in the direction of greater administrative power for females in those areas, numerous constituencies of women would spring up with precisely that end in view. Given democratic recruitment, that is, positions of service and authority would come to be filled by the solicitations of one kind of affected group or another, rather than being most open, as now, to ambitous individuals representing primarily their own desires. This change from the job as an individual good to the job as a locus for the fulfillment of specific community needs would be accomplished without any "quotas" whatsoever.

As for merit, whether its requirements are real or fancied, it should always be judged (to combine Aristotle with Bentham) by those who know their own interests best—the diners at the feast, the patients of the surgeon, the dwellers in the house. If the people persisted in nominating incompetents and dolts for technically exigent positions then no one would suffer the consequences more than themselves in the end, as they would come to realize: learning by doing. The technocratic ideology, contrarily, is based on assiduous cultivation among the public, by experts, of the belief that every day in every way society is in such a state of crisis that learning by doing is impossible. Unless the experts are given free rein, without interference, machines will run amok, explosives will explode, the economy will grind to a halt, and nuclear war will instantly break out. Thus a kind of surplus value is extracted from citizen-clients, who surrender a part of their personal capabilities to enhance the creative opportunities and powers of those who monopolize the term, "professional." The message that this form of exploitation is necessary is thrust on a worldwide public by the spokespersons for estimable professions, without exception.

Those professions however, to revert to my earlier catalogue of those who rule but are not ruled, also contain thousands of architects who design buildings with windows that won't open, doctors who prescribe unnecessary drugs in the interest of pharmaceutical companies, teachers who dislike children, economists who can neither predict nor understand inflation or depression, scientific administrators whose public statements about the problems of nuclear power are without exception false, and political elites who manage consistently to arrange costly wars in the wrong place at the wrong time. Theirs is a message designed to prevent democracy from happening; the only way to test its validity is to open up positions of responsibility to those communities (through their representatives) on whose behalf that responsibility is supposed to be exercised.

# VI

The appropriate mix among formal electoral representation, communal delegation, professionally administered recruitment under external controls, appointment by lot, and town-meeting democracy, is no concern of this essay. As I have said at several junctures, in deference to the fundamental principle that the end of democracy is to make effective public choice possible, such questions can only be answered by the same people who create a democratic social order in the first place. My purpose here is only to point to some of the tools that may be of use in that task of invention; that can be put at the disposal of the body politic without effects on it more predictably harmful than those it now endures.

Of course at no time in an ordinarily sane community will every conscious person wish to be either choosing a representative or engaging in some more direct form of political activity. The vision of those classical theorists and neoclassical theorists from Aristotle to Hannah Arendt, who believed strongly in the life of political participation but distrusted most potential participants, has a certain truth to it: political life, or life in general, would become unmanageable if everyone were at all times publicly engaged in doing and being done.[11] I have attempted to describe a social order that provides refuges from political life for individuals; that has distance as well as immersion built into it, by virtue of its multiplicity of representative and participatory roles, and its plurality of institutions within which to earn a living.

On the other hand, the permanent and total exclusion of any competent person (in the legal sense) from the realm of action must lead to some form or other of tyranny, which is no less so for being called "democracy," "polyarchy," or "representative government." No act of choice can be imputed to political nonactors except in a political system that rewards the activism of all equally. The hallmark of a politically egalitarian society is not that everyone runs around doing political things all the time, but that anyone can engage in citizenship activities when struck by the need or the interest, with as much chance of success as anyone else. Where the philosophy of political equality departs from Aristotle and Arendt, then, is in its insistence that everyone is potentially an active citizen, and has the rights and duties of such, regardless of whether the potentiality is being realized at any given moment. The egalitarian, that is, need in no way deny the traditional conservative's assertion that human beings are imperfect. The egalitarian, rather, draws from that assertion, and from its corollary that government ought to be restrained, the radically contradictory conclusion that all citizens ought to be empowered to engage equally in the actions that constitute political restraint. For as all are imperfect, none is worthy of a privileged position of rule, compared to any other.

# Notes

[1] Throughout, my discussion of representation in its varying shades of meaning is informed by Hanna Fenichel Pitkin, *The Concept of Representation* (Berkeley: University of California Press, 1972), though I have attached a normative and metaphorical content that she more or less avoids, to certain modes of representation that we both discuss.

[2] No one has told us more about town meeting democracy than Jane Mansbridge, *Beyond Adversary Democracy* (New York: Basic Books, 1980).

[3] Joseph Schumpeter, *Capitalism, Socialism, and Democracy*, Chs. 21–23; and Walter Lippman, *The Phantom Public* (New York: Harcourt Brace, 1925).

[4] See the criticisms by David Vogel, "On 'Democratic Investment,'" *democracy*, vol. 2 no. 3 (July 1982), pp. 135–41. For an analysis of participation in the local school board elections in Ocean-Hill Brownsville that takes a different view, see Philip Green, "Decentralization, Community Control, and Revolution: Reflections on Ocean Hill-Brownsville," in Philip Green and Sanford Levinson, eds., *Power and Community: Dissenting Essays in Political Science* (New York: Pantheon Books, 1969), pp. 266–68.

[5] Again, for a thoroughly persuasive argument for the irreplaceability of the parliamentary institutions of what I've called "the shadow world of politics," I'm deeply indebted to Carmen Sirianni, especially his "Councils and Parliaments: The Problems of Dual Power and Democracy in Comparative Perspective," *Politics and Society*, vol. 12 no. 1 (1983), pp. 83–123.

[6] *The Civil War in France*, in Marx and Engels, *Selected Works*, Volume I (Moscow: Foreign Languages Publishing House, 1962), pp. 519–20; Hannah Arendt, *On Revolution* (New York: Viking Press, 1963), Ch. 6.

[7] In A.S.P. Woodhouse, ed., *Puritanism and Liberty* (London: J.M. Dent, 1938), pp. 74–5. I learned much about the Levellers from the Smith College Senior Thesis of Mary Bridget ("Molly") Burke, "The Levellers Vindicated: Or A Discourse Shewing That Obligation Stemmeth Only From Mutual Consent to the Lawes, and That The People Are The Only Trew Judge of The Justness Thereof" (Northampton, Mass.: 1976).

[8] Jurgen Habermas speaks of the "dimension in which the sciences practice reflection. In this dimension they critically account to themselves, in forms originally employed by philosophy, both for the most general implications of their presuppositions for ways of viewing the world and for their relation to practice. This dimension must not be closed off," he adds, by the politicization of inquiry. See Habermas, *Toward A Rational Society: Student Protest, Science, and Politics*, trans. by Jeremy J. Shapiro (Boston: Beacon Press, 1970), pp. 8ff.

[9] For a further discussion of this point, see my *The Pursuit of Inequality*, pp. 188–96.

[10] *The Republic of Plato*, trans. by Francis M. Cornford (New York: Oxford University Press, 1945), I, 340. Other translators of *The Republic* give a less explicit rendering of the argument in this passage, but in all renderings the point is essentially the same.

[11] *The Politics of Aristotle*, ed. and trans. by Ernest Barker (New York: Oxford University Press, 1958), III, xi, 1282a; and Hannah Arendt, op. cit.

# 10

# THE RIGHTS OF EQUALS

## I

The notion of representation and participation described in the previous chapter is intended to give weight to, among other things, the idea of equal individual and group rights. That idea is liberalism's most significant, but also most endangered contribution to the theory and practice of popular government. Our rights make up an endangered species because we have only a defensive and only an individualistic conception of them. The defense of rights in its purest formulation is meant to protect the weak against the strong, the helpless against the powerful, and the governed against the governing. That is ultimately a hopeless task, for we are really saying that the inert should be protected against the active by protectors drawn from among the active themselves. That is equal right as charity, and though the system of political charity is not without its glories (who can read *Gideon's Trumpet* without feeling its emotional tug at the heartstrings?),[1] it bears the same relationship to the political system in general as the soup kitchen bears to a capitalist economy.

Democratic representation and participation, contrarily, abolish the distinction between the acted and the acted-upon, by making the actions of leaders legitimate only through the active self-mobilization of communities. In addition, the multiplication of levels of representation and participation, within which people can find allies and spokespersons, will often prevent conflicts between individuals or groups and society as a whole from constantly becoming final showdowns, and will thus also provide an institutionalized, positive protection against the overwhelming forces of centralized power. In that context, then, we may hope to give real substance to the abstract and often alienable rights of liberal individualism: to describe instead the fundamental rights of equal citizens. In so doing we must comprehend both those rights which are incorporated in the doctrines and practices of traditional liberalism, and those which necessarily go beyond its understanding of equal right to a broader interpretation.

This enterprise may seem puzzling to some readers, admittedly, given the emphasis I have placed on public ownership and control of the means of production, communal self-sufficiency, and equality in the division of labor and the distribution of rewards. It is a long-established tradition on the Left, especially the Marxian Left, to treat questions of civil liberty and civil right casually, as though they are a legacy of bourgeois individualism that will disappear when the material order that gives rise to them disappears.

That attitude, however, is badly shortsighted. That individuality is grounded in sociality, as Marx insisted, is beyond question; that different social formations will engender different kinds of individuals equally so. But to repeat what I have argued earlier, to rest everything on the expectation of universal human liberation is utopian in the worst sense. To imagine that a general commitment to social cooperation rather than to atomistic individualism will eliminate the tension between individual psyche and social order, between individual need and collective conscience, is simply to indulge in a play on words. Except among those who live the simplest kind of prehistorical existence, and perhaps not even among them, there is not the faintest evidence, or reason to believe, that that tension should ever vanish; that it is anything but real, deep, and irremediable. From this perspective, then, to discuss the idea of equality without considering the protection of individual and group rights, would be irresponsible.

We can see that this is so, in fact, by merely taking up the most obvious, logically and practically prior question, that must be settled before we can coherently conceptualize the notion of a community: who are to be considered its citizens in a world of endless geographical and social mobility? That is to say, resolution of a fundamental question of right necessarily precedes any attempt even to frame the argument that the strict communalist would like to defend. And since few of the differentiations that generate the problem of rights require anything more than mere mobility for their inspiration, on this ground alone we are justified in treating the liberal idea of right as an essential component of any egalitarian social theory.

From the standpoint of a democratic egalitarianism, then, we must begin by confronting the most serious problem of citizenship that is visible in the pseudodemocratic world of today: the existence of those second-class citizens or more properly noncitizens (known as "aliens") who are present by the thousands or millions in all capitalist societies. How would an egalitarian regime define citizenship so as to avoid duplicating our own sorry record on this, the most primary issue of all?

Who are the citizens of a democracy? The only justifiable answer is, any persons living and working in it who have not specifically chosen to be, exclusively, citizens of somewhere else. The prerequisite of any defensible notion of democratic citizenship is that if we as citizens want to make use of other people's talents or energies— and that is exactly what we are doing when we hire them to perform labor we do not want to perform ourselves—then we owe them the option of sharing our citizenship. To have a class of rightless aliens in our midst would be no different than having a class of janitors and maids in our midst.

A democratic society must offer resident aliens the right to become citizens. Otherwise its inhabitants will be simply hiring a reserve army of labor to which they have no obligations, thereby making a mockery of the democratic division of labor. As for those who reject the offer, the minimal obligation they would thereafter be owed would be due process and equal protection of the laws. They would also be owed the protection of treaties with their jurisdictions of origin in which the right they would or wouldn't have would be definitively established. A democratic community may define itself as narrowly as it pleases, but then it has to do its own work. (Of course, in a fully democratic world, communities that refused citizenship to immigrant aliens who were doing useful labor would probably have to pay a premium for their services: which would be fair enough.)

Moreover, any exclusivist definition of citizenship by any community of any size, immediately establishes the presumption that it considers itself a sovereign community, acknowledges no other sovereignty over it, and expects none of the benefits and protections that accrue from belonging to some larger sovereign entity. Within any larger sovereign jurisdiction (claiming "the monopoly of the legitimate use of force within a given territory"), be it as large as the United States or as tiny as Luxembourg, incorporated communities can neither exclude fellow citizens from entry, nor deny them equal rights, without effectively seceding from the larger commonwealth. Democratic societies probably ought to recognize a right to secession; they cannot recognize a right of local or regional authorities to impose unequal treatment on equal citizens of the whole.[2]

These requirements are fairly straightforward: they tell us how citizenship would be established among a community of equals. So too is the initial definition of the fundamental political rights of those citizens. Again, except in a community so unified that politics had disappeared from it altogether, the rights of political equals have to be defined: and any such essay in definition must take us well into the traditional liberal worldview.

Thus, it cannot be assumed or taken for granted but has to be stated that in addition to the right of participation in any regularly institutionalized version of participatory or representative politics, the right to freedom of intellectual or spiritual expression in all its forms, to freedom of association, and to completely open government, must also be enshrined by any regime that is meant to be democratic in the full sense of the word. By that we have to mean more than a merely intangible commitment. The rights that underpin political equality ought to be constitutionally recognized and, where necessary, legislatively articulated rights in a regime of political equals; else the commitment to political equality is mere vapor.

Even though these traditional liberal rights are insufficient to buttress the practices of democratic equality in and of themselves, they are still fundamental to it in a way that the other components of egalitarianism are not. That is because these rights are constitutive of equal citizenship itself. We do not need to justify them by claiming that they are prerequisite to some other fundamental rights; or by appealing to natural right, whatever that might be and whoever or whatever might be its author; or by appealing to social utility, a la John Stuart Mill. Freedom of speech, association, and political participation are not essential rights because they lead to, support, undergird, or otherwise buttress the activity of democracy; they are essential rights because they *are* the activity of democracy.

The operational behavior of democratic politics consists of activity in which people with sometimes mutual but also sometimes conflicting interests, talk to and argue with each other about the best way to implement and manage those interests; form coalitions based on their differing conclusions, if their conclusions do indeed differ; and choose spokespersons to assert those conclusions and choose definitively among them. The fundamental rights of a democracy is a shorthand expression for this behavior. In this respect, the activities that require protection for the associational activities of individuals or minority groups on the one hand, and the justification of majority rule on the other, are the identical activities. When it comes to political rights we do not need to choose between the two conceptions, for they both impose the same requirements. (With the exception of the rights of individual conscience. Civil disobedience, the public activity that stems from the exercise of those rights when they have been legally proscribed, probably ought to be legally validated by any decent regime, in the form of a legislative recognition of the right of conscientious refusal. By this I mean only the conscientious refusal to inflict injury on others.)

It is usually thought to be a difficulty in this approach to the rights of democratic citizens that we must decide whether or not these rights are to be absolute. The alleged difficulty is spurious, though. There are all sorts of perfectly obvious ways in which fundamental rights may be subject to abridgement and still remain fundamental. They may come into conflict with other fundamental rights: libelous free speech versus the right of privacy; the right of free press versus the right to a fair trial. Or fundamental democratic rights may come into conflict with each other, as when demonstrators or counter-demonstrators provoke a riot against each other; or when the right of teachers to be free of censorship in their teaching conflicts with the right of parents to exercise democratic community control over the education of their children.

Or there may be disagreement about what constitutes the exercise of a protected right, properly interpreted: is obscenity, or the wearing of armbands, or the advertisement of commodities for sale really "speech"? Is it an instance of peaceable assembly to parade in uniforms carrying weapons? There is no way in which the most unregenerately libertarian philosophy provides a definitive resolution to any of these dilemmas, except perhaps the conflict between teachers and parents. Any settlement of such conflicts will be both right and wrong, and only courts of law can decide authoritatively on which side the balance ought to weigh most heavily. In none of these instances, that is, is the issue of absolute rights properly raised.

It is very definitely raised, however, when we consider the issue of censorship, and here the notion of equal political rights requires elaboration. What is totally incompatible with any democratic constitution is the assertion of some alleged general social interest, in the name of which the rights of some democratic citizens are to be repressed. On utilitarian grounds the would-be censor is always able to justify the repression of this or that statement or idea or movement: the potential harm to the polity from its expression outweighs the potential benefit of the expression. But the philosophy of equal rights is not a utilitarian philosophy, and this kind of balancing test is wholly inappropriate among democratic citizens. We do not enshrine the fundamental rights of expression and association because they are good for us but because, as I have said, they constitute part of what we mean by democratic equality. Minority right is not an afterthought we tack onto democracy after we have secured its fundamental institution of majority rule. In some nations that may seem to have been the historical order of things, but it is not the philosophical order. Once we have understood the necessity of a notion of rights for any conception of a society of political equals, we then appreciate that without majority rule we don't have democracy, and without minority right we don't have it either.

It follows from that assertion, moreover, that where the two modes of social determination apparently come into genuine conflict, either the majority must concede to the minority, or some independent judge must decide between them; but the majority itself cannot rightfully rule. The philosophy of democratic equality that gives the majority the right to make rules is the very same philosophy that gives minorities the right to claim constitutional protections. If the latter claim fails because of some supposedly negative social utility it may entail, so too could the former. There is no necessary relationship between utilitarian thinking and majoritarianism, and a majority that surrendered the legitimacy of someone else's constitutional protections to the demands of some claimed necessity would by that token have surrendered the legitimacy of its own protections. Where supposed utility or one party's moral preference takes precedence over constitutional rights, that is not the striking of a balance but an assertion that might makes right. The definitive version of social utility or social ethics at any given moment is nothing but the version of those who have the power to make their view stick: and they may not always be the majority.

Therefore, in an egalitarian, democratic society founded on the notion of equal rights, it is a self-contradiction for its jurisprudence to recognize as potentially criminal such offenses as seditious libel, or conspiracy to advocate anything at all, or the publication of dangerous materials with an intent to harm the national security, etc. One further complication, however, is instantly suggested by this approach to the rights of democratic citizens. Does the right to engage in the normal activities of equal citizenship extend to those who, had they the power to do so, would abolish those rights for those they disagree with or disapprove of? Do antidemocrats deserve rights in a democracy?[3]

We seem to be caught in a paradox. The principle of political freedom for all is one of the fundamental principles of political equality. No one should be allowed to advocate the denial of that freedom to anyone. But if the principle of political freedom is one of the fundamental principles of political equality, then the minority of people who disagree with that fundamental principle should not be deprived of their inalienable right to disagree with it.

On the one side of this paradox, it is possible to contemplate the careful crafting of some piece of legislation making it an offense to, say, advocate deprivation of the equal rights of a religious or racial minority and to contemplate the use of that legislation to suppress what would otherwise be the legitimate associational activities of some recrudescent group of Klansmen in an otherwise egalitarian society. On the other side, any serious counterrevolution of that kind seems remarkably unlikely to occur in a society that has endorsed a far-ranging democratic revolution in the first place. The obvious unlikelihood of such an occurrence suggests that it ought to be enough to proscribe the actual criminal or suppressive behaviors themselves: deprivation of rights, criminal conspiracy, and so forth. (The U.S. Civil Rights Act of 1866, though it has rarely been used as it might have been used, is a good model of this kind.)

Advocacy, association, participation, then—all acts constitutive of democratic political life—ought never to be suppressed per se. In a democracy the only acceptable grounds for the suppression of free association and participation could be (to use a much misused phrase in its proper context) a "clear and present danger"—as interpreted by the public authorities *and* ratified by the courts—that otherwise legitimate expressions of political behavior are about to turn into forbidden acts of harmful and criminal deprivation.[4] With this sole exception, all the manifold ways in which one or more of the citizens of an egalitarian regime can express themselves, or can associate together to advance their interests or ideas, ought to be constitutionally embedded and protected wherever and whenever they occur.

# II

To identify the fundamental political rights in an egalitarian regime is only to begin the discussion of rights. An equally crucial question is, how ought those rights to be defended against the possibility that on occasion, in one community or another or even in a nation as a whole, a majority temporarily inflamed by the passions of war, or of prejudice, or of xenophobia, or of economic interest, will attempt to withhold those rights from the objects of their passion? Here we are asking not how the aggressions of some conspiratorial antidemocratic faction can be contained, but what can be done when we ourselves have temporarily become the antidemocrats?

In no liberal capitalist society have economic or military elites ever attempted to dismantle legitimated popular institutions and substitute for them the rule of sheer domination. Absent a really convulsive crisis, we can be fairly sure that they never will. In that sense the trajectory of contemporary societies toward democracy is truly progressive, and cannot be halted at any step along the way without at least the temporary acquiescence of a majority itself.

By contrast, the idea of minority right—of protection against majorities—is very problematic, both historically and philosophically, despite what I've said about its intrinsic relationship to democracy. And indeed, the sad history of invasions of minority right by aggressive majorities is directly related to the more abstract problem of philosophical justification.

Ordinarily, we do not deny legitimacy to the outcome of a vote or a debate or a meeting merely because that outcome differs from what we would have advocated, or did advocate. What the majority does may not always be right, but as long as constitutional rules are not violated it is always legitimate. If, in an egalitarian polity, the majority decided to desocialize public enterprise, more steadfast egalitarians might criticize this action as an error that would soon lead to the undermining of political equality itself; but they would not think the action was an illegitimate outcome of the institutions of political equality. That is the inescapable paradox of democracy in any imaginable version whatsoever.

I have throughout insisted that empowerment to engage equally in civic activity is also fundamental to the notion of political equality. It is true that the means of empowerment are different from the fundamental political rights. The latter are constitutive of democracy itself and thus need no further justification. Contrarily, I have had to give an instrumentalist justification for the economic and social rights of equal citizenship. The necessity for that kind of justification does not, however, make those rights of empowerment less fundamental. Without these empowerments, the political guarantees of the democratic regime will degenerate, as they have among us, into merely formal provisions and pious slogans, vitiated by underlying and determinative realities of class and caste. The political rights of equal citizenship will not in practice be equally available to truly equal citizens unless those rights are buttressed, again at the level of constitutional guarantee, by the commitment to genuinely equal social opportunity and economic security that I have summed up as constrained inequality, the democratic division of labor, reproductive rights, and a public sector of communal enterprises that is truly available to and supportive of all who need or desire its support. That is, before the guarantee of individual rights can be meaningful, the collective right of every member of the community to be an equal member of the community must also be guaranteed. Only when this right is understood as a fundamental constitutional right, will the linkage between an expectation of benefits and of docility, servility, and obedience finally disappear.

Fully equal opportunity in this sense means more than equal opportunity; it means equal treatment. But here we encounter the ultimate problem for egalitarians. For the ideal of equal treatment in an egalitarian society is more than merely procedural. Equal treatment has a substantive content in addition to an administrative or legislative method. In an egalitarian society equal treatment has a purpose: to ensure that the outputs of government— of public order or collective action in the broadest sense—do not discriminate among persons in such a way as to deprive some of them of access to or enjoyment of the possibilities, privileges, and amenities available within the social order.

The problem for egalitarians is that although the justifications of majority rule and minority right are basically the same justification in the realm of political association, that is not so in the realm of economic and social behavior: of communal identity. In this latter realm, fair procedures and just outcomes may conflict with each other. At this point, the thrust of the discussion of political equality undergoes a decisive shift.

Much of the notion of political equality I have been developing so far is, I think, similar to the intuitions of most of the democracy-seeking citizens of the liberal capitalist societies, even those who would consider it utopian to carry the logic of that notion as far as I have taken it. The recognition that how we order or reorder economic structures is crucially related to the achievement of political equality is also quite common. Thus, even though there is considerable varia-tion from one society to another in beliefs about whether or how that reordering ought to be accomplished, it still makes both logical and practical political sense to argue the essential and necessary intimacy between the two kinds of equality. The form of the argument is that a democratic division of labor, for example, would be in the interests of the majority, both in and of itself; and more importantly, that it would support institutions of political equality that are in the universal interest.

That mode of argument cannot as easily be used on behalf of the claim of minorities to the rights of equal opportunity or equal treat-ment, however. There are all sorts of easily imaginable cases, even in an egalitarian polity, where claimants on behalf of equal opportunity or equal treatment would properly be satisfied with nothing less than the particular outcome they had demanded, and could rightfully consider any other outcome illegitimate; even if it were produced by a majority decision and even though it satisfied the needs or interests of an overwhelming majority.

Thus, for example, even though discrimination against racial and ethnic minorities must ultimately disappear within a truly democratic division of labor, their members may still disproportionately bear some relevant burden of past discrimination. They might therefore demand compensatory assistance on one hand, or exemption from certain standard requirements on the other in order to make good the reality of the promise of genuinely equal opportunity. That, of course, is the kind of claim that has constantly been made in American society and often upheld by the Supreme Court.

By the same token, we can imagine a whole array of behaviors that could only be addressed coherently if the constitution of political equality, as interpreted by prescribed organs of judicial review, incorporated some general proscription of them. Even in an egalitarian polity we can imagine attempts to remove homosexual men or women from the classroom; to deprive resident aliens of civil rights; to erect public facilities without sufficient access for the handicapped; to build a new road through or impose some other disamenity on a neighborhood inhabited largely by members of some minority group rather than the majority; to treat one language rather than another as the official language of public social discourse; or to penalize the communicants of a religion by treating their sacred practices as mere secular deviations from some allegedly appropriate attitude toward work. Even within the democratically organized division of labor in production itself, we might encounter efforts to prevent exceptional women from engaging in certain activities defined as dangerous to the well-being of women in general, or stereotyped on some other grounds as belonging properly to men; and so on.

Nor can we happily presume that the intuitions of most people will come down in favor of the special protection of minority interests of this kind, when a real conflict is posed between themselves. We cannot presume on some helpful notion of false consciousness, according to which people would support the equal treatment of minorities if they knew what was really good for themselves. Wholly leaving aside the ethical and epistemological status of false consciousness, we cannot confidently assert the value of a complete rather than merely formal notion of equal opportunity and equal treatment to the average, conventional, heterosexual, white worker (male or even female). Where others (capitalists) are the barrier to equality, that is one thing; where oneselves (the democratic majority) are identified as the barrier by some group socially defined as "outsiders," that is quite another: the consequentialist appeal no longer applies.

And yet, with the exception of a claim for compensation, the exemplary cases I have imagined above are not even arguable by an egalitarian. They all represent outright denials of equal treatment or equal opportunity; of the bedrock principle of political equality that no policy is likely to receive more or less support merely by virtue of the nature of the social interests it represents. In that respect an expansive equal protection of the laws doctrine (such as is asserted in the 14th Amendment to the American Constitution) is as essential to the constitution of political equality as are the more conventionally upheld rights of free association.

Here at last the egalitarian cannot possibly stand on the principle that what people really want is what is really right. At this point, therefore, fidelity to the ideal of political equality compels me to desert the mode of discourse that relies on persuading people that if they desire some end, they ought also to desire some intermediate steps that are logically and realistically entailed by it. The only possible argument on behalf of an unequivocal defense of minority rights is not that political equality correctly understood *logically* entails minority rights (as I have insisted until now), but that political equality correctly understood *rightfully* entails minority rights. The democrat defends substantive minority rights not because the notion of democracy requires that defense but because any notion of democracy that spurned that defense would be unworthy. All our consequentialist arguments—that if I don't defend minority rights now I may find myself in some oppressed minority later; that a nation cannot exist half slave and half free; that the repudiation of any democratic value sets us on a dangerous slippery slope; that there will be less crime and more communal happiness where there is no social discrimination; etc.—are true, but they do not suffice. In the end, the egalitarian can only stand on an appeal to moral reason, not practical reason. If we can free ourselves from our own fears, interests, and prejudices, this is what we really mean by democratic equality.

It is impossible to go farther. It is only possible to assume that that appeal can be made persuasively, and somehow gain acceptance. Beyond that assumption, we can only talk not about why, but how to defend minority rights in an egalitarian polity.

## III

The ultimate line of defense of minority rights in a democratic regime ought to be obvious to Americans, for it is that nation's most signal contribution to political thought and practice: constitutionalism, as realized through a system of judicial review immunized from popular assault. Judicial review based on constitutional doctrine can only be one among many ways of settling disputes in democratic societies. There will always be conflicts, even immensely bitter conflicts, that will not be resolvable by appeal to principles, and may not even be susceptible of peaceful resolution. This could be true, for example, of conflicts among equal citizens who have, however, widely disparate attitudes toward the use of natural resources, the preservation of natural landscapes, the rights of animals and their human keepers, the proper balance between pedestrian and vehicular traffic, etc. In fact, if there were no minorities at all, the institutions of adversary democracy still would be strained to the utmost.

Judicial review, though, is a peculiarly appropriate method for the defense of minority rights. It is unfortunate, therefore, that judicial review, epitomized in this particular activity of the federal courts, has come to have quite a narrow meaning in the context of American constitutional law. Here we must give it broader scope. A system of judicial review for an egalitarian polity might include, and probably should include, not only a court system, but a proliferation throughout communities and organizations of such institutions as the grievance committee, the ombudsperson, the independent adminis-trative review board, and so on. The key to the successful functioning of all such entities is that they have the power to define formally pro-tected rights within the ambit of their authority, and that they be immune from replacement by members of the community whom they may frustrate or offend. The members of courts deciding on constitutional issues should be appointed or elected for long fixed terms, if not for life. Ombudspersons or review boards should be chosen by constituencies of the agencies they are going to oversee rather than the agencies themselves, and should be removable only by those constituencies.

Most democrats have no trouble with the notion of ombudsmen, grievance procedures, and administrative review. Judicial review, on the other hand, has been one of the most contested of political inno-vations since John Marshall first thrust it upon an unhappy Thomas Jefferson. Jefferson is a much greater name in the history of demo-cratic thought than John Marshall. Thus both theorists and popular writers committed to what they have called "democracy," have continually denounced American-style judicial review as elitist and antidemocratic.[5]

However, if a fundamental rule of political equality is the inculcation and preservation of minority rights, and if political equality is the organizing principle of democracy, then the institution of judicial review to protect those rights and that equality is not antidemocratic but is the essence of democracy. No one really questions this when the right to vote is at stake. The real disagreement is not about the nature of judicial review but the nature of democracy: not how to protect fundamental rights, but which rights are fundamental. Conversely, if we accept the understanding of democratic equality proposed here, we will also accept that judicial review of acts allegedly injurious to the social opportunities of minorities is as legitimate and necessary as judicial review of acts allegedly aimed at the deprivation of someone's political liberty.[6]

It may be, of course, that in a society where everyone learns the first principles of democratic constitutionalism as the fundamental content of everyday life, judicial review could be performed by randomly chosen citizens (appellate juries, so to speak) rather than legal specialists. I do not think that argument could be made unambivalently by anyone who has ever confronted the intricacies of trying to decide, say, whether a tax levied by Pennsylvania on liquor imported from New Jersey ought to be considered an interference with commerce; but perhaps in a real democracy social and economic intercourse would be, as Marx imagined, more transparent. Even so, the principle of insulation of those who perform any version of judicial review from the community out of which they have originally emerged is, or ought to be, privileged.

The notion of neighborhood courts trying and punishing offenses like child abuse or misuse of a partner's assets is a good democratic proposal. That the jurors will have to go back and live among their neighbors after their term of service, and may therefore be afraid to reach decisions that would be unpopular with their neighbors, is exactly what we are after: ordinary law should represent the common daily understandings of the community within which it is applied. Constitutional law, per contra, should represent the common permanent understandings of the community within which it is applied, and these may easily be forgotten by communities temporarily possessed of some antidemocratic or inegalitarian sentiment. Only citizens who are neither chosen by a community, nor responsible to it for their performance in office, are in a position to defy its temporary will, without fear or favor, as the need for the enforcement of constitutional protections may arise. What Rousseau said about the legislator who gives a people their constitution—that ideally he ought to be a foreigner, with no personal stake in the kinds of laws that they adopt, and able to leave as soon as the constitution has been laid down—is in a less dramatic way true of appellate judges as well. Judges, ombudspersons, etc., ought not to be foreigners but they ought to be safely detached from public control if they are to monitor the one area of social behavior over which any temporary public ought not to have ultimate control: the maintenance of democratic principles.

It is indeed tempting to insist, contrarily, that having made an egalitarian revolution and installed a regime in which civic equality would be treated in all educational institutions as the primary value, we should not have to worry about the possibility of majority tyranny against which judicial review is designed to guard us. That temptation should be disregarded. The history of the United States by itself offers enough evidence of the ability of communities and nations dedicatedly espousing the rhetoric of equality at the same time to persuade themselves that if only some group of people defined as troublemaking aliens could be disposed of, life would be better for everyone else.

No doubt, tolerance ought to be immediately recognizable as a virtue in an egalitarian regime: especially an egalitarian regime in which what an intellectual must conceive of as the enlightening effects of a common liberal education should be freely available to all. In a relatively classless society people ought not to be subject either to the sadism of brute power or to the sadomasochism of powerlessness; citizens who are brought up to treat each other as equals ought to internalize the ideal of minority rights as easily as they do that of majority rule. These are all comforting thoughts. Still, Tocqueville and Freud warn us compellingly against accepting them unquestioningly, even after we have imagined ourselves in a realm in which males and females have equally and cooperatively shared in the nurturance of future citizens.[7] We hardly know enough about the psychology of labelling certain behaviors as deviant, perceiving others as fitting the label, and then proceeding to treat them differentially, that we can feel free to make any secure judgments about the relative behavior in these respects of the inhabitants of one kind of society or another. What we do know is not especially reassuring. We seem to be very adept at fearing nonconformity, and the source of those fears, when they are manifested, often seems to lie at least as much in the unknowable psyche as it does in the more observable and 'manipulable social order. An appropriate civic education is the first line of defense for a stable democratic regime; but we cannot assume that it would suffice. In any event there are conflicting models of what constitutes a democratic educational system. Ought its purpose be to unite communities, strengthen families, or liberate children? Soidisant democratic arguments are possible on behalf of all these approaches, but they may be incompatible with each other and generate serious social divisions.[8]

We must reach a similar conclusion about the prospect that some kind of formal recognition of the right of communal resistance, which seems to follow logically from the notion that in an egalitarian society authorizations and powers emerge from communities, might constitute a satisfactory protection against majority tyranny. There are some examples of communal or regional resistance, on behalf of individuals or minorities, in American History: from the state of Wisconsin's effective protection of fugitive slaves against the reach of the Fugitive Slave Act to the State of Massachusetts' ineffectual attempt to nullify the impact of conscription on its own citizens during the Vietnam War. However, aside from the question of whether communal resistance can ever succeed in the absence of real secession, we have to recognize that local communities are not only a potential bastion of defense against generalized oppression: often they are the oppressors themselves. In an egalitarian but pluralistic society the ability and desire of relatively homogenous and self-governing communities to be oppressive of deviant intruders in their midsts might even be enhanced.

Thus, it must be reasserted that we cannot assume the issue of minority or individual rights will disappear even in an egalitarian regime. Democratic education and communal solidarity will never be sufficient to ensure the protection of those rights; and only the institution of judicial review has the fullest potential for accomplishing that task; the mere notion of rights by itself, no matter how deeply embedded in the collective consciousness, cannot be sufficient.

## IV

To this point, though, this is still to speak of defensive measures only; of negative liberty. Democratic theory, as we have seen, commands much more than that. And although the entire body of this essay has defined a positive, empowering notion of opportunity there is also a second, somewhat different aspect of empowerment that I have not yet done more than hint at, and that has to be elaborated as a necessary addition to the discussion of genuinely equal opportunity.

The fundamental constitutive rights of democracy are not all exactly alike. The rights of association, participation, representation, are quite simple to implement. Once we have authorized them and clarified what we mean by them, there is really little further that needs to be done. In addition to the negative prohibition against restrictions on them, they require only free public space for their exercise, and some kind of rudimentary technology for transmitting the results of that exercise from one place to another. In the electronic era the process of transmission may be quicker than it was in, say, the eighteenth century, but it is not better or freer or more equal; and it is neither more nor less available to all people, in principle, than were pen, paper, and a coach and horses in that earlier era.

The right of speech, which we should more generally refer to as the right of communication, is different. Full and free public discussion and debate is an absolute prerequisite to any process of democratic decision making. And in this realm technology not only makes a difference, it makes a decisive difference. If ideas are communicated on paper, then to be without access to a printing press may be to be effectively prohibited from expressing them. If ideas are communicated along coaxial cables, lack of access to a television studio will have the same effect. The democratic guarantee of the vote requires only the legitimation of political competition to realize itself; the democratic guarantee of participation and representation requires only the existence and legal protection of autonomous communities and groups; the democratic guarantee of equal protection requires a climate of tolerance and the protection of securely independent judicial institutions. But the democratic guarantee of free speech, free press, and full public discussion requires more than protection, legitimation, or tolerance. It requires actual access to the means of communication; without that it is empty. By positive liberty or empowerment here I mean to restate the democratic requirement suggested by the late A.J. Liebling's famous epigram, "What good is a free press if you don't have one?"

What might this requirement mean in practice? The first approximation of an answer to that question may seem drastic, or even drastically simple-minded, but it is unarguable nonetheless. Democratic equality requires the dismantling of the entire structure of monopolized mass communication—newspaper chains, nationwide network television, mass-market book publishers—that we have come to take for granted as the very heart of consumer civilization itself.

Whoever controls the image in a world dominated by the mass communication of images ultimately controls that world.[9] That is so because the very structure of mass media of communication is incompatible with the structure of democratic citizenship itself: of genuine representation, of nonalienated and mutual linkage, and of continuing rotation in role and responsibility, between those who represent and those who are represented. There is no way that the controllers of the mass image can ever be representative of any constituency or can ever engage in anything but alienating communication.

The mass-produced image abstracts from, negates, and distorts the actual images that particular human beings have of their world, and then returns the alienated image to them as though it were their own. Lacking the technical, or technological facility to produce the competing images of our own understanding of the world, we are all reduced to being a consumer of someone else's worldview. If for a moment we think (with apologies) of the social decisions that make up collective life as commodities, then a citizen is someone who produces those commodities, at least his or her share of them. I do not have to make my own shoes or build my own home to be a full-fledged citizen; but the person who simply consumes the commodity of social life is a pseudocitizen.

Images are not just any commodity. In the absence of resistance, of the carefully thought-out production of counterimages, they are authoritative; they irradiate, so to speak, the field of potentially autonomous communication. I am implicated in no fundamental political or social contradiction when I accept that a Florsheim shoe is really a shoe, an ingot from Bethlehem Steel is really an ingot. But if I accept that Archie Bunker is really a human being or that *Time's* depersonalized account of this week's events is the authoritative account, then I am necessarily surrendering my own experience of what is human, to a concocted experience that is necessarily a lie and a sham. It is a lie and a sham because we cannot obtain a mass audience by communicating true particulars, except in the rarest of circumstances; and yet this lie and sham is also more vivid, more real, than my own devalued experience. At the very best, our own local knowledge of what social life is all about is always going to be competing with the grander, more global, more compellingly expressed knowledge of someone else: of a dominant class.

Moreover, to have representatives to the world of mass communications is useless. What will they represent, other than what they represent today—the presence of censorship, of resistance to particular kinds of stereotyping, etc.? All that can accomplish is a further cleansing of the mass image, usually making it even more abstracted from reality, and robbing us of the one dialectical element in our relationship with the mass image: our ability to be made angry by it. What our representatives can never do, neither in this world nor in a more democratic one, is substitute our particular truths for the mass untruth, for then we would no longer be dealing with a medium of mass communication.

As for the democratic pluralist solution, by itself it will not do either. Given the existence of a culturally authoritative mass communications medium, the thousand local flowers that bloom in its shadow will either be infiltrated by it (that is already happening to cable television in the U.S.) or imitate it, but less authoritatively, catering to minority tastes that it ignores.[10] Suppose that somehow we do genuinely open ourselves to the communication of our experience by the people of one region, locality, or neighborhood to another. That would still just be a democratic undercurrent, a democratic counterculture, in an antidemocratic milieu. That's a prescription for marginal reform in a pseudodemocracy and perhaps valuable for that purpose; but as to real democracy, a prescription for abandoning it.

All social formations decay, and an egalitarian formation may well decay even quicker than others. If there is one overriding meaning to life in a democracy, though, it has to be that participating in the shared production of products and of culture is what is easy and can be accomplished by any ordinary person; whereas to subvert public life on behalf of some elite's imperial vision requires the saboteur to be extraordinarily scheming and manipulative, and pathologically ambitious. Democratic pluralism can countenance almost any set of organizational arrangements, perhaps; but it cannot countenance any arrangement whereby communal democracy is the counterculture, and alienated mass pseudodemocracy is the normative culture.

How images, whether in one's home on a screen, in a collective gathering place, in print or on a newswire, should be best collocated and communicated, is a topic that would require an entirely separate discussion. At the minimum, however, we obviously have to talk about making sure that the technology of print and picture media are widely available to individuals or groups among the public, through the sharing of technical facilities and distribution networks; and through the maintenance of enough channels of public communication to ensure that no single private entrepreneur or public corporation could dominate discussion anywhere. This is another area, clearly, where several desirable principles must exist in an uneasy balance. The value of being able to generate knowledge or images of events of national or even global interest to disparate regions and localities exists side by side with the requirement that authority and power to control their distribution be decentralized. The requirement of cooperative social ownership of communications media, in order to ensure the equal access for and thus the empowerment of the voices of all citizens, exists side by side with the equally democratic necessities that there be free room for private competition with community institutions that will inevitably fail to satisfy all needs; and that there be constitutional protection for the expression of dissident views, and for minority access to the tools of communication that might be denied by a monolithic public voice.

The reference to private competition especially requires further explication, for that is a proposition that in this realm has traditionally been ignored or denigrated by socialists, egalitarians, and advocates of community control. It will not do to substitute community control of the means of communication for either the dominated mass market model or the centralized state control model and think that we have accomplished something. If all printing presses, television equipment, and so forth, were owned by local publics, who or what would guarantee access to those means of communication for dissidents, nonconformists, and the like? Judicial review alone is not a satisfactory answer, for that is the last line of defense of our rights. In an egalitarian society, any litigant who appears before the ultimate tribunal demanding equal access to some community newspaper will by then have undergone so much struggle, obloquy, and perhaps ostriciza-tion that triumph seems hardly worthwhile. Liebling's rhetorical ques-tion is as relevant for the advocates of community control, or of work-place democracy, as it is for advocates of the free market.

This might not seem to be a crucial issue if we conceive of all com-munities as essentially little pluralist republics, but that too would be an error. Madison was surely right to argue that the larger the scope of a polity, the more diverse and more balanced will be the interests contained within it; the smaller in scope, the greater the potential for majority tyranny.[11] We expect, for example, that some kinds of sec-tarian groups will aggressively reject all external influence and opin-ion; despite that, it would not concern us greatly if some such group owned its own printing press or television channel, etc., to which no one else had access. But a town can be really nothing more than a politically incorporated sect, and the exclusivity that had not upset us in the first instance would be quite disturbing. (This has happened, for example, in the town of Antelope, Oregon, which has been taken over by the followers of Bhagwan Shree Rajneesh. To say that the remain-ing inhabitants of Antelope who are not members of the sect feel that local tolerance is in question, would be to put it mildly.)

In a different way, the same thing can be true of a workplace, where eccentric or inconvenient ideas about how the work ought or ought not to be done can be treated by the majority as brutally as is a member of the lumpenproletariat by the police force. In both cases, conscientious dissent is probably more easily sustained before a court of strangers constituted by an impersonal medium of commun-ication than in the intimate community. This might well be true of protest against all the potential forms of discrimination I have alluded to in this chapter. Thus, the kind of decentralization of political authority that must accompany any effort at equal self-government poses the question of how freedom of communication for all is to be ensured, perhaps even more starkly than it is posed among us now.

The market for communication of ideas, moreover, is the one market that ought to be entirely and truly free. Neither corporate oli-gopolies nor state nor local monopolies in the means of communica-tion are compatible with democratic equality. This is a positive argu-ment for what I have heretofore only negatively defended as accept-able: the existence of independent personal accumulation not based on the exploitation of involuntary labor, nor monopolistic extortion from involuntary consumers. A democratic system of communications must do more than make room for local control and individual right of access; it must encourage and protect a genuine pluralism in the sources of access. A democratic constitution, therefore, ought to provide special protection for and encouragement of the private as well as communal ownership of the means of communication in particular. This might be done via either tax incentives of programs of direct subsidy or in some other manner. However it is done, the principle of maintaining a privileged position for the publication and communication of ideas and images by independent persons or groups has to be part of the central philosophy of democratic political equality, and constitutionally protected.

# V

Finally, we must distinguish the democratic version of equal opportunity from the classical liberal argument for the free market.

At various times throughout these pages, I have referred to an apparent multitude of rights pertaining to democratic opportunity: the right to own and operate a private, nonmonopolistic business free of unfair competition; the right to be secure in the guarantee of a socially standard reward for the performance of socially valued tasks; the right of access to all agencies of self or civic improvement; and the right to work but also the right to strike against the conditions of work. Above all, though I have not mentioned it specifically, a right to own personal property, or, more broadly speaking, to have a full share in the communal life, is the general right that stands behind all of these. Thus, though my language may seem at times to suggest a traditional individualistic notion of property right, what I have in mind is far from that. The emphasis on socially valued tasks, on civic improvement, and on communal life, as well as the earlier treatment of the division of labor in production and reproduction, must make it clear that the egalitarian does not conceive of property right in the same way as does the classical liberal individualist.

Thus, for example, abolition of the free market for labor, as I have proposed abolishing it—by implementing the right to work for a standard wage in the public sector, and by defining the right to work as a right of access not only to the job but to associated institutions of civic and self-improvement—would make it difficult to amass immense accumulations of wealth based on the exploitation of massed, involuntary labor. From the standpoint of rights theory, what is important about this prospect is that it requires no invasion of individual property rights. Egalitarians need not propose to forbid would-be entrepreneurs to hire labor on their own terms; we need only propose to create public institutions that would make it unnecessary for people to allow themselves to be hired for labor on someone else's terms.

The second condition that has sustained accumulation in the regime of corporate capitalism is suggested by the very term itself: the creation and legalization of the limited-liability corporation as the major instrument of accumulation. Like the free market for labor, the limited liability corporation is entirely the creation of the capitalist state itself. Again, to limit the scope of the limited liability corporation to public enterprise (or to private enterprises employing no more than a certain number of workers, or having no more than a certain number of shareholders or a certain amount of outstanding stock), would be to demolish the legal underpinnings of capitalist property right without depriving any individual of any natural, individual right.

Just what kind of property right, then, ought an egalitarian polity to recognize and protect?

Let us again imagine a paradigm case, the case of John Doe who works hard for many years, saving money from his earned income until he has put aside enough money to buy outright a piece of land and physical plant and equipment, and to hire some workers. All this is in order to produce a product, "Doepowder," that he has personally invented in his spare time: a product with effluents so noxious that they contaminate for decades any organic matter in which they come in contact. The same product, however, does have the beneficial and inestimable side-effect of alleviating some dreaded disease. The society in which John Doe lives and works wants the cure and is prepared to pay a price for it: but not any price. (The case is paradigmatic in that some people will take this view of almost any industry you can name.) Criminal repression of his work is therefore effectively out of the question, but some kind of public control is clearly necessary: some kind of regulation that, if it is to be effective, will have the result of greatly inconveniencing Doe and considerably increasing the price of Doepowder. How can we justify this?

It is immediately obvious that we cannot answer this question by saying that Doe has a right to use his property as he will. If my happiness, or my liberty to live as I please, or my human right in my own healthy body and the healthy bodies of my family, are infringed on by Doe's activities, then we do not have a "private right" against public intervention. We have instead nothing more or less than one private right against another. In a democracy, simply, government will intervene when the number of people who think their rights are being infringed on by the unregulated use of property is greater than the number of people who want to use their property without regulation. All these rights are equal in the eye of humans or nature. To say that the right of one can outweigh the right of 50 is to repudiate democracy and to institute not individual right but minority tyranny. Absolute property right, therefore, rather than being constitutive of democracy, as are the rights of speech, voting, etc., would actually be subversive of it.

Nor can the idea of nonintervention be rescued by contrasting, as do some free-market theorists, monetary compensation paid to the victims of externalities, or the imposition of monetary disincentives on the creators of externalities, with the supposedly more obnoxious regulation or prohibition of those same externalities. As a practical matter, it may sometimes be true that the method of compensation is more effective than the method of regulation, and on such occasions a majority may choose to implement compensatory procedures. As a matter of alleged principle, though, the method is unacceptable.[12]

I do not want to be poisoned and then compensated for being poisoned—that is, bribed to accept the event. Nor do I want a producer to be free to choose between poisoning me at a great expense and not poisoning me at a lesser expense. That kind of free choice is only acceptable to me if a jail term lies at the end of it. Moreover, monetary arrangements are in any event not noncoercive of the producers of externalities. They merely involve different agents of coercion: courts, to decide who is owed how much; administrative tribunals or investigatory bodies, to decide what has actually happened, why, and whose fault it is. If we first decide to let the environmental chips fall where they may, and let the parties to these relationships sue or be sued, society eventually will be constituted as an endless inquisition: half of us would be lawyers and the other half either plaintiffs or defendants. This is social disorder masquerading as economic theory.

Furthermore, the truism that not all side-effect costs (or benefits) can be measured is, like most truisms, true. If, for example, we were to ask pregnant women exposed to Doepowder residue to put a price on the wellbeing of their unborn children, we would ask them to treat the community's supposedly deepest values with the contempt that prostitutes have for their clients. The only thing worse than offering such a bribe would be accepting it. Enough of that and we finally have a civilization of people who despise each other as much as they love money.

In the same way, conflicts will often arise, not between a proprietor and the public, but within the productive enterprise itself. Once John Doe hires any workers at all to do anything at all, it is impossible to ignore as a question (rather than a dogma) who of the many people involved in the making of Doepowder can rightfully exercise the internal authority of proprietorship and management. That is, as against workers in an enterprise, what power does a proprietor have as of right?

The answer is none. The illusion that owners or managers have some rightful power is given only by the antecedent social fact that owners and workers have different legal positions in capitalist societies and thus different amounts of bargaining power (though this relationship has been gradually changing during the past century). If Doe's workers—making the realistic assumption that he does not carry out the entire production process himself—demand a say in the ordering of that process, and occupy his plant when he refuses, what recourse as of right does he have against them?

In capitalist societies, he can usually call on the police to come and forcibly evict the workers, on the grounds that his property is being transgressed against. But he can only do that because there is a prior social agreement that he has not first transgressed against the workers by ordering them around, refusing to bargain with them, and threatening their livelihoods. If these things were considered illegal, the workers could say that by staying on the scene they were merely protecting their property rights against a potentially criminal threat until public authority arrives to give them official protection. He would only have a right not to be occupied, in other words, if the state had granted him a particular, privileged legal status as opposed to all others that are in a working relationship with the Doepowder plant. But then it would not be a state of equals.

The fact is that legal obligations come about only through social agreement. The owner of a productive enterprise—that is, the person or persons whose initial investment brought it into being or whose continuing investments of capital maintain its operation—is therefore dependent on social convention, and social convention alone, for the defense of his or her prerogatives. If a society has arrived at a consensus that industrial authority should be allocated on an egalitarian foundation, then John Doe has no right to expect any other arrangement. Once we consider worker's jobs, or their ability to share in a community's life, to be as much their property and thus as much subject to the protection of right, as any other physical thing or piece of paper or intangible idea, it becomes clear that as between workers and an employer we have, not natural right against coercive force, but right against right.

The idea that invested capital conveys rights over others that mere life and work do not is simply the self-serving ideology of old-fashioned capitalism. Just as in the case of the regulation of externalities, if we live with any state at all, minimal or extended, centralized or decentralized, we live with the prospect that our particular mode of conduct may be interfered with in the interest of the health, safety, or welfare of those we live with. To object to interference in toto is to say no more than that we wish to live entirely alone.

# VI

What then is the practical difference between these two versions of fundamental economic rights? In an egalitarian regime, property right of a kind would certainly demand constitutional protection. Given a democratic definition of property, though, neither unalloyed accumulation, nor the unrestrained use of capital, could be considered appropriate extensions of that right.

Property right in a democracy should certainly encompass a citizen's right to own and use a business free of unfair restraint. It should also entail some restraints on the power of a democratic majority rightfully to socialize the property of any private or independent entrepreneur. Could any momentary collection of workers right-fully turn the privately-owned workplace at which they were working into a worker-owned workplace without further ado?

The response we ought to have to proposals for the nationalization of, say, the Chrysler Corporation is that, questions of compensation aside, that agglomeration of productive activities belongs to no one in John Locke's sense; thus there is no offense to our sense of justice in such proposals. But our primordial sense of justice is precisely what would be offended, it seems to me, if the burgeoning backyard indus-try of a few friends who had pioneered a new kind of microcomputer, or a grocery store that developed a booming business by staying open late and stocking exceptionally attractive or unusual goods, were to be expropriated from their owners at the moment they began to make their mark on society. This latter case quite apparently illustrates Locke's version of the labor theory of value at the moment when that theory still genuinely illuminates what we might call a natural right, not yet distorted by the corruptions of state subsidy, market monopoly, the manipulations of financial wealth, the impersonal giantism of corporate capital, and the exploitation of labor.

Locke's labor theory, as Marx suggested, is in fact more of a cri-tique than a defense of modern corporate property, which is owned in large part by people who've never worked on it, and worked on by people who derive no ownership therefrom. It is thus quite apposite to our example, even if our technologically knowledgeable friends, or our au courant provisioners, must rely on hired labor to develop their conception to the point of sale and social appropriation; as long as that labor has hired itself out to them on a truly voluntary basis. The simply held and personally worked on property of the small businessperson, in other words, is assimilable (as large-scale cor-porate property is not) to the moral intention that Locke, and all seri-ous defenders of the natural rights of labor, had in mind.

On the other hand, our democratic version of justice would be equally offended if profits from this kind of personal business property could be used to buy up other people's personal businesses, creating local monopolies and also falsifying the proposition that people deserve that which they have worked on with their own hands; or if it could be dissolved at the will of the owners when they got tired of it and had made enough to retire on.

This conjunction of variants of injustice, then—the natural injustice of sequestering truly private property and the social injustice of being able to use it in an anti-social manner—combine to suggest a simple principle. In an egalitarian regime, private, noncorporate productive property ought to belong to those who have created it themselves and worked on it themselves (even if others also have worked on it); and it ought to stop belonging to them when they stop working on it. (I use the term "productive" here as a shorthand term for economically active property, not only meaning it literally but also comprehending by it property used in distribution, the conveying of services, etc.)

At that point, if children or other members of their families have also been associated with the enterprise in a working capacity, it would perhaps be rightful for them to have the first option to take over legal ownership of the enterprise. Otherwise, for appropriate compensation it might devolve to the associated workers, the community, the nation, the world, or nobody at all, pending an agreed-upon disposition of it; or it might be sold to another private entrepreneur. Any of these outcomes surely would be legitimate in an egalitarian regime.

However, as I have suggested, in an egalitarian regime the rights of small-business property will still be limited by capitalism's standards. That must be so, since equal citizens will also recognize property right as encompassing the right to hold a job on good behavior; to withhold labor in order to ensure socially acceptable treatment on the job (the right to strike); to make sustainable claims on a standard social reward and the accepted agencies of public provision; and to have an equal share in the ownership (that is to say the enjoyment) of public property. Unlike the associational or communicative rights, therefore, "property rights" so defined would necessarily always be in potential conflict with each other or subject to taxation or restraint to support and maintain each other—not as a matter of happenstance (as when free speech becomes libelous or interferes with fair trials) but as a matter of that very definition. No use of property could be countenanced that would deprive some citizens of an equal chance to pursue their own versions of happiness, their own equal opportunity, together or singly, for that would be to turn equal right against itself. Since, in an egalitarian society, being an employer of other people's labor could not convey any special legal rights that one's employees did not also possess, a private employer could never be in the position to rightfully call upon the public authorities to settle a work dispute (unless laws against personal injury, the destruction of property, etc., were being violated; or unless a majority of the enterprise's work force were on the employer's side).

Thus, those who wished to choose the life of private entrepreneurship could only do so on the understanding that they would never be able to call upon the forces of law and order to discipline employees who try to change their working conditions; as well as in the knowledge that there would be no pool of the unemployed from which they could draw strikebreakers if the need ever arose. In that sense would-be entrepreneurs would also make a sacrifice in entering on the chancy business of free enterprise: they would take a risk that they would not be able to have their own way. That risk might be more than balanced by the circumstances that being an entrepreneur would become otherwise less risky, in that failure would leave them no worse off than anyone employed in the public sector, the guarantees of which would apply to them as well. Individual risk taking aimed at private advantage may indeed be more likely to occur when we are all protected by a secure floor: the existence of the socially standard guarantee.[13]

In capitalist societies, let us remember, small businesses constantly close, go bankrupt, suffer from the depredations of competing monopolists or oligopolists, and are unable to get support from banks or other lending institutions. In many ways to start a small business may be a worse fate than to enter on a skilled trade; certainly the failure rate is higher.[14] That so many people persist under such conditions (as they do under the even more restrictive conditions of Communist society) suggests that their activity represents a human ambition as genuine as any other. A democratic society, in fact, would be more truly democratic if it adopted constitutional protections for the rights of individual entrepreneurs as for workers, protecting them even or especially against what could otherwise be the monopolistic competition of public enterprises themselves. Small business could thus achieve in an egalitarian social order what it has never been able to obtain under capitalism: equal right.

As to personal property, in the traditionally accepted sense of the word, the standards of the American Constitution—that "private property ought not to be taken for public use without just compensation," and that no person should be deprived of property "without due process of law"—are perfectly compatible with a regime of democratic political equality. That can be so, though, if those standards are understood to protect only truly personal property in addition to truly individual entrepreneurship: the kind of property that can really be the subject of a claim of universal rights.

When we say that something is a universal right, as distinguished from a socially conferred privilege, we mean that it is in principle available to all persons, either individually or as members of a sharing community, and no one's invocation of it necessarily requires withholding it from others. My exercise of the right to vote does not deprive anyone else of their right to vote; indeed, the individual exercises of that right are mutually supportive of a collective right. So too with the other democratic rights. My free speech does not deprive you of your free speech, or anyone else of theirs. That I am a Jew in no way prevents you from being a Christian; that I publish a pamphlet in no way prevents you from doing the same. The same principle applies to property rights: to the kind of pursuit of property that enhances a person's life rather than an organization's power; that in the words of John Locke's proviso leaves "enough and as good in common for others";[15] and that entails no assertion of a right to control or regulate another's use of his or her time, or to impose generalized costs on one's neighbors. As for the accumulation of property for wealth, any society of equal citizens would also equally understand that the just compensation we receive for the public taking that appears in the guise of taxation and regulation, is the compensation of living in a society that is free of class conflict, and that is recognized as just and thus worthy of loyalty by those who inhabit it. That kind of public taking stands in need of no further justification.

Admittedly, that prohibition against confiscation is not compatible with the transition from pseudodemocratic capitalism to the regime of political equality, since that transition cannot take place without the revolutionary confiscation of wealth; the expropriation of certain property rights; and the use of tax revenues to finance the new and necessarily redistributive institutions of the democratic division of labor. Thus any egalitarian proposal must answer as well the argument that expropriation deprives individuals of the fruits of their labor that belong to them as of right.

Non-Marxist economists are probably on strong ground in asserting that the founder or organizer or underwriter of an enterprise does something different from what is done by labor, in Marx's sense of that word. The question, however, is what they deserve for this work; how much more they deserve; and why? How are we to tell?

What is certain, again, is that an argument about rights will not suffice here. According to that argument, whatever people get for whatever reasons, as long as they have acted within the law they have a right to keep; it would be a violation of natural human rights to take it from them coercively. To take from one group of people on behalf of another group, merely in order to create a better society, is to treat those people as instruments, as a means to someone else's ends; and that is a violation of a moral law.

Yet, no one really believes that people really deserve everything they have at any given moment; the way in which they got it is an absolutely crucial indicator of their desert. Nor will it do to say that as long as accumulation occurred under color of law it was justified. Accumulation based on slave labor took place in Nazi Germany; accumulation based on total coercion of labor takes place in the Soviet Union; accumulation based on semislave labor takes place in the Republic of South Africa. All of these accumulation processes have proceeded under the color of law.

Clearly, to say this would be perverse. What we believe instead is that people deserve to keep legitimately accumulated property, but they don't deserve to keep ill-gotten gains. And both legitimate accumulation and ill-gotten gains (like crime itself) can only be socially defined. From time to time those definitions are changed, and when they are, and previously accepted behavior is condemned as immoral or proscribed as illegal, so do rights change also. Thus, one important antecedent condition of the rise of capitalism in Great Britain was the confiscation of church lands in the sixteenth century—lands that were quite a large proportion of total land holdings in the British Isles. The expropriation of the commons by the gentry, and of the Scottish Highland clans by the English aristocracy and Crown, were also crucial aspects of that process.

In the United States, sources of property and wealth as various as the confiscation of Tory property during and after the revolution, the intensive exploitation of slave labor and then repudiation of slavery, and the expropriation of land from the Native American communities, all involved redefinitions of socially acceptable methods of accumulation. All these are historical examples of redistribution at work.

That is not to say that our definitions of legitimate and ill-gotten gains must be totally relativistic, susceptible to the whim of any passing armed force or moral majority. Within reason, though, if the ways in which labor is now organized, profits defined, controlled, and deployed, and wealth consequently amassed, come to seem illegitimate to the democratic majority, it will have every right to treat these as activities that should not have been rewarded to begin with, and from which the accumulated reward can retrospectively be withdrawn.

I emphasize, within reason. Not every such determination would itself be legitimate, even if made by a majority. Whatever property rights are going to be recognized in an egalitarian society have to be attached to all its citizens who agree to live in that society peaceably. Prudence as well, dictates that the smallest possible number of people be treated in a purely expropriative manner. More importantly, morality requires that no one be deprived of the right to earn as much of a living as possible under the changed understanding of what it means to earn a living; and that no one be deprived of any more property or property rights than is necessary to effectuate the construction of institutions of civic equality. The only way to avoid permanent legitimation of the illegitimate in this respect, would be for it to be generally understood that the transition from capitalism involved the uncompensated socialization only of a kind of corporate property that would no longer exist after the transition had been completed.

Thus egalitarians ought to have a doctrine of property rights, but unless we really believe that the capitalist definition of property rights is the only natural or god-given definition, there is no reason why we must submit to the outcome of capitalist social relations as an outcome to go forever unrectified.

Otherwise, in an egalitarian society, all the rights of the pursuit of happiness that I have adverted to throughout this discussion could be and ought to be protected. Their most signal protection, beyond the institution of constitutionalism based on judicial review, would be the social fact that, unlike the rights of corporate capital, they would be available to any citizen who chose to pursue them; and it would thus be in everyone's interest that they be protected. But private property

right in the essential means of production, as we have understood it
in the capitalist regime, is in no way available to everyone or in
everyone's interest, and thus does not stand on the same footing as
the fundamental rights that are constitutive of egalitarian democracy
itself. Only of a society in which those rights are protected, but that
single right is not, will we be able to say that individuals truly are
equally able to express their legitimate life's desires; and those desires
truly are equally capable of being realized.

## Notes

[1] Anthony Lewis, *Gideon's Trumpet* (New York: Random House, 1964).

[2] For a fuller treatment of this point, see Michael Walzer's *Spheres of Justice*, ch. 2.
I have relied heavily on Walzer's discussion, though I do not come to his conclusion.

[3] Carl Auerbach makes the best argument against rights for antidemocrats, in "The
Communist Control Act of 1954: A Proposed Legal-Political Theory of Free Speech,"
23 *University of Chicago Law Review* 173 (1954); and David Spitz the best counterargument, in his *Democracy and the Challenge of Power* (New York: Columbia
University Press, 1958), especially ch. 4.

[4] See Justice Douglas' dissent in *Dennis v. U.S.*, 341 U.S. 494, 591–598 (1951),
for what is still the best statement of how the clear-and-present danger test should be
used as a test of action rather than speech.

[5] The classic statement on "judicial elitism" is Louis B. Boudin, *Government by
Judiciary* (New York: Goodwin, 1932), 2 volumes.

[6] Michael Walzer makes a contrary argument in "Philosophy and Democracy," *Political Theory*, vol. 9 no. 3 (August 1981), pp. 379–400. I have tried to give reasons for
treating equal opportunity rights as fundamental to democratic equality; I do not think
that Walzer gives satisfactory reasons to the contrary. Rather he seems not to recognize
that political rights without social guarantees are often hollow.

[7] Alexis de Tocqueville, *Democracy in America*, ed. by Phillips Bradley (New York:
Vintage Books, 1954), vol. II, Book II, Chapter 1; and Sigmund Freud, *Group Psychology and the Analysis of the Ego*, in *The Standard Edition of the Complete Psychological Works of Sigmund Freud*, ed. James Strachey (London: Hogarth Press,
1953), vol. 18, pp. 78–80.

[8] I have adopted this point from "States and Schooling," an as-yet unpublished
paper by Amy Gutmann of Princeton University that is the best available discussion of
this subject.

[9] Cf., Herbert Schiller, *Communication and Cultural Domination*, 2nd ed. (New
York: Pantheon Books, 1978).

[10] See Todd Gitlin, "New Video Technology: Pluralism or Banality," *democracy*,
vol. 1 no. 4 (October 1981), pp. 60–76; Ralph Lee Smith, "CATV: Its Impact on
Existing Technologies and Institutions," in George Gerbner et al., eds. *Communications Technology and Social Policy* (New York: Wiley Interscience, 1973). Smith
concluded that "Faced with a new technology, our institutions seem incapable of
implementing any concept of the public interest other than the accomodation of
economic interests. The numerous services that broad-band (cable) systems can bring
to city governments, to city school systems, and to poor and disadvantaged popula-
tions of our inner cities, the contributions that they can make to a revived sense of

community through the creation of local and community broadcasting services, and the role that they can play in alleviating the profound feeling of voicelessness, through abundant channels and open access for the presentation of all views—these are sacrificed in order that the economic interests of small groups will not be disturbed." Nothing has happened since 1973 to cast doubt on that generalization. See, e.g., Kenneth C. Laudon, *Communications Technology and Democratic Participation* (New York: Praeger, 1977), especially ch. 6. ("Briefly, there is no mass market for the kind of [participatory] citizen technology we have outlined. It is unlikely, then, that large corporations will put resources into the development of devices required for an authentic citizen technology."). And see also Schiller, *Who Knows? Information in the Age of the Fortune 500* (Norwood, New Jersey: Ablex Press, 1982).

[11] Cf., Grant McConnell, *Private Power and American Democracy* (New York: Alfred A. Knopf, 1966), especially Chs. 4 and 5. This is still the classic treatment of size and tolerance.

[12] For a judicious treatment of this issue, see Steven Kelman, *Regulating America, Regulating Sweden: A Comparative Study of Occupational Safety and Health Policy* (Cambridge, Mass.: M.I.T. Press, 1981); and *What Price Incentives? Economists and the Environment* (Boston: Auburn House, 1981). The 1982 attempted declaration of bankruptcy by the Manville Corporation, solely in order to escape from litigation aimed at securing compensation for illness incurred by those working with its product (asbestos), exposed once and for all the absurd pretentiousness of the notion that a satisfactory system of compensation for civil wrongs can exist in some pure essence outside the realm of state intervention and regulation.

[13] This is the argument made by R.H. Tawney in Chapter 9 of his *The Acquisitive Society:* "Economic fear may secure the minimum effort needed to escape economic penalties. What, however, has made progress possible in the past, and what, it may be suggested, matters in the world to-day, is not the bare minimum which is required to avoid actual want, but the capacity of men to bring to bear upon their tasks a degree of energy, which, while it can be stimulated by economic incentives, yields results far in excess of any which are necessary merely to avoid the extremes of hunger or destitution." Tawney, op. cit., p. 159.

[14] In 1980, business bankruptcies were 7.9 percent of new business incorporations; unemployment among "craft and kindred workers" was officially 6.6 percent. Compare Table 661 in the *Statistical Abstract of the United States,* U.S. Department of Commerce, Bureau of the Census (Washington, D.C.: U.S. Government Printing Office, 1981), with Table A-32, p. 548, of *Labor Force Statistics Derived From the Current Population Survey: A Databook, Volume I,* U.S. Department of Labor, Bureau of Labor Statistics (Washington, D.C.: U.S. Government Printing Office, 1982). Evidently, this comparison bears only tangentially on the reference in the text, since there are no figures available which state the odds, for an individual, of starting a small business and going bankrupt, or of entering a skilled trade and becoming unemployed, over a given period of years. The figures are suggestive, however.

[15] Locke, *Second Treatise on Government,* ed. Thomas P. Peardon (New York: Bobbs-Merril, 1952), para. 27.

# Part 4

## *Conclusion*

# 11

# PROGRAM FOR A FUTURE THAT WILL BE HERE SOONER THAN WE THINK

---

## I

Above all else, Marx has taught us that any complete social theory must offer not only a critique and a projection, but also a strategy for implementing our projections by dynamic interventions into the historical process. In the absence of any strategic analysis, we easily fall prey to moralism, utopianism, or at best simple irrelevance.

In Marx's sense of the term, the social theory I have laid out here is incomplete (he would have said "unscientific") for I cannot propose more than the merest sketch of a strategic program. That is not an idiosyncratic failure on my part. Once we acknowledge that the proletariat will not be and in fact never has been what Marx thought it would be—the historic bearer of the real needs of all humans—then theories of political mobilization, like the programs they are supposed to implement, become little more than wish lists.

Given that limitation, I have already gone as far as a theorist without a movement can go in describing the essentials of a mass movement for democratic equality. In the American milieu, the necessary components of that movement are broadly obvious. They include a continued effort to radicalize and mobilize professionals, and to gain access to or control of new communications technologies, in order to challenge the dominant ideology of pseudodemocratic capitalism; a massive drive for reunionization, concentrating especially on working women and minorities, and on the new white-collar (and public service) class; the development of solidary ties with other national labor movements, the better to resist the transnational corporations that are now moving capital freely from regulative to more hospitable environments; recognition of the centrality of the feminist agenda, including reproductive rights, physical security and economic independence for women, and child-care support; the forging of unity between middleclass ecological activists and blue-collar workers concerned with occupational health and safety issues; a concerted effort (which will be the most difficult of all) to do away with all institutionalized forms of racial inequality; and above all the articulation of an egalitarian philosophy of domestic reform and genuine internationalism, in place of the pseudopopulist currents of militant nationalism and nuclear adventurism.

Organizationally, the historical logic of all these efforts is that they should lead first to the continued development of those activist communities that mobilize themselves around their immediate concerns through solidary modes of participation, and that choose their public representatives democratically and organically. (In the U.S. the National Council of Neighborhood Women, and in the German Federal Republic the Green Party, are exemplary.) Thereafter, those initially separated communities of protest and change need to perceive the common link between their particular concerns and a necessary, general transformation of public agendas and public spaces. Expressing together an egalitarian, radically transformative version of human need, they can then begin to create a collective culture that will turn hitherto abstract and isolated efforts at legitimation (such as this one) into the philosophical justifications of a mass movement. In the penultimate stage, then, what has been a decentralized plurality of community movements must eventuate in the creation of progressive caucuses, alliances, and ultimately dominant coalitions within the major American reformist institutions: the Democratic Party (or some replacement therefor, if that eventuality comes to pass), and the trade union movement.

At this point, though, strategy has long since become armchair strategy and must give way to program—which, at least, can be and usually is produced from armchairs. And here I can be more definite, for the outlines of an egalitarian program are clear. An egalitarian program for any period consists of policy proposals that have, taken together, the effect of bringing equality closer; of restributing power and resources, and empowering citizenship. Innate wariness, and a decent respect for the immense inertia of history, lead me to formulate this fairly specific program for a very unspecified future. I could call it a program for the nineteen-nineties, or for the twenty-first century. I call it instead a program "for a future that will be here sooner than we think." That, I am certain, is true; and in any event anticipation is my purpose.

## II

My summation of the ideas presented in this book is put forward in a spirit both practical and utopian.[1] I do not know if it is utopian to hope for their full institutionalization during the lifetime of anyone reading this book, but it would certainly be wildly optimistic. On the other hand, I hope here to be able to suggest that we can in actuality imagine significant policy changes relevant to an advanced industrial (or post-industrial) civilization; changes which at one and the same time would address current social needs and yearnings, and yet would clearly lead in the direction of democratic equality. This summation, therefore, will consist of such proposals, and an elucidation of their relationship to the institutions of democratic equality.

The very partial program briefly presented here is designed to suggest an egalitarian alternative to both liberalism and conservatism; but within certain crucial limits. First, this is a program for Americans, and is thus geographically, culturally, and historically particular. Writing in Great Britain, for example, I would emphasize the abolition of what the British call public schools, and of the peerage and the monarchy as well. In the U.S., to pursue this example, the politics of schooling are quite different. Due to the nature of American religious pluralism, the private vs. public quarrel is often cast in the argumentative mode of assimilationism vs. acculturationism, or populism vs. liberalism, or fairness vs. monopoly, rather than elite vs. mass (as may still be the relevant focus for a British discussion). Thus, I have no proposal to abolish private schools in the U.S., for such a proposal would not only be irrelevant; it would be offensive.

To be sure, I have tried not to fall into the trap of taking "American" to be definitively circumscribed by its most longstanding meanings until this very moment, and by nothing else at all. That several of the proposals sketched out below would be unconstitutional according to current understandings worries me not at all, since by that defensive standard of philosophizing we are still back in the 1880s enacting "Mr. Herbert Spencer's *Social Statics.*" The point is not to surrender to existing dominant tendencies in American culture—the point is to change it, not to understand it (as the philosophers have already done). The point is rather to understand the particular problems that are set for social policy within the context of American culture, and the historical strengths and weaknesses, within that context, of various ways of implementing policy.

Secondly, I have tried not simply to reiterate here comments that I have already made throughout the main body of this essay. I have also avoided making suggestions about certain questions of policy that have already been much discussed, such as programs for national health insurance, childcare support, flextime, affirmative action, reindustrialization, nationalization of the energy giants, public control of investment banking, and so forth.[2] The proposals that follow are somewhat less familiar, on the whole, though not by any means all original with me; my intended contribution is to put them within a novel, and egalitarian, framework.

If an ultimate desire of public opinion in our pseudodemocracy is for real democracy, for political equality, as I believe it is; and if political equality demands, as I have argued here, dramatic and drastic alterations in the capitalist divison of labor and the social relations of production, as well as new forms of political accountability; then we must demonstrate that relationship, in actions as well as in words. The proposals that follow, then, are intended to demonstrate how we can make at least modest inroads on existing structures of class, caste, and elite domination, while responding to the political agenda that either exists now, or is likely to exist (in the U.S.) sooner than we think: once Reaganism's "creative destruction" has run its course.

# III

The novel version of full employment that, in my conception, underpins the democratic division of labor, cannot be coherently pursued at all until the conventional Keynesian commitment to full employment has been reinstated as the heart of macroeconomic policy. The U.S. is moving quite deliberately in the opposite direction, to the point where policymakers now contemplate with equanimity the spectacle of a permanent reserve army of labor amounting to 10 percent or more of an already minimally defined labor force. That development would seem to make discussion of macroeconomic policies for full employment an exercise in irrelevance. On the other hand, the spirit of these "utopian essays and practical proposals" leads us to see even the most disastrous social tendency not only as a misfortune but also as an opportunity: for every crisis is in fact both. The acceptance of mass employment leads ineluctably to the demand that unemployment as an acceptable policy option be repudiated. Already full employment legislation with teeth in it has been introduced in the House of Representatives (in 1982); though nothing immediate will come of that or any similar legislative initiatives, we can be sure that the topic will remain on the American political agenda as far into the future as we can foresee. That being the case, it is not my intention here to suggest a fullscale macroeconomic program, but instead to suggest some egalitarian considerations that ought to inform any program for reemployment, the maintenance of full employment, and ultimately an approach to the democratic division of labor.

1. *Social Cost Accounting and Democratic Planning.*   We begin with fundamentals. Beyond all the particular prescriptions for democratic equality that may be found in these pages, the heart of the matter is my assertion that social goods, the goods of equal citizenship, can be valued as we now value the individual consumption of commodities. Although no such method of valuation yet exists for us, the method of social planning and evaluation known as social cost accounting offers an approximation that we can use as a fruitful, potentially revolutionizing starting point.

What we mean by social cost accounting, is that all business enterprises above a certain size ought to be required by law to carry on their books as income *all* the external and internal public costs of their way of conducting the enterprise: from the costs to abutters of cleaning up a toxified environment, to the costs to the national health care budget of treating job-related illness; and so forth. Those books, completely open to the representatives of either interested groups from among the public or of the workers themselves, would thus be treated as public accounts of a publicly distributed good (or ill). In the words of two proponents of this method:

> (B)y creating or retaining jobs, a social cost-benefit approach results in capturing the gains of not having to provide as much unemployment insurance, general relief, and crime control; to settle as many insurance claims; to incur such exorbitant health costs; nor to levy such high tax rates. Many jobs are sacrificed today because the costs enumerated above are borne by the public sector, rather than by the private investors whose decisions are responsible for them.[3]

Thus, spurious revenues—revenues that exist only because someone else has been made to absorb the costs of production—could then be confiscated, that is, taxed away at the rate of 100 percent. By the same token, external benefits that have not been paid for by their consumers ought to decrease the tax liability of an enterprise by the same amount. Thus, we could come to value the social product by social rather than socially neutral market standards, without seriously damaging the free market in the sale and purchase of desired commodities. The public would gain a twofold capability: to be able to assess the actual social performance of a private enterprise; and to be able to exert influence on private actors to perform in a socially acceptable fashion. Perhaps the most interesting aspect of this proposal is that it contemplates no immediate interference with the fundamental rights of private ownership, since even the existing accounting conventions—what constitutes a profit or a loss, an asset or a debit—are already purely social.

*2. The Reserve Army of Labor.* With this background in mind, we can begin to consider egalitarian social policy in a new light. For example, the egalitarian approach to the labor market within a pseudodemocratic social formation has two essential components. First, work should be shared. No one who wants to work should be out of work while others are doing what is defined as remunerative full-time work. Second, it ought to be against the law to disemploy any person who has not yet secured alternative employment at a satisfactory wage. What might this mean in practice? It means that firms should be permitted to declare particular workers "surplus" or "redundant," if that is really what they are; but should also be compelled to continue to employ those redundant workers at a marginally unproductive rate while they look for other work (or undergo retraining).

How could this cost possibly be borne, however? The method of social cost accounting shows us precisely how to rationalize such social costs. The cost to the firm of supporting redundant workers would be entered as an offset to those external social costs for which the firm was being made to account. Society as a whole (that is, all of those other persons receiving satisfactory incomes for doing work socially defined as valuable) would then have an incentive to search for new avenues of productive employment or to find better ways to distribute the benefits of improved technology. In either case, particular capitalist firms would continue to have an incentive to look for labor-saving technology; workers would have an incentive to cooperate in that process; and the true human costs of that progress would have to be appreciated and borne by all. Obviously this kind of program would be fatuous if all it could accomplish would be to build permanent, uncontrollable wage-push inflation into the economic order. To repeat, I cannot undertake an entire macroeconomic analysis here, but certain requirements—such as that the jobs we create through either redistribution or government spending must entail socially productive work—are obvious. Egalitarians, however, have an appreciation of "productive" that goes beyond contemporary neoconservative understandings according to which only what is privately acquisitive is worthy of that description. Egalitarians recognize that, for example, improvement in the productive capacities of workers (their health, education, housing, etc.); an increase in worldwide demand through redistribution in less developed countries; changes in the sectoral composition of production (especially away from military production); the creation of an environment more hospitable to human life; and the development of productive techniques that are less dependent on expensive or scarce inputs (e.g., cogeneration of energy, or reliance on solar rather than nuclear power sources), also may potentially increase the productivity of a given segment of the labor force.

These comments are, admittedly, rather grandly general; and there are certain peculiarly American difficulties that they hardly touch at all. Most tragically, the implicit contempt for human possibility that now informs all established versions of macroeconomic policy has led us to the point at which millions of permanent conscripts in the reserve army (especially though not exclusively among black people) now live as though they were inmates of an open concentration camp (the oxymoron is deliberate). The results in individual pathology and communal breakdown are all too predictable.

We may have passed beyond the pale, to a realm of racial oppression from which there is no returning. However, if we ever can cooperate with each other to think about the rehabilitation of an underclass, many of whose members are too far gone in their exclusion to be reached by the indirect manpower policies of macroeconomics, the path we must take is clear in principle. The pattern of intergenerational pathology can only be broken by removing its cause—hopelessness—without equivocation. By "without equivocation" I mean that that perfectly reasonable hopelessness must be replaced not by some abstractly urged, and thus instantly discredited hopefulness; but by the certainty of a well-rewarded future.

What this prescription implies is that we will have to compel private corporations or the public sector to be the guarantors of social reward to the children of the underclass, from infancy onward. That guarantee, to be believable, would have to be virtually absolute, or at least contingent only upon the good behavior associated with satisfactory progress through the various levels of schooling in the normal way.[4] The costs of this program to a particular corporation would, again, be treated as an offset against the various assessments imposed on it by the principles of social cost accounting. The development of wasted human capital would be demanded of private corporate capital, but would also be recompensed: exactly what a privatized, asocial free market can never accomplish.

In this case, what I have so briefly described hardly attains the status of a proposal, practical or otherwise. However, readers who wish to pursue this suggestion further may fruitfully begin, perhaps, by contrasting it with Edward Banfield's 13 "feasible measures" in his essay on "What Can Be Done?" about the underclass in American cities.[5] All of Banfield's proposals are aimed either at expanding formal opportunity via macroeconomic policy, or at changing the behavior of the (so-called "lower class") people at whom they are aimed, through coercion of themselves or their families. On one hand, better choices are to be offered those still capable of making them. As for the rest, those members of the underclass who have already virtually fallen out of the mainstream for good, their own behavior is presumed by him to be the problem. The victims must make themselves more acceptable to their victimizers in order to be relieved of their victimization; they must change their ways in order to change their fate. In contrast, I assume that our humanly destructive social and economic arrangements pose the problem in the first instance; that these, and those of us who benefit the most from them, are the most appropriate subjects of the coercion that will be neces-sary to end such a deeply embedded social deformation. We change the behavior of individuals (unless we think that the poor or the black or whoever are by nature more evil than the rest of us) by building new social structures that make the attractions of constructive behavior, and the promise of a genuine reward for it, plainly visible and decisively unbreakable. But here for the moment invention ceases and we must move on.

3. *Constrained Inequality: Incomes Policy.*    The tragedy of the reserve army of labor aside, structured economic inequality in the U.S. remains extreme. Although policymakers have so far shown little stomach for attacking that structure, the opportunity for doing just that is, again, necessarily going to be before us. As it already is every-where else in the advanced capitalist world, the question of an incomes policy (price and wage controls) is soon likely to be on the political agenda in the United States. The stop-go approach of first inducing inflation through government expenditures demanded by various interest groups, and then inducing depression through cut-backs in those same expenditures, has clearly reached a dead end, though its death throes may be prolonged. The question will be not whether an incomes policy, but what kind; and particularly, what kind of policy toward wages, salaries, and differentials.

In order to treat this question intelligently, we must begin with appropriate assumptions. What is necessary is to stop looking for microcauses of inequality and consider the social system itself for a moment. Within that system, there is a sharply graded and differen-tiated hierarchy of earned and unearned incomes, from the billionaire's inheritance to the handicapped person's welfare pittance. Does "family background," say, explain the inheritance, and "bad luck" or "genes" the pittance? Of course not. What explains both the difference and the incredible scope of the difference are the legal and social relations of capitalism.

The social system of capitalism guarantees first that property can be inherited in almost unlimited amounts. Second, the stratification system of capitalism takes the form of a steeply graded pyramid, not because that's the way people are naturally, but because that's the way the employers of labor, with some help from trade unions, have successfully chosen to distribute wages and salaries. Thus, there are always millions of people suffering from inadequate levels of income through no fault of their own, performing reasonably well at jobs that do not pay reasonably well. At the same time, a relative handful benefit from undeserved levels of income through no real merit of their own, other than that they happen to have procured the kind of job or property that pays well.

That is our version of the way in which liberal capitalism has been institutionalized. From the point of view of capitalism itself, the additional group inequality that has been visited on various peoples is unjustifiable in any straightforward economic sense, in that it is purely discriminatory. To overcome the effects of that pure discrimination we need primarily to eliminate its effects by adopting appropriate compensatory programs of affirmative action combined with a meaningful commitment to full employment in the traditional sense. Even at that, though, our notion of equal opportunity would still conjoin social mobility with a good deal of class stratification and an immense amount of economic differentiation, due to our perverse way of stratifying earnings.

From this perspective, we can see that an egalitarian incomes policy offers a much more promising path to minimally decent levels of general economic sufficiency than do reactive social programs that are constructed as though extremes of inequality resulted from a series of discrete social problems (or "natural" disabilities). The proposal I have suggested above, for rehabilitating the permanent underclass (or at least its children) applies only to the extreme end of the ladder of inequality. Most remaining inequality has to be tackled by tackling the scale of wages and salaries itself. Any incomes policy will have at least some egalitarian tendency, as long as the gap between the best off and the worst off in American society otherwise continues to widen, as is now happening. However, some incomes policies would be more egalitarian than others. The heart of a really egalitarian incomes policy has to be: (l) a prohibition on all increases in real wages, except for those persons earning below the national median income (or, since the median income in the U.S. is strikingly low, perhaps persons earning up to a certain amount above the median income); (2) a sharp increase in taxes on high incomes and especially on unearned wealth. The result ought initially to be to create an effective national ceiling of something in the very low hundreds of thousands of dollars of income after taxes. Any such incomes legislation should also have built into it an automatic response to "bracket creep," to prevent gains for those below the wage-increase barrier from being promptly taxed away. The best way to do this, and also the most equitable income tax system generally, would be to have a flat-rate tax for all those at or below the median (or other fixed national limit), together with a high uniform standard deduction to ensure progressivity.

Serious progressivity would then be limited to incomes above the median or fixed limit, and ought to be moderated except at the extreme. Progressive taxation as an approach to the genuine redistribution of income is ultimately much inferior to a strong incomes policy. It is not just that redistributive taxation contradicts the dominant ethos of capitalism. Much more crucially, progressive income taxation gradually comes to seem an affliction to everyone but the very poor, in that it affects not just the wealthy but all workers and citizens who succeed in raising their incomes during the life cycle. Certainly the differential treatment for capital gains, tax sheltering, and other forms of tax favoritism that benefit mostly the wealthy, ought to be closed by any egalitarian legislation. But that aside, even progressive taxation combined with tax reform—the closing of loopholes—is not a very promising strategy politically, in that again all of us except for the very poor benefit from at least one and usually several more of those loopholes.

In sum, the differences between median incomes and most above-median incomes are not really so great, and the most common loopholes are not really that regressive in their effects. It is only in the top 1, 2, or 5 percent of incomes that economic inequality really becomes so gross as to be incompatible with equal citizenship; and that is where the redistributive component of progressive taxation ought to be most heavily concentrated, in order to give effect to a redistributive incomes policy.

# IV

It is not difficult to imagine that the question of an incomes policy will soon be on the American political agenda; it already has been there, and the implementation of a prices and incomes policy insured the reelection of a president in 1972. It is more difficult to imagine how the more traditionally socialist agenda of public ownership of the means of production, planning production for use rather than for profit, and so forth, might become salient in an atmosphere that has so far been almost totally hostile to such notions. We need to imagine policies that will constitute preparation for whatever degree of public control the public will ultimately come to see as the essential underpinning of democratic equality.

If we cannot have a socialized economy overnight then we have to set our sights lower. It is the incentives to action rather than the total institutional structure surrounding them that must first be changed. To the extent that capitalists go on existing, and governing, in a social formation that is on its way to becoming noncapitalist, they must be compelled to begin to behave as though they were public representatives rather than private owners.

Codetermination on the European model, therefore, is not by itself likely to accomplish this; it is a stabilizing and integrating but only slightly democratizing or socializing force. What is necessary is to change the framework within which profit and loss are calculated, or the actual items that come to be entered under the headings of "profit" and "loss," and to make this change in such a way that it reflects underlying social realities and has real social consequences. The discussion of social cost accounting already tells us how to do this; the following proposals primarily extend the scope of that method, or at least of the informing principle implicit in it, to the question of ownership of the means of production.

4. The Means of Production.   Two obvious rules for determining whether a private corporate enterprise ought to be subjected to public takeover have already been widely discussed; they follow from the general principle I have enunciated earlier, that the public control of enterprise is contingent on the expression of a public interest in the conduct of the enterprise. Thus private corporate enterprises requiring public subsidization of any kind ought to be compelled to add public representatives to their boards; "no subsidization without representation" should be the economic democrat's slogan.

Correlatively, the abandonment of a working plant by any corporate management ought to be the signal for its assignment to some kind of cooperative public ownership. The weight of the competing interests, although not expressed via the mechanism of legislation, is still self-evident in this situation. In the case of corporate flight private management is effectively agreeing that it no longer has a private interest in the particular productive plant at risk. The only question for democrats then becomes whether the public has an interest; if so, we have established that the public interest is stronger than the private, and can look for ways to have the parent company, as it ought to, assume the burden of risk. If the operation were truly a lemon, the public should be able to recoup its losses. If not, a public enterprise will have been created where a public interest truly exists and a private interest does not.

Despite my caveat, this proposal by itself seems to raise the specter of "lemon socialism," the convenient arrangement whereby the public picks up corporate lemons and private enterprise retains the plums. That arrangement is convenient only for private enterprise, since its ultimate result is to give public enterprise even more of a bad name than it already has. Thus no program for dealing with the means of production is satisfactory (for democrats) unless it provides a method for extending public access to the plums as well, with at least equal force. Again, the technique of social cost accounting promises to do this. We can see on reflection that these various planks in the democratic program for the productive sector overlap. That is, the most clear-cut candidates for public rescue and thus the beginnings of public control are likely to be those enterprises that have been landed with the most burdensome assessments of social costs incurred through unsafe or environmentally damaging operations. The simple rule should be that subsidized relief from the confiscatory tax on external costs, like any other kind of subsidy, triggers public cooptation into management. No doubt some enterprises may be both noncompetitive and externally costly: true lemons. But on the whole there's no reason why the worst imposers of external costs should also be numbered among the declining industries of any given epoch. Thus, the combination of social cost accounting with the principle of "no subsidization without representation" ought naturally to bring about public control of those enterprises in which there is, in an objective sense, the greatest public interest: those which affect us most decisively in the very enjoyment and reproduction of our lives.

*5. Democratic Planning and Democratic Representation.*    As to who could evaluate social costs and benefits, the answer follows, self-evidently, from the conception of democratic representation: any group of people nominated and elected for that purpose by whoever constitute themselves as an interested constituency. Now costs and benefits are evaluated by totally removed, nonresponsible, and non-responsive managers. Even a weakly articulated public constituency would provide more democratic accountability than none at all.

In the same way, representation on corporate boards in the name of a public interest, as well as representation on local or regional bodies that contemplate the takeover of abandoned productive plant, should also be dictated by the same principles of democratic selection. The more numerous the enterprises we subject to some version of the representative principle, the more a real world of representation will begin to make inroads on its phantasmic variant. The more we multiply such bodies of representatives within the structures of production and planning, the more commonplace will become the institutional devices for choosing them, and the less likely it will be that they will degenerate into a condition of insulated elitism. Democratic participation has to become a habit if democracy is to be realized, and it can only become a habit if opportunity exists to engage in it habitually. It will certainly never be realized if we limit its exercise to the choice of leaders from among the insiders of distant political parties that are accountable only in the most vacuous sense of that term.

# V

As with egalitarian labor market policies, and public control of the means of production, an approach toward realization of the democratic division of labor must proceed by inscribing its costs and benefits within existing institutions of production and accumulation. On the basis of what I have suggested so far, the most fruitful way to proceed here ought to be obvious: it is to encourage and reward contributions of private, hierarchical, nondemocratic enterprise to the development of the democratic division of labor.

6. *The Democratic Division of Labor.* The democratic division of labor, as I have described it, is based fundamentally on the reintegration of education and work. The obvious requirement for implementing the first steps toward a democratic division of labor within a not-yet-democratic social formation is to attach training to work. Whether by legislative compulsion or through the use of tax incentives or

credits, every corporate employer above a certain size ought to be turned into an educator or a subsidizer of education.

To put the core of training, retraining, and continuing education programs anywhere but within the productive sector itself would be to make them an alternative to work, and thus, in most cases attractive only to the already unemployed (who will be unlikely to take advantage of them). Within the productive sector, education and training should be attached to the employment of wage workers as a matter of course.

As to the costs of such a program, the corporate sector could probably bear it. If to do so would weaken the nation's position in the international trading economy too dangerously, then perhaps there would have to be compensation from the public purse according to understood ground rules. But that should only be a last resort. On the whole the only subsidy corporations should receive for performing this function is to be granted an offset against tax burdens they have already incurred by imposing externalities on the public. Profit flows from business and financial institutions are the best available source of ready income in advanced capitalist societies. Most of the time, to subsidize the corporate sector is robbing Peter to pay Paul, and we should rather think of the training/education enterprise as an added cost of doing business assessed on the sector that can best afford to incur that cost.

To sum up this discussion of the public control of private enterprise, then, the problem of gradualism in systemic economic change can be restated as follows. As we move away from capitalism toward a truly mixed democratic economy, we face a dilemma. If public planners, however chosen, intervene in the operations of an essentially market economy, they introduce a different set of rules for calculating and evaluating social costs and gain than those the market is used to and relies on. The result is likely to be distortion of information flows and decision making within the market context, thus weakening the performance of a system most of us will still depend on, in what must often seem to be an irrationally interventionist manner. Alternatively, public planners will tacitly surrender their authority to the needs of those private decision-makers whose actions still govern the market according to an older and more rigorously institutionalized set of rules. The proposals outlined above are designed fundamentally to alter the kind of information that comes to private market

actors, by changing customs and procedures, so that the information
that comes to them will look like the same kind of information on
which a democratically planning public would also base its decisions
about potential costs and gains. Thus no matter the pace at which,
or the scale on which, the socialization of enterprise proceeds, it will
be preceded and so accompanied by the equivalent, necessary altera-
tion in the rules by which we all, perforce, value what is made, sold,
and bought.

*7. The Democratic Division of Labor, Continued.*   The above proposal for attacking the capitalist division of labor would probably have
the primary effect of attenuating the technical division of labor in the
blue-collar sector. Its social impact, therefore, is likely to be limited to
the realization that workplace democracy can to some extent replace
workplace hierarchy. There is more at stake than that in the idea of
the democratic division of labor, though, especially as we confront
the seemingly intractable division between tasks that are intellectually
complex and those that are not. The effort to democratize that aspect
of the division of labor will always have to go forward on many fronts,
and will probably be endless. In several respects, the most likely place
to begin that effort is not within industry itself, but within institutions
of higher education.

The significance of academic institutions in this respect is that by
virtue of the task they are assigned to perform, and the way in which
they are expected to perform it, they are the most operationally flexible, the least oriented toward normal profit rate constraints (which are
quite different from and more stringent than simple balance sheet
constraints), and the most intrinsically idealistic of our major social
institutions.

More to the point, it is academics who are now primary carriers of
the message of equality. This is in no way to endorse the proposition
of neoconservative ideologues, that academic intellectuals form an
elitist left-wing conspiracy against the instinctively more conservative
people. For it is equally true that academics are primary carriers of
the message of inequality. Academics, along with journalists of the
various communications media, are the main carriers of every ideological message. To say that is to do no more than to describe the
social division of labor in advanced industrial societies; not to criticize
or expose anybody.

There is, however, a peculiarity of academic egalitarianism that has to be recognized. Inegalitarians incur no responsibility but to look out for their own interests and reward those who follow their preachments. Egalitarians, contrarily, do incur the responsibility of behaving according to at least some minimal standard of moral consistency. Democracy is one quality that most definitely begins at home. As a matter both of tactics and of right, academic egalitarians have to look closely at their own world of work while issuing grandiose pronunciamentos about economic democracy or the democratic division of labor.

Within the academy, the most signal manifestation of the social division of labor is not the division between tenures and nontenured faculty; or between students and faculty generally.

Rather, as every secretary, cleaning person, or groundskeeper knows, it is the division between all faculty and students and administration on one hand, and all members of the support staff on the other, that really manifests class lines in the academy. As institutions grow larger and more bureaucratic, administrators as representatives of the trustees also tend to confront faculty as a separate class; that is a secondary division compared to the primary one between all mental and all material laborers in the academic world, but it has a symbolic importance in that it signifies, to all observers, the full complicity of higher education with the larger social system.

What kind of reorganization, then, would begin to establish the principles of the democratic division of labor at institutions of higher education, in such a way that the genuine commitment of academic egalitarians would be visible to the outside world? Two proposals constitute a minimal egalitarian program.

1. To confront the secondary but symbolically significant class division between administration and faculty, the policymaking staff at all institutions of higher education (e.g., registrars, deans, financial officers and the like), ought to teach part-time in the ordinary course of events; and all teachers ought to do some kind of administrative work in their ordinary course of events. The point is not to destroy the boundary between administration and teaching totally (though that is probably the ultimate goal), but to weaken it: to demonstrate that it exists purely for the sake of convenience, and convenience can live with alterations in the received mode of operation. What is required,

to restate one of the central themes of this essay, is to attack the notion of the administration or management of other people as a career, to which the manager is admitted and from which the managed are barred.

2. More fundamentally, the single most decisive requirement for the democratization of higher education is the requirement that all support staff, white collar or blue collar, be guaranteed, in the normal course of events as part of their job descriptions, the best education that the institution at which they work can offer them; or alternatively, the education that best equips them to be promoted, either within the institution or elsewhere in the world of work, to the next most professionalized or responsible level of work available to persons of their interests or talents. (Their children ought also to be granted whatever privileges and benefits the children of faculty receive.) Everyone who is not a teacher or administrator at an institution of higher education ought to be considered one of its students; and the purpose of such institutions ought to be prepare every one of their students to graduate (or to cooperate with neighboring institutions in doing this).

## VI

The proposals that I have so far spelled out all have as their aim the creation of a more egalitarian social system. However, as I argued at the beginning of this essay, the ideal of social egalitarianism is best advanced on the grounds that it establishes precedent conditions for the more ultimate democratic goal of political equality. At the same time political equality, as we have seen, is much more than merely a residue of egalitarian social arrangements: it poses its own crucial problems, which must be solved in their own right. The remaining proposals, then, address the issue of political equality directly.

8. *Political Equality: the Shadow World.*   The most dramatic obstacle to the realization of democratic representation in the United States today is the almost indescribable, and daily growing power of sheer money in the electoral system. Until and unless the system's insatiable demand for money can be quenched, it will be ridiculous even to talk about pseudodemocracy (for which we will come to feel a certain nostalgia), let alone the real thing: elective oligarchy will be our future.[6] The solution must initially be found within the political

system itself, and if we do not find it soon it will be too late: for the redistribution of wealth can only be achieved by political action, and before very long the existing distribution of wealth is going to render the system within which legitimate action takes place totally impenetrable.

Heretofore, despite every indication of the complete fruitlessness of their endeavor, political reformers have continued to try to oppose the power of money by preventing those who have it from spending it. That is pointless: and so completely pointless that a cynic might be led to believe that such reforms are very carefully designed to accomplish nothing.

The simple fact is that in a particular social formation it is impossible to prohibit the most ordinary, legitimate, and dominant form of social behavior. In our social formation that behavior consists of spending money to buy what you want. So overwhelming is the dominance of that variant of human behavior that it has proven impossible for us to prevent the purchase of pornography, or narcotics, or street prostitution, even though those commodities are for the most part bought by disreputable people from other disreputable people. It is all the more absurd to think we can prohibit the purchase of political candidacies by the most reputable, most powerful, and most authoritative members of the social order. The kind of immense effort it would take to police the flow of political money would require treating the electoral system as though it were actually a subversive criminal enterprise. That is not going to happen, anymore than white collar crime is suddenly going to be treated with the urgency that radicals are always calling for, in a society that counts on white collar criminals for fulfilling our most important material needs. People who have millions of dollars to spend on political candidacies are not going to be prevented from spending them, one way or the other. The stunning inappropriateness with which both conservative Supreme Court justices and liberal members of the Board of the American Civil Liberties Union treat campaign expenditures as a quintessential variant of free speech, demonstrates how deeply we have inscribed the fetishism of commodities at the center of our cultural unconscious.

However, calls for the public financing of political campaigns are also insufficient, and for a similar reason. The American electorate is not looking for a new sphere in which to spend several billion dollars of tax revenues; nor are the inhabitants of the most privatized social formation in the modern world likely to be very happy, in the absence of appropriate preparations, about the socialization of what is in many ways the most philosophically private sphere of all.

These two comments set the boundary of our problem. Since we cannot effectively prohibit the spending of large sums of money on politics, nor legitimize the spending of those large sums of money on the public account, we have drastically to diminish the cost of political campaigns. There is no other solution. In order to begin to control the power of money in politics, and thus preserve those few avenues toward political equality that now exist, we have to deprive money of the commodity it will otherwise so successfully pursue.

Once having stated this requirement for a solution, we can then easily perceive the terms of the solution. Most political campaign money is now spent on one commodity and one commodity only: television advertising. In fact television as a tool of political campaigning has two helpful characteristics from our perspective. Not only is it incredibly expensive; it also provides a commodity (television time) which very few people think of as something they have an individual right to appropriate or make use of, unlike other tokens of support for a candidate. The power of television in political campaigns, which is really the power of money in political campaigns, is thus ripe for overthrow, and the way to overthrow it is self-evident: to prohibit the selling of television time, by public licencees, to candidates for political office or their supporters. What is not for sale, it is no invasion of liberty to be unable to buy.

Correlatively with the banning of paid political advertising on television, we should also then open up television (especially public television) to speeches and public appearances by all candidates, free of charge. Thus, no candidate would be deprived of the opportunity to communicate with voters, no individual would be deprived of the opportunity to support a candidate (except that the candidates would not require nearly as much support), and at the same time we would have begun to recapture the political system in a way relevant to the modern age of technology. It might then even be feasible to provide public support for the remaining expenses of election campaigns (transportation, direct mail, etc.) In any event, there is no other way to begin to get the shadow world of pseudodemocracy under our control.

*9. Political Equality: Participation and Representation.*    To shatter the facade of pseudodemocracy is hardly enough, though. Not only must we resist the cultural imperialism of the shadow world and its spurious claims; we must also strive to create a democratic political culture at the same time. It would take another book to describe and analyze all the myriad ways in which we will have to do this.[7] Certain quite disparate requirements, such as the continued importance of affirmative action criteria in all mass-based democratic organizations, the necessity of abolishing television networks and newspaper chains, and the importance of coalition building among democratically organized grass-roots groups, are obvious. Here I want instead to describe, as examples rather than as an inclusive program, three paths toward political equality that are perhaps not so obvious.

1. Democratic Representation and Trade Union Democracy.

Despite the decline of blue-collar work as the central life experience under capitalism, any democratic movement must and will be based on a trade union component. Trade unionism remains the most powerful tool of mass organizing; many groups that appear to be substituting some different principle of organization for unionism are in fact extending it in new areas (the white-collar women's organization 9 to 5, for example). American trade unions, however, are notoriously undemocratic, with few exceptions; and it is impossible to build democracy on an autocratic base.

The problem of union autocracy is a very serious one for the American Left, then. It is not going to be solved, however, by casting anathemas at union officials for their undemocratic behavior. Nor, more unfortunately, can union democracy be brought into being simply by the multiplication of outside support for union insurgents, for outside support is very suspect within union ranks. In any event, to call for the support of self-styled democratic insurgencies in trade unions, though important as a demonstration of democratic good faith, ultimately misses the point. There would be no difficulty for democratic theory, after all, if insurgents usually won. The fact is, though, that they usually lose; and not all the references we can compile to unequal financing, leadership muscle, and so on, satisfactorily explain why union members, given a chance to vote for a (democratic) change, do not take it.

Let us therefore recast the way in which we usually look at the question of union democracy. Insurgents usually lose elections: if we assume that unionists are reasonably informed citizens making reasonably intelligent judgments how are we to explain their apparent preference for autocracy?

There is, I think, a perfectly reasonable explanation. Democratic insurgents usually lose because trade unions have no powers that they (the insurgents) would be especially skilled at exercising. What American union leaders mostly do is negotiate contracts with the representatives of businesses. The negotiators on the business side are about as democratic as the average general—and indeed in some industries often deploy a barely concealed willingness to resort to one or another version of force if negotiations fail. They are autocrats, and sometimes they (or their professional union-busting help) are little better than thug autocrats. And that, of course, is who can deal with them best. Trade unionists are not rejecting democracy or equality when they reject insurgents; they are registering a preference for known toughness, because that is, in their experience, the most desirable leadership characteristic of all.

What democrats want to do, therefore, is not to attempt to legislate internal democracy in unions. Given the individualist assumptions of pseudodemocracy any such legislation is bound to carry in its wake provisions that will militate against union or labor movement solidarity by preventing union leaders from acting as representatives in the larger political world. This has been the case, for instance, with both the Taft-Hartley and the Landrum-Griffin Acts. Egalitarians do not want the state to be neutral toward collective action, but to encourage and support it. Thus, the goal of democratic legislation ought to be to provide new powers and responsibilities for union representatives that are not dependent on class compromise; on an ability to restore order and renew productivity on terms that have been in large part set by the recalcitrance of capitalists.

Concretely, one of the most significant contributions that reformist legislation can make to the revitalization of the labor movement in the U.S. would be the delegation of health and safety inspection and enforcement powers on one hand; and responsibility for overseeing the mitigation of external environmental costs to the workers themselves on the other hand. In most cases where a workplace is organized it will be union leaders, or persons chosen through the union electoral system, who will be put in charge of that procedure. Where unionization has not yet occurred, there will be a new incentive to it,

since disciplined organization is required to carry out such tasks effectively. And union leaders will then have a crucial task to perform: a
task that will not just consist of negotiating with the autocrats of the
ruling class. They will be representing the expressed needs of their
constituents on behalf of an overriding public policy. The
authorization of that public policy will legitimize their determinations
regardless of, or even despite, the wishes of their employers. Moreover, given the existence of the method of social cost accounting
described above, the externally and internally generated public costs
of the work process will be assessed on the enterprise. Workers will
thus have to make informed decisions about the trade-offs they wish
to make among those costs and their take-home wages.

Thus, instead of being merely hard-fisted negotiators, union leaders
will also have to be representatives and educators: workers will have
to articulate their needs to their leaders, and those leaders will have to
explain the possibilities and costs of action to the workers. This relationship will necessitate an entirely different kind of leadership. In the
heart of the trade union movement, where democratic activism must
begin and must ultimately take hold, the structural requirements for a
nascent democracy rather than for autocracy, will have come into
being.

2. Direct Democracy.

As I argued in Chapter 9, genuine direct democracy (as opposed to
mass democracy) actually multiplies channels of democratic
representation. One goal of egalitarians ought therefore to be to
search for policy arenas in which the institutions of direct democracy,
and thus of democratic representation, may be realized. It is a happy
coincidence that the most plausible modality of direct democracy is
ideally designed for policymaking in what will for many decades be
one of the most crucial of all policy arenas: the arena of energy policy
formation.

It is perfectly obvious that most people, even most well-educated
people, are incapable of analyzing the trade-offs implicit in various
energy mixes. For inegalitarians that statement signals the end of the
discussion; for egalitarians, it is only the beginning. Our collective
inadequacy need not be taken as the excuse for trained experts to
trade opaquely phrased arguments in elite venues that are closed to
citizens. Instead, democrats will insist that the function of experts in
this policy arena is to educate the public to the point where it is capa-

ble of participating in the decision-making process in an informed manner. Citizens need only be educated well enough to choose representatives who will be able to make an intelligent presentation of their interests, to negotiate those expressed interests with other representatives, and then to return a policy proposal to their consti- tuents for some kind of authorization. As the outcome of dialogue with constituents, for example, decentralized regional power authori- ties could make energy-related decisions consistent with the informed wishes of the majority of those constituents, as well as with the vetos cast by communities that have been given the authority to resist the external imposition of unacceptable costs. The decentralized authori- ties or communities might then have to petition the central govern- ment, or energy authority, for certain kinds of subsidy, relief, etc.; the central authorities in turn might have to mandate special taxes or other kinds of assessment to make the desired policy economically feasible. At that point, potentially, the dialogue would recommence. Thus, the market would truly be determining production policies and costs; but marketplace determinations would result from the demo- cratically expressed desires of citizens rather than the competitive anarchy of grossly unequal economic actors.

In the arena of energy policy, the main subsidy provided by govern- ment should be the provision of forums for public education and the defraying of its cost. The outcome of that process will almost cer- tainly be less expensive than the outcomes of the secretive, monopo- listic decision-making process from which our energy policies now devolve.[8] With respect to the future of nuclear power, though, what- ever else democrats have to say about it as an energy source, it has already become perfectly clear that like nuclear war, nuclear power will be too dangerous to leave in the hands of the people. As or if it proliferates, the national security state will have finally entered the most daily aspect of our lives. Any technology that can justify an administrative proposal to seek prison terms of up to 20 years for anyone who allows access to information that might ''provide impor- tant insights into nuclear material production and processing'' is a technology that every democrat must inspect from a political rather than a merely technical standpoint.[9]

3. Political Equality and the Nuclear State.

Nuclear power, of course, presents only one aspect of the most frightening contemporary event of all: the development of the nuclear state.

The nuclear state is the final revelation (unless there are yet more hideous revelations to come) of the national security state: the state in which all decisions and all institutions are ultimately subordinated to the decisions and institutions that national security elites consider necessary for preservation of that evanescent frame of mind known as national security. The national security sector, as we might call it, is the first line of defense, and the deepest line of defense, for all that is centralizing, monopolizing, and antidemocratic in corporate capitalism. Both class subordination and elite domination are rationalized, bolstered, and emphasized by commitment to the priority of security or defense.

As to class structure, the criterion of success in international competition effectively commands, in any nation that pursues that course, the disciplining of the domestic labor force, and indeed the suppression of all unruly elements that might weaken, through their activities, the nation's trading position or the credibility of its military might. Even more decisively, the national security state absolutely predicates elite domination of all socially determinative decision making.

The principle of the military chain-of-command may be useful for armies, but it is literally incompatible with even the tamest forms of representation: in the United States most of our so-called representatives are actually barred from knowledge about, penetration of, or influence on immense areas of policymaking. More insidiously, the national security state is a state in which the embrace of the military principle, and thus of antidemocratic hierarchy, is all-consuming. Supporting leaders and taking orders becomes the preferred form of political participation; the principle of "need to know" gradually substitutes itself for the principle of freedom of speech, as do secret intelligence activities for democratically made public policy. Where arguments about policy can be ended with the statement that "Your President knows best," that "he" has information unavailable to you and that thus your views (whoever you are) must be totally devalued, there democracy has come to an end.

There is yet an even more profound reason why, for us at least, the nuclear state is the most dangerous enemy of democratic promise. Americans notoriously display more cynicism about government, and thus about the value of public agency and collective social action of any kind, than the citizens of other advanced capitalist societies. Our condition of political privatization is hard enough to overcome under any circumstances. The nature of the nuclear state makes that task all the more difficult.

Our cynicism about government, that is, is intensified by our deep, though deflected, popular dissatisfaction with the extent of our public spending on the world's most gigantic and yet most futile military force. A seemingly widespread consensus about the need for greater and greater military spending has obscured the profoundly alienating effect that an elephantine military budget has upon civic consciousness in the nuclear age. For now as never before, the kind of criticism that is typically levelled at the welfare mess is doubly applicable to the military establishment. Dollars spent on defense could often as well be burned in the streets. The purpose of these expenditures is not to win wars. The United States has not sought to win a war since 1945. Nor does all our military might make other world powers behave as we would like them to behave. U.S. military strength has accomplished almost nothing in the past 35 years, and the United States' influence over the actions of other nations is steadily diminishing (though its economic influence remains immense). Nor can military spending provide a greater sense of national security. Beyond the basic requirements of minimum nuclear deterrence, its upkeep and renewal, additions to a nuclear arsenal contribute nothing to making people feel more secure. In fact, they have the opposite effect. First, they incite actual or potential enemies to enlarge their own arsenals. Second, since the only possible justification for further additions to an arsenal capable of destroying the world many times over is that despite the arsenal we are alleged not to be secure, the precondition of increases in the military budget is always a carefully orchestrated increment to the national sense of insecurity. Thus, underlying the clamor for more government spending for national defense is the growing awareness that more and more equals less and less.

The program of joy through strength is thus doomed to failure. Assuming we can avoid a nuclear holocaust, all that will come of more nuclear madness is more anxiety. The time is ripe for a concerted attack on the whole notion of security through supernuclearism. The elements of a rational military strategy, based on a minimal nuclear deterrent and a reduced commitment to being the Pinkertons of the Third World, will cost hundreds of billions of dollars less than what the Reagan administration (at this writing) has in store for the mid-1980s and after. An attack on this, the most debilitating kind of big government, will be an important step toward restoring the viability of the idea of collective political action.[10]

In this respect, all the proposals I have put forth here are deliberately and necessarily linked. Constrained inequality, the democratic division of labor, and political equality develop from and depend on each other. But there is little point in thinking about them at all if we do not immediately act to prevent the fatal hardening of democracy's arteries; to forestall the triumph of the nuclear state. The search for equality is a series of struggles on all fronts; not one can be divorced from the others.

## VII

All these proposals aside, it might well be said that we live in an age of which benevolent despotism would seem to be the most hopeful outcome; how can I or anyone maunder on about the struggle for equality, genuine democracy, and all the rest?

To put it another way, how do we explain the electoral resurgence of an apparently discredited conservatism, and the near disintegration of an apparently triumphant Keynesian liberalism, throughout the advanced capitalist world? That question is especially poignant for capitalism's critics, given that conservatism still shows no capacity in its own right to master the pains of the boom-bust cycle, and break the logjam of stagflation. Why is it then suddenly in such good repute?

The answer to that question may seem paradoxical; it is actually simple, as most paradoxes are. During the long upswing of the postwar period—the epoch that effectively ended with the Oil Embargo of 1973—social democratic or welfarist parties came to power virtually everywhere by placing all their bets on the success of capitalism. Capitalists would continue to accumulate, and they would accumulate enough that social democratic redistribution could be painless. Conservatives, contrarily, staked their reputations on the failure of socialism; first in Eastern Europe, then in the mixed economies of the West. What happened is that conservatives made the better bet. In the long run, to be pessimistic during an upswing is better than to be optimistic. It's not necessary to be cynical to note that nothing works very well for long. Conservatives were therefore on solid ground when they insisted that nothing would work for long except their panacea, which had the inestimable virtue of having failed so badly when last tried that no one had thought to resurrect it within the living memory of most people.

Whereas conservatives have been consistently single-minded in their rejection of everything but free market capitalism, social democrats and liberals have been trapped by their own double-mindedness about capitalism. For the reformist Left everywhere, the great postwar recovery was a gigantic illusion; it should be the Left's last illusion. At the moment it seems that capitalism with a stony face is the best that conservatism has to substitute for capitalism with a human face. And if that is the case, then the Left in the West must give up its tacit, paralyzing reliance on capitalism's sputtering engine of accumulation if it is to recover lost ground, let alone start a forward movement.

Revolutionary transformation (for that is what I am ultimately proposing) requires for its realization not only a moment of historical crisis but also a change in consciousness. The new consciousness must be prepared to effect the transformation and to extend it, and thus, that new consciousness must be able not only to diagnose the crisis, but to perceive and implement an alternative way of doing things. In the end, therefore, reformist interventions such as I've tried to articulate here are insufficient in and of themselves. Critics of capitalist pseudodemocracy must suggest a new, less wasteful way of generating productivity; of accumulating and reproducing the material foundations of material well-being. These proposals are intended only to start us in that direction; the entire book defines the new mode of social life. And even at that, to return to the question of strategy and mobilization, this book and these proposals exist, for now at least, within the realm of ideas alone, and not of action. That is as it has to be, unfortunately. The philosophers can only interpret the world in our various ways; someone else will have to change it.

# Notes

[1] My conjoining of "utopian" and "practical" is borrowed, with profound gratitude, from Paul Goodman's collection of essays, *Utopian Essays and Practical Proposals* (New York: Random House, 1962). The political philosopher will, I suspect, perceive the egalitarianism expressed throughout this work as representing an uneasy amalgam of Rousseau, Marx, and Mill. My understanding, however, of the appropriate method for *doing* democracy has been influenced by Goodman more than anyone else.

[2] A good place to begin is with Samuel Bowles, David M. Gordon and Thomas E. Weisskopf, *Beyond the Waste Land* (New York: Doubleday, 1983); and Barry Bluestone and Bennett Harrison, *The Deindustrialization of America* (New York: Basic Books, 1982).

[3] See note 6 to Chapter 7.

[4] Given the distribution of learning disabilities, low IQ, etc., in the United States, the only ground on which the inegalitarian can deny that it is possible to train any children for normal accomplishment, under the right circumstances, is to adopt a racist theory of the genetic determination of intelligence. See Green, *The Pursuit of Inequality,* chs. 2–4.

[5] Edward Banfield, *The Unheavenly City Revisited* (Boston: Little, Brown, 1974), Ch. 11.

[6] The most trenchant description of the contemporary relationship between money and politics is Elizabeth Drew's two-part series on "Politics and Money," in *The New Yorker*, vol. LVIII (December 6, 1982 and December 13, 1982).

[7] See, for example, Stanley Aronowitz's "Socialism and Beyond: Remaking the American Left, Part II" *Socialist Review*. No. 69, vol. 13 no. 3 (May-June 1983),; Harry C. Boyte, *The Backyard Revolution: Understanding the New Citizens Movement* (Philadelphia: Temple University Press, 1981); Albert and Hahnel, *Unorthodox Marxism*; and Michael Albert, *What Is To Be Undone: A Modern Revolutionary Discussion of Classical Left Ideologies* (New York: Porter Sargent, 1976).

[8] See, for example, Robert Sherrill, *The Oil Follies of 1970–80* (New York: Doubleday/Anchor, 1983).

[9] This language is from an administrative regulation proposed by the Reagan administration in the summer of 1983; see the *New York Times* for August 18, for the comments quoted on the next page.

[10] I've discussed this point in my "Redeeming Government," *The Nation*, vol. 233 no. 20 (December 12, 1981), pp. 626ff. On the conception of the nuclear state in general, see Richard Falk and Robert J. Lifton, *Indefensible Weapons: The Political and Psychological Case Against Nuclearism* (New York: Basic Books, 1983).

# 12

# THE PURSUIT OF EQUALITY

What is the substance of democratic politics? Democratic politics is the effort of any group of people, aware that they have diverse interests, needs, and conceptions of the good, and acknowledging that diversity as legitimate, to reach a mutually acceptable compromise of those interests, needs, and conceptions of the good. The outcome, or compromise, is mutually acceptable because it has been reached by procedures that have previously been agreed-upon as fair. However, deeply inscribed conflicts of class and caste stretch the search for mutuality and fairness to the breaking point, since the outcome of a neutral decision-making process among unequals is always suspect. Or, alternatively, in the presence of those kinds of conflict the political process is reduced to a sham, in a fearful attempt to avoid testing the limits of conflict. Either way, a people so divided are unlikely to find a resolution of conflict through procedures that are suitable to political equality.

The discussion of social equality in Part II of this book was essentially a discussion of how to overcome underlying conflicts of class against class, caste against caste, and class against caste, by creating a relatively classless (and casteless) society:, and thus, a genuine collectivity with a genuinely collective interest in peaceful conflict resolution. To be sure, we would not thereby eliminate all forms of social conflict but we would reduce them to more manageable proportions. Class conflict as we know it is especially destructive, in that its logical outcome is the attempt by each or every class to penetrate the state apparatus, and dominate the state for its own aggressive or defensive purposes. (The conflict of castes and especially the sexes, for the most part, results not in unending attempts to penetrate or seize the state but in the injustice of perpetual domination.) The attainment of social equality would render this entire cycle of aggression and defense unnecessary, and thus make possible the meaningful version of equal, democratic citizenship that I have described in Part III.

In the end, I can make only three claims on behalf of this vision; but they are important claims.

First, what I have been advocating so far is a coherent notion of real political and social equality, as opposed both to communitarian ideals which are really attainable only in the small scale, and to the traditional liberal, but pseudodemocratic, conceptions. Moreover, this notion shares with both of those ideals the one underlying theme they have in common, and that any democratic ideal must share. The liberal conception of the autonomous citizen, the communitarian conception of the freely cooperating citizen, and the egalitarian conception of the equal citizen are all founded on the proposition that the good political life emerges only from the positive, active decisions of equally choosing human beings; never from their submission to the constraints of some impersonal fate that dominates them, but that a separate class among them is itself able to dominate. It has to be explicit in any democratic theory that we may, for example, lose a war together and still be equal citizens together in defeat; but that to be subjected, without real agreement, to another's power over us within our own community is to become pseudocitizens.

Second, while this notion of political equality places the underlying democratic ideal within a more coherent descriptive framework, it is also what most people really have in mind when they say they believe in democracy or self-government. In some pseudodemocracies today the official political sphere claims the public-spirited energies of more citizens; in some (as our own), less. Almost everywhere in the so-called democratic world, though, resignation and alienation are the responses of the average citizen to claims that government is of, by, or even for the people. The purpose of democratic theory today should be to explain that resignation and alienation, and to offer a vision that the citizens of pseudodemocracies may come to see as a viable alternative.

Finally, we should take note of Aristotle's well-known formulations on citizenship, in which he says that "the good citizen must possess the knowledge and the capacity requisite for ruling as well as being ruled . . ."[1] It is typical of contemporary democratic theories to ignore the second half of Aristotle's formulation, about the capacity for "being ruled." We ought not to ignore it.

Behind all other aspects of genuine citizenship, there must stand, in a larger sense, the development of our capacity to appreciate the existence of a public good that on at least some occasions transcends individual or group interests—even our own. Without that capacity, generalized throughout the polity, political equality or democratic self-government will instantly self-destruct (as is close to happening among us today). Doubtless my use of phrases like "the good society" or "conceptions of the good" can only be suggestive and not indicative. For historical reasons too familiar to need restating, the languages both of ordinary discourse and of technical philosophy have not been able to make much sense out of notions of "the good," whether emanating from nature, god, or history, for several hundred years. But then, the kind of society in which those languages have been spoken has been so marked by the spirit of competition rather than the spirit of cooperation that we cannot expect otherwise.

In that circumstance, it would be the height of academic irrelevance to attempt to derive the moral premises implicit in the argument of this book from some overriding ethical theory that is allegedly grounded in objective foundations. It may be impossible to establish in any decisive way that democracy is good for us; it may very well be that a majority of people will always prefer the passive consumption of commodities to the active engagements of citizenship.

It is possible, though, to point to what seems very clearly to be an intimate relationship between our acceptance of inequality, and our inability to find for ourselves a satisfying notion of the public good even as we are apparently searching for it. Can a new conception of the public good, or new conceptions of the public good, emerge from the pursuit of political equality, alternatively? Admittedly the answer to that question is not self-evident. It is impossible for anyone engaged in serious reflection about the nature of social order to gainsay Rousseau's observation that stable political community is impossible in the absence of some version of what he called "civil religion." (A sacred theology will do as well, but it is very unlikely to be egalitarian.) If we strip away the authoritarian aspects of Rousseau's conception—enforced patriotism, enforced religiosity, and censorship—we can then note the centrality of what he called the "single . . . negative dogma" of the civil religion: "intolerance," which is to be forbidden.[2] Rousseau meant by this injunction only intolerance in its institutionalized, theocratic mode, but we have learned since that there are all too many forms of intolerance other than the religious. As de Tocqueville observed about American society, egalitarianism itself may be one of them: "The majority," he wrote, "exists in the perpetual utterance of self-applause," and therefore "freedom of opinion does not exist in America." Democratic republics may succumb to that form of tyranny in which "the body is left free, and the soul is enslaved."[3] The civil religion of democracy can only be democracy; and egalitarian society can only be founded on a general belief in the appropriateness and virtue of an active egalitarianism: of people acting collectively toward a common goal. But if at the same time egalitarianism does not mean an equal respect for neighbors and fellow citizens in their differences from oneself, as well as their fundamental similarity as active, human, moral agents, then de Tocqueville's fears will be borne out. It is the doctrine of equal participation in representative government, conjoined with the notion of constitutionally embedded equal rights (including positive rights of equal access to the means of wellbeing) that together may square what seems to be an unsquarable circle; that might support the development of a body of citizens who, with equal freedom, freely embrace the doctrine of their equal and active liberty together.

No doubt it must be said of my concrete proposals, and the larger vision that stands behind them, what I have said of the alternatives: nothing works for long. But by positing a new vision rather than variations on a tired old theme, we may at the very least wrench the dialectic of philosophy and policy sharply away from the morass of meanspiritedness, futility, and mortal danger in which it is now mired. To do that, we must demonstrate our concrete willingness to stand on the proposition that the best hope for a stable and peaceful human existence is not envy, greed, competition, and inequality; but instead, cooperation, public spiritedness, and the sentiment of equality.

I can offer only this speculation. To the extent that different communities of potential citizens are not differentiated and alienated from each other by the fear, envy, and antagonism between classes, sexes, and races that grow out of having totally different life chances; and to the extent also that representatives and those they represent share a communal rather than an alienated relationship: to that extent the notion of a lived public good may be at least imaginable. Ultimately, that is the only argument for the democratic ideal.

# Notes

[1]  *The Politics,* III, iv, 1277b.

[2]  Jean-Jaques Rousseau, *On the Social Contract,* ed. by Roger D. Masters, trans. by Judith R. Masters (New York: St. Martin's Press, 1978), p. 131 (Book IV, Ch. VIII.)

[3]  In *Democracy in America,* V. 1, pp. 274–75.

# INDEX

tion). 259
Nozick, Robert, 63–66, 78
Nuclear weapons, and democracy, 263–65

Ocean-Hill Brownsville, 185, 200
Occupational health and safety, 35, 36, 260
Old-age insurance, 69
*On Revolution,* 187

Paris Commune, the, 186–87
Participation: in Capitalist societies, 83; and democracy, 181–85, 203–4, 211, 252; and leisure time, 82, 89
Petty bourgeoisie. *See* Small business
Philanthropy, 65
Planning: democratic, 94–96, 133–34, 141, 144–49, 164, 244; and the market, 68, 262; public, 43, 123, 165, 253–54
Political equality: definition of, 170–74; demand for, 4–7; and the means of production, 117–37; and planning, 144–49; policies for, 256–65; and rights, 206–10; and social equality, 6–7, 23–24, 62, 170, 212. *See also* Democracy
Pollution. *See* External diseconomies
Populism, 3, 124, 128
Poverty, 19, 63
Press, freedom of the. *See* Mass communications, media of
Privilege, 22, 83, 93
Professional managerial class (PMC), 14, 16, 19
Professionalism. *See* Experts
Profit, role of, 39–40, 42–46, 150–51
Property. *See* Means of production; Rights
Protestantism, 158
Pseudodemocracy, 1–3, 7, 17–18, 22–23, 143, 156, 182, 256, 259; definition of, 3

Racial inequality: costs of, 34, 46, 240; in the division of labor, 14; and majority rule, 212–14; in the U.S., 245–47. *See also* Discrimination
Rajneesh, Bhagwan Shree, 223
Reaganism (and Reaganomics), 21, 142, 242, 265
Referendum. *See* Direct democracy

Religion: and Democracy, 158–59
Representation: compared to pseudorepresentation, 175–79, 181–82; and democracy, 173, 175–200, 203–4, 250–52, 261
*Republic of Plato,* 195–96
Resources: misallocation of, 37–48, 152–60; public allocation of, 66–70, 78, 119–20; scarcity of, 60–61, 147
Revolution. *See* Social transformation
Reward: differentiations in, 70–77
Rights: of Antidemocrats, 209–10; of communication, 219–24; conflict between 207–10, 226, 230–32; and equality, 76–77, 203–24; and individualism, 104, 224; the Left and, 204; of minorities, 99, 173–74, 208–18; of property, 224–35, 244; reproductive, 103–5, 211; as universal, 232, 234
Risk, 231, 236
Rockefeller family, 64–65
Rohaytn, Felix, 48
Roman Catholicism, 158
Rotation in office, 188–91
Rousseau, Jean-Jacques, 17, 63, 96, 124, 180, 184, 193, 195, 217, 266; on the general will, 174; on tolerance, 271–72

Sacrifice: in Capitalist societies, 45–48, 143–44, 161, 178; in a democracy, 161–62
Schumpeter, Joseph, 142, 161, 180
Secession, 106
Sex role stereotyping, 97, 109, 213
Small business, 125–31; rights of, 230–36
Smith, Adam, 150
Social class. *See* Class
Social cost accounting, 144–45, 243–45, 246, 251
Social democracy, 143–44, 150, 265–66
Social equality, 7–10, 269; definition of, 170; as fundamental, 211; and political equality, 6–7, 23–24
Socialism, 125; authoritarian, 118; democratic, 7, 10, 118; market, 7, 151; prospects for, 250
Socialists: Democratic, 9; traditional, 8, 118
Social justice, 77
Social transformation: and Capitalism,